Table of Contents

Omaha, Nebraska

Introduction
- Context of the Problem
- Purpose of this Black Paper
- Background of the Study
- Research Question to be Examined
- Limitations
- Significance of the Study

Citizen Participation: A Review of the Literature
Methodology
Design Method
Research Question
Minorities in the Community Development Process: Omaha Overview

Introduction
The Community Development Process
Phase 1: Planning, Self-Reliance and Segregation
Phase 2: Planning, North Omaha & the Federal Government
- Minorities and Urban Renewal
- 1975 – Community Development Block Grants Come to Omaha
- Development Formation in North Omaha

Phase 3: Contemporary Planning and Minority Input
- North Omaha Community Development
- Omaha By Design

Getting Minorities Involved in Community Development
- Increasing Minority Participation: Proposals

Expanding the scope of traditional planning
Emphasis on value of minority input
CDBG week
Minority Input Development Conference(s)
Community benefits agreements
Participation allotments
The New Public Service approach
Citizen panels
Capacity building
Human capital development business investments
Involvement of higher education
Involvement of African-American church

- ## What Black Organizations and Leadership Can Do

Summary and Conclusions
References

<u>Keys to Empowerment</u>

Introduction

Key: Avoid External Definition
- The White View of Race: The Omaha World Herald

Key: Define, at the Outset, What "Empowerment" Is
- African-American Empowerment Network
- Understand the "Politics" of Race and Reality in Omaha: The Conclusions of the 1997 Race Commission Study
- Mentoring: Passing the Baton
- Core Issues: Directions for "Empowerment Network"

Key: Avoid Pacification/Placation Approaches
- North Omaha Community Development
- North Omaha Rebuilding Committee
- NorthStar

Key: Define "Development" In Your Own Image and Interests

Key: Know Your Enemy

- Internal Opposition: Provocateurs and Race Traitors

Key: Three Approaches to Neighborhood Development?

- Neighborhood Maintenance Approach
- Social Work Approach
- Political Activist Approach

Key: Connect Community Work With "Re-Education
Key: Define Leadership Types -- Urban Models as a Basis for Black Political
Action -- A Theory and Prospective Paradigms

- Concentric Zone Model Community Leadership Paradigm
- Sector Model Community Leadership Paradigm
- Multiple Nuclei Model Community Leadership Paradigm

Conclusion
References

Anticipatory Repudiation: The Omaha Example

Introduction
Anticipatory Repudiation, Omaha and CDBG
Evidence of the Failure of CDBG in Omaha
References

Closing Remarks

INTRODUCTION

This book, like all of my texts, offers critique and commentary of those
institutions and cornerstone organizations that play pivotal roles in impacting upon

the black community. Most books about these institutions are descriptive and consist of fluff pieces outlining the well-meaning "programs," and "projects" that are employed that are aimed at helping the disadvantaged but for some reason always fail. But of course, any failure is immediately attributed to the people and never to the institutions. In other words, those who are ghettoized are victimized twice: one for being victims and a second time for being stupid enough to believe that the system really gives a damn about them.

This book, *Urban Planning, Community Development and the Systematic Abuse of African-American Communities: Contextual Appraisal, Commentary and Critique*, hopes to inspire and evoke change in the existing approaches, paradigms and praxis being created and promoted by urban planners, developers and contractors. It is because of these groups, following the decisions and "master plans" laid out by mayors and others, that have under-developed black communities all over America. With the help of handpicked lackeys and ministers, this is the best way to describe how on-going abject poverty has been perpetuated and maintained.

The book consists of chapters made up of papers that I have written over the years. When combined I believe that this is about as comprehensive a work that has been written that addresses race, urban discrimination, code enforcement and related issues that deal with the on-going segregation and compartmentalization that continue to plague this society and as a result, continues to do harm to minority communities (ghetto, barrio, reservation) all over America.

The first section, "The Social Aspects of Urban Renewal: From 1958 to 2012" is essentially a review of an article that provides the history of a program that did much harm to black areas in the name of "development." It is a critical race theory approach and addresses the roles that planning and "white privilege" play in justifying the white flight to suburbia and the on-going "experiments" that were performed on the ghetto, with urban renewal being the blanket name applied to white incursions, impositions and re-configuration of the ghetto.

The second section, "Legal Aspects of Urban Planning," shows the role that laws have played in buttressing the segregation, redlining, steering, blockbusting, restrictive covenants and other ploys that were used to create and maintain the ghetto. Also in this section is important information on the role of zoning and code enforcement, and various "housing programs" that made tens of millions of dollars for developers and planners and left black communities oftentimes too weak to do anything but wander.

The third sections deals with so-called "minority participation" in these various programs and how planning departments pimp and placate the masses through various "master plans" on their way to maintaining racial segregation. The target city is Omaha, Nebraska, a hick town that has bilked its black community of

50,000 out of just over $250 million dollars since 1975. As long as the black community continues to be labeled a "pocket of poverty", the city of Omaha can qualify for free grant money from the federal government, promising to use the funding to "help the poor negroes" but instead spending it on downtown skylines, westward development, suburban growth and the hiring of individuals who live nowhere near the black community. The section also includes way to get people of color more involved in the citizen participation process.

Section four is titled, "Keys to Empowerment," and defines the term "empowerment" because it is a buzzword that is often used by those who are encroaching (invading) black communities in the name of "development." Understanding the role that the media and "fake studies" play in justifying the incursions is very important and will be addressed, as well key pitfalls to avoid such as shill nonprofit organizations that are set up aimed at doing the bidding of the city while fronting as "community-based organizations" and an examination of three approaches for neighborhood development: the neighborhood maintenance approach, the social work approach and the political activist approach.

Various long-term urban planning models will also be explained.

The fifth and final section addresses what I call "anticipatory repudiation." In a nutshell, it is also known as an anticipatory breach, and is a term in the law of contracts that describes a declaration by the promising party to a contract that he or she does not intend to live up to his or her obligations under the contract." (Wikipedia, 2017). In this context the various cities that receive Federal funding and then refuse to do right by black communities are in violation and as a result should be "repudiated" by both the funding source as well as the neglected victims.

THE SOCIAL ASPECTS OF URBAN RENEWAL: FROM 1958 to 2012:

INTRODUCTION

I've been a fan and student of urban planning ever since I entered into a program while a student at the University of Nebraska at Omaha and went on to receive both a Bachelor's and a Master's in the area. From there I went into other areas – urban education, sociology, black studies – but my academic accomplishments won me a scholarship from the Department of Housing and Urban Development enabling me to enter the Urban and Regional Planning Department at the University of Iowa. Although I only stayed one year, I learned a great deal, enough to peak my interests in the area and to read everything I could on the subject, from utopian planning, land use planning and zoning codifications to gentrification, social planning and a plethora of other areas.

I am not only an urbanologist, but also a Critical Race Theorist. I will explain this paradigm in the next section of this paper. At this point it should suffice to point out that this particular paper is a response to and critique to an article written in 1958 by Armin A. Roemer who, at the time, was the Assistant director for the Detroit City Planning Commission. The inspiration behind my interest is the time period: a time when America was much more racially and residentially segregated than it is today, and a time when urban renewal and other considerations for "helping the negroes" were still in their embryonic stages.

The fact is, I hold urban planners largely responsible for that segregated state of affairs, which for a time was backed by federal law, I work to challenge and critique those attitudes which shape the thinking behind the types of articles that served as the basis for policy which, in turn, led to the thinking of many of today's city and neighborhood planners.

This paper addresses the paradigm used to analyze the writings of Roehm, who penned the article on urban renewal. In this paper I quote, for one Aguirre (2000) who explains that critical race theory is important because CRT writings use first person accounts –as I do – and they are also characterized by frequent use of the first person, storytelling, narrative, allegory, interdisciplinary treatment of law, and the unapologetic use of creativity. My view is that by personalizing and talking directly TO the people, I can get this otherwise complex information out to them and they, in turn, can arm themselves with this information and no longer fall for the "urban planning rope-a-dope that has been inflicted upon them for decades.

I follow up the section on critical race theory with a brief explanation of planning and "white privilege." It is important that the readers of this document understand that what is taking place in these cities and as a result, in our communities, is by design. It is planned – and it has a racial basis. White privilege is a "well-kept secret" when it comes to the technical orientations of urban planning documents and presentations. And yet, as I also state later, if you look around communities across America and then visit the planning departments, the lily-whiteness of these departments makes it clear that what is produced has nothing to do with having a social conscience that includes people of color. How, I ask, are you going to sit around a meeting table with all white people (and maybe one or two scared minorities who won't speak up, lest they lose their jobs) and map out a strategy that is going to help black people? The arrogance that such an approach embodies is the epitome of what "white privilege" is all about.

The discussion and analysis of the social aspects of urban renewal, from a perspective of a paper written by an urban planner in 1958, is what this paper is all about. It provides us with historical context and a foundation for better understanding what is taking place around us to this very day. Today's planners are an extension, and the "political protégés" of the earlier planners. These people want to talk about the central city as a slum and pay homage to "urban renewal" even when their very words contradict any "successes" that urban renewal was supposed to have bought about.

CRITICAL RACE THEORY

Those of us who know have a responsibility to act on what we know. In the case of urban planners, there are so few of us who are African-American and those who are may not be conscious or "black" in terms of their priorities. In fact, most planning departments around the nation have a token black representative who views black people and the black community with the same types of disdain-and-how-dare you as their white counterparts.

I am a critical race theorist, because we take that which is important to address and make it palatable for the public, turning it into a "story" of sorts. If we can personalize these important issues, this will hopefully motivate more people to take action.

Tate (1997) writes,

> Critical race theorists recognize that the way public problems are defined can influence how laws and policies area constructed and interpreted. One purpose of legal story telling by Bell and other critical race scholars is to engage the reader in democratic deliberation concerning the ironies and contradictions associated with laws constructed to appease White self-interest rather than address notions of equity.

According to Tate, borrowing from Derrick Bell (one of the founders of Critical Race Theory), the goal of critical race theory is NOT to "provide a social formula that would solve either all or an of the racist issues that beset the country" but to "review those issues in ALL their political and economic dimensions, and from that vantage point enable lawyers and lay people to determine where we might go from here" (p. 211). More importantly, *"The goal, for us … was not to guarantee an end to racism, but to work forcefully toward that end"* (p. 211).

This statement, in itself, makes total sense. I recall when Afrocentrism first burst upon the scene, and before that it was the concept and conviction of "black power." None of these were really solutions, but they were played off as being "the answer" to not only the question of black liberation but also bringing an end to racism. In Bell's statement, as quoted by Tate, I find an honesty about both the process and the end result. And it is refreshing: to work forcefully toward that end. And in the final analysis, knowing how the system functions, isn't that really all we can do?

The story of black people is the story of what America is about, stripped of all of its pomp and impious ceremony. That is why Critical Race Theory, if taught as a major educational theory (and not just a minority viewpoint or paradigm) can go a long way to getting people to begin LISTENING to what black folks have to say in everyday language. What is said about critical race theory in education applies, not only in the classroom, but in our analysis of the world around us:

> Critical race theory in education is defined as a framework or set of basic perspectives, methods, and pedagogy … that seeks to identify, analyze and transform those structural, cultural, and interpersonal aspects of education that maintain the marginal position and subordination of [African American and Latino] students. Critical Race Theory asks such questions as: What role do schools, school processes, and school structures play in the maintenance of racial, ethnic, and gender subordination? (Lynn, 1999: 608).

Aguirre (2000) provides a functional definition of critical race theory in the following excerpt:

> The most distinguishing feature of CRT writings is the use of stories or first-person accounts … [C]ritical race theory writings … are characterized by frequent use of the first person, storytelling, narrative, allegory, interdisciplinary treatment of law, and the unapologetic use of creativity … Critical race theorists use storytelling as a methodological tool for giving voice to marginalized persons and their communities. They tell stories that challenge the majority's stories in which it constructs for itself … a form of shared reality in which its own superior position is seen as natural … As a result, critical race theorists focus on giving voice to marginalized persons and communities because they are suppressed in the majority's stories (p. 3).

That is why throughout this paper you will see me referring to black people as "us" and others as "them." This brings us to the urban planner and the "social aspects" of what it takes to become a planner, especially as those planning models relate to, and are imposed on, black people. This has been a long-time trend and I've traced the mentality behind the formation of a number of programs (model cities, urban renewal, HOPE VI, etc.) and most of them are rooted in a negative framework: viewing black people as a "problem" that has to be fixed, repaired or mended. The same approach is therefore held when it comes to addressing the communities that "these people" (blacks) live in.

With this as our conceptual and analytic foundation (critical race theory), I now address the article on social aspects of urban renewal and use that article as a basis and bastion of analyzing the white approach to dealing with communities of color while at the same time attempting to make it appear as if race is somehow incidental and that they (whites) have the solution to the problems of communities of color. But first, a brief overview of "white privilege" and the role that it plays on planning departments, planning visions and planning programs all over the United States.

PLANNING AND "WHITE PRIVILEGE"

White privilege. They don't see it, but we do. Just by being white in a white-dominate society, many of them (I say MOST) get opportunities that people of color have to either work hard for or will never receive. This is a social fact. What is it? DeNeisha Manuel (1999) simply describes it as, *"a set of unearned invisible advantages held by white people simply because they are white."* Kendall Clark, in referring to white privilege as a social relation, defines it as, "a right, advantage, or immunity granted to or enjoyed by white persons beyond the common advantage of all others; an exemption in many particular cases from certain burdens or liabilities." He adds that it is also, "a privileged position; the possession of an advantage white persons enjoy over non-white persons" (Clark, 2003).

Take this mentality into a field as technical and potentially powerful as urban planning, and you have a recipe for white nationalism and black exclusion. This is what the history of urban planning has shown, despite its claims of having a concern about "social planning." But again, remember that *Plessy v. Ferguson* – the law that made racial segregation in public accommodations legal – was a matter of "social planning as well. But look who it benefited!

Peggy McIntosh publishes what black people knew all along, in an article called, "White Privilege: Unpacking the Invisible Knapsack." In part, she wrote,

> I think whites are carefully taught not to recognize white
> privilege, as males are taught not to recognize male privilege.
> So I have begun in an untutored way to ask what it is like to
> have white privilege. I come to see white privilege as an
> invisible package of unearned assets that I can count on
> cashing in each day, but about which I was "meant" to remain
> oblivious. White privilege is like an invisible weightless

knapsack of special provisions, maps, passports, codebooks, visas, clothes, tools and blank checks (McIntosh, 1988).

Continuing, McIntosh cogently contends,

> I see a pattern running through the matrix of white privilege, a pattern of assumptions which were passed on to me as a white person. There was one main piece of cultural turf; it was my own turf, and I was among those who could control the turf. My skin color was an asset for any move I was educated to want to make. I could think of myself as belonging in major ways, and of making social systems work for me. I could freely disparage, fear, neglect, or be oblivious to anything outside of the dominant cultural forms. Being of the main culture, I could also criticize it fairly freely (McIntosh, 1988).

I offer that along with being an urban planner, a deep-seated hatred of black people and the poor must be a part of the skill-set. I arrive at this conclusion based on what urban planning, in all of its forms, has produced. I am an historian and around this nation I see black people in ghettos and Latinos in the barrios. I see Native Americans on reservations. I don't consider this to be a quirk; it is a result of social planning with an emphasis on isolating and containing black people while at the same time, creating a "heaven on earth" for white residents.

While privilege is a norm, and that is why they do not feel guilty when they realize that their cities and towns have an "area for the negroes," a "black community" or a "ghetto slum." They have been able to convince themselves that "those people just want to be around their own," and they pass these myths down to their children. If urban planners wanted to address poverty, they would ask people who are affected by it. Instead, armed with a giant can of "denial," they approach it as an issue to be maintained, because the poorer a community is, the more Federal money the city qualifies for year after year after year.

If you look around communities across America and then visit the planning departments, the lily-whiteness of these departments makes it clear that what is produced has nothing to do with having a social conscience that includes people of color. As the saying goes, "what goes in is what comes out." How are you going to sit around a meeting table with all white people (and maybe one or two scared minorities who won't speak up, lest they lose their jobs) and map out a strategy that is going to help black people? The arrogance that such an approach embodies is the epitome of what "white privilege" is all about.

SOCIAL ASPECTS OF URBAN RENEWAL: A CRITIQUE

This article was written in 1958 and as such, there are going to be some issues that appear, in retrospect, to be naïve. But even in that, projections and predictions are made and they are rooted in the way that people of color – blacks – were treated and thought about during that time. This is an excellent way to show how race and the formation of black communities are, therefore, congruent.

The article begins:

> The more large-scale and comprehensive city planning becomes, the more it must be concerned with social problems. Twenty years ago the city planner was generally regarded as a visionary, as a man who planned dream cities' that probably would never — because of practical difficulties involved — become actuality. Ten years ago the city planner was recognized as a somewhat more practical person. He bad succeeded in setting up zoning ordinances and master plans for future land use. In the 1950s, however, the city planner bas become a man of action. Many of his ideas have become fertile; many of his plans have changed the face of the city and the lives of its citizens (Roemer, 1958).

There are certain assumptions that are made in the preceding paragraph that are matters of conjecture and opinion instead of fact. Let me point out a few of them.

According to Roemer, the larger the comprehensive planning is, the more "it must be concerned with" social problems. This is more of an ideal than it is an expression of the way things operate in the world of reality. These people plan based on what they know, and what they know is isolationism, rejection and segregation – when it comes to black people. Any "social problem" that exists, especially during the writing of this article, was always blamed on us: unemployment, low median housing value, low median income, teen pregnancy, single parent family hood, crime, drugs, and so on. This is scapegoating at its finest and black people have always been convenient scapegoats because we were too powerless to respond to criticisms and during that time, any response at all was almost tantamount to a death wish.

The reason why "city planners" were regarded as visionaries was due more to their education and impressive credentials than to any commitment they had to creating a city that would be inclusive. In fact, a city planner is no different than any other white man with a college degree: they see their background, knowledge base and skill set as nothing more than a way to extend their own belief systems. Therefore, if he's majored in business, his business principles include excluding black people; if he's majored in engineering, he wants to design things that are going to benefit his people; if he's majored in religion, then his religious teaches him that blacks are evil and whites are put here by God to "civilize" them.

The city planner designs cities so that those considered "problems" are separated from the majority. As Rothwell & Massey (2009) convincingly contend,

> In areas where the races are more integrated, for example, homeowners may be politically unable or less willing to impose exclusionary zoning laws. Conversely, if most Whites live in suburbs and most African-Americans live in central cities, then Whites may not only be able but quite eager to impose zoning restrictions to preserve that arrangement.

The segregated properties are usually located in the least desirable areas (based on surveys of and needs expressed by whites). That is why in many older cities you find black people near "the bottoms" (the body of water than tended to flood); near the industrial areas where the smog can be found; close to railroad tracks and the like. The city planner during those times was more concerned about high population density for the poor and black and in that way, we were compartmentalized in small apartments, "rooms" or one bedroom houses. The higher the population density in the "black area" (also known as the slums, the ghetto, the urban core and more recently, the war zone), the more land left to design leisure activities for whites.

What is "visionary" about perpetuating racism? Planning dreamscapes is easy to do when you have the backing of people that have money and you don't have to worry about any form of resistance or any lobbying or special interest groups. And that's the way it was in the 1950s: we were on our way, but still pretty much humble to a fault. And the urban planner was one of the people that took full advantage of it.

So when Roemer writes that ten years later, "the city planner was recognized as a somewhat more practical person. He bad succeeded in setting up zoning ordinances and master plans for future land use," how is this any different once the variable of "race" has been interjected into the equation? In my view, the reason why the status of the city planner "evolved" from visionary to more practical was because of his roles: more black people were coming into the city and as a result, more perceived "social problems" were on his plate. His "master plans" and "zoning ordinances" had to be framed in such a way as to exclude black people while making it appear as if there was no "selective discrimination," "redlining" or "steering" taking place.

Then came the 1950s and the planner "has become a man of action." A man of action in the 1950s meant responding to the new kind of "negro" that was migrating from the South to the North. The "action" was not physical, but ideological and structural. Since the article is written in the present tense, Roemer, speaking from 1958, explains that the ideas of the planner during that period, "have become fertile; many of his plans have changed the face of the city and the lives of its citizens.

The use of a term like "social responsibilities" is really a euphemism for "damage control" or, more appropriately, "negro containment." Planners think about what is in the best interests of those with the most money and status; in other words, other white folks. For instance, n their analysis, Cutler and Glaeser (1997) found evidence that decentralized White racism, as revealed in housing preferences, perpetuated contemporary segregation in U.S. metropolitan areas. In other words, segregated situations are where the white majority feel the most comfortable: blacks in the central city, white folks in the suburbs.

Roemer almost admits as much in the following excerpt:

> Consequently the city planner bas become increasingly aware of the social responsibilities inherent in his work. He knows that the land use decisions are helping to shape the human emotions and relationships of the future. Thus the planner, who set out with an awareness of economic, physical, and aesthetic needs, bas of necessity become deeply concerned, too, with social needs. There are, of course, many social factors to be considered in zoning decisions (Roemer, 1958).

If "social responsibility" was "inherent" in his work, *the planner would have been doing it all along; it would have been a part of his job description.* The fact is, social responsibility was created by the influx of the low-income whites as well as the blacks who came into the city – the city had to have a brand new "approach." But a racist is always going to look out for the best interests of the power elite first and foremost. So when Roemer writes that the planner, "knows that the land use decisions are helping to shape the human emotions and relationships of the future," he knows that this shaping is going to take place with major racial and class decisions as his guide.

That is why Roemer adds that, "the planner, who set out with an awareness of economic, physical, and aesthetic needs, has of necessity become deeply concerned, too, with social needs. Were his intentions honorable from the outset, that social needs element could have been incorporated along with his "economic" considerations. But those who created these cities (after stealing the land) wanted monuments and tributes to whiteness and white nationalism. That is why those from places across the sea have counterparts here in America with the name "new" in front of them: "New" York, "New" Amsterdam, "New" England and so on. The social needs of the many outweigh the social needs of the few, that is, when the needs of the few were even given any consideration at all.

And they did it through zoning and the manipulation of the housing stock. The zoning decisions that were made took into consideration a number of social factors. Throughout the twentieth century, affluent Whites have taken political actions to separate themselves spatially from perceived out-groups—first Southern and Eastern European immigrants, then African-Americans, and most recently Hispanics, but always the lower classes. Some experts see class exclusion as the primary motive for zoning. But Massey and others (Stelly, 1992; Stelly, 2002; Fogelson, 2005) point out obvious racist motivations in the history of U.S. housing policy. Over the years, as one set of discriminatory barriers was eliminated by civil rights legislation and court decisions, new barriers were erected, yielding what Rothwell and Massey (2009) refer to as a "moving target" of discriminatory mechanisms.

And it is through zoning codes, manipulation of the housing stock, bank redlining and steering, and covert forms of discrimination by landlords that served to maintain the segregated state of affairs. *In all this, the city planner stood by and did nothing about the social aspects of race relations – he simply catered to the needs of the majority by providing more structures, streets, sewers and accommodations that served to make segregation safe, secure and acceptable.*

Roemer continues:

> Large retail stores, machine shops, and other commercial enterprises that encroach on residential areas have a blighting effect first on property values, second on social values. Approximately 100,000 houses in the aging core of Detroit have been blighted because of unplanned, helter-skelter land uses. The people who live in this area have suffered, too. it is generally conceded. The planner, therefore, must lay out future residential sections so that they may remain economically and socially stable. Nonconforming land uses in older, deteriorating neighborhoods must be eliminated wherever possible (Roemer, 1958)

As an urban planner myself, I know that based on what I have studied, some of what was written above is not universally true or applicable.

For instance, Roemer claims that, "large retail stores, machine shops, and other commercial enterprises that encroach on residential areas have a blighting effect first on property values, second on social values." That is what mixed-zoning is for and that is why when a major business is coming into an area, they must first approach the city council and the city planning department and make a presentation to show what value a particular business will have on an area. If not that, then they must go to the state legislature and request what is called a "variance," that is, an exception to the existing zoning for that area to enable the business to enter a residential area.

So yes, businesses to impact on a residential area – in a positive way for the most part. They provide jobs and they generate other forms of economic development. Look at the strategy that Wal-Mart uses. Even when they seek to encroach on areas where they are not liked, they appear before the city council with two things: plans and promises. They say they'll create jobs and that the store they build will complement the surrounding area. The community turns out to oppose it because it will crush the smaller businesses and the mom and pop stores. Wal-Mart then meets behind closed doors with the decision makers, greases a few palms (which they have been caught doing on several occasions), gets the approval they need and they start building.

Economic development-related arguments are the arguments that are used when these businesses seek to bid on a piece of land and construct that business. In many cases the city will recruit such businesses and offer them tax breaks and other incentives to move wherever they want. Machine shops are another story, and they usually have to go where the land is cheap, which is why the oily, greasy, dirty buildings and surrounding dirt that these shops are located on are usually found in the black community or the Latino area of town.

The "blighting effect" has since been addressed by these planners, who have now turned a "blight designation" into big business. Through abusing what is called the "blight designation" and applying it to any part of the city that they wish – even well-to-do areas – these planners can then bring in developers and use Tax Incremental Financing (TIFs) as incentives to build, build and build. They can ignore the black community, which has all the blight that anyone could need, and reserve the designations for those areas where they (the city power structure and investors) can make the most money. Planning and its "social responsibilities" have changed, alright: for the worse.

And Roemer outlines the method of operation in this statement that, "The planner, therefore, must lay out future residential sections so that they may remain economically and socially stable. Nonconforming land uses in older, deteriorating neighborhoods must be eliminated wherever possible." Take note of a prospective double standard: the "future residential section" gets the benefit of the doubt even though it is still in an undeveloped state! Even while incomplete, this is an area whose future is taken into consideration and as they are laid out, positive approaches toward development are taken into consideration.

Now look at the wording used to describe the older areas of the city – where black people reside. If the land uses in the older sections exist, it is because of these planners! The residents didn't alter or change the zoning in the area! The planner thinks "race first" whether he admits it or not; that which he produces, along with his colleagues, establishes this to be a fact. Put more subtly by way of Roemer,

> The planner recognizes today that there are social ramifications in every move be makes. Planning for commercial and industrial land uses goes deep into the heart of a community. The planning affects economic health, and economic health or illness sets off a social chain reaction (Roemer, 1958).

Why do only commercial and industrial planning ventures "go deep into the heart of a community"? What about residential planning? It is in this area where the houses that those employees live their lives, is it not? The social ramifications come into play when planners give priority to commercial ventures and to residential ventures only when those residences are located on the urban fringe or the suburbs. The amount of discretion that these people have, and their ability to cover it up with technical language inclusive of zoning codes, land use utilization lingo, and general bullshit, is the key to the segregation that is the end result of these so-called "socially conscious" planning experts.

> Equally important is the problem of relocating families and individuals displaced by civic improvements. Here there are both economic and interracial factors to be weighed. Most families live in a given area because of a complex of economic and social constraints. These families are not entirely free to move elsewhere. Planners must make certain, therefore, that suitable housing in a suitable environment is available to each displaced family (Roemer, 1958).

When families are mentioned, what is it about? It's about relocating them. Roemer writes about "individuals displaced by civic improvements" as if it is no big deal. You are talking about taking people out of their homes for a "public good" that may or may not even include them. Even Roemer has to admit that in such a case, "both economic and interracial factors" have to be weighed. And why not? The areas being pillaged and the people who are being relocated and displaced are, most of the time, people of color!

The proof is in his own statement that, "These families are not entirely free to move elsewhere." And why is that? First of all, it's because of their race, especially during the time period that Roemer's article is discussing. Today it's about race and finances: that is why affordable housing is being placed on the urban fringe to entice and induce the poor to "move out of the ghetto" so that whites can come back into the area with the development money that has been allocated because of the poverty of that area, and begin re-designing that area – and their lives.

To make his case, Roemer uses the city of Detroit:

> We believe that Detroit offers an interesting and valuable case study for the observation of processes of social changes set in motion by national housing policies, particularly the program set forth in the Housing Acts of 1949 and 1954 and now referred to as the Urban Renewal Program. The Housing Act of 1949 for the first time offered federal assistance to local governments for acquisition and clearance or land which was to be resold for private rebuilding. Under the formula established in this act the federal government repays the city of Detroit two-thirds of the net cost of the acquisition, clearance, **and** preparation for resale (emphasis original) (Roemer, 1958)

An "interesting and valuable case study?" Roemer is either misinformed or intentionally lying. A number of urban historians will tell you that during the 1950s – the period that Roemer is writing about, Detroit faced incredibly trying times, to put it mildly. Kenneth Stahl, author of *The Great Rebellion: A Socio-economic Analysis of the 1967 Detroit Riot,* had this to say about the Motor City:

> While many may feel that the 1960s were the pivotal decade in Detroit, the 1950s *provided many secondary causes which helped grease the skids of anger and give it a final push towards rebellion.* The three-headed monster of *urban renewal, interstates* and economic recession vastly altered the landscape of Detroit in the 1950s and would loom large as a socio-economic minefield that would cause the city to blow up in 1967 (Stahl, 2009).

This is evidence that the planners, a part of the city administration, played major roles in the decline of Detroit. An article that appeared earlier this year (2012) said that Detroit's population had declined some 250,000 in the past several years:

> Finally, these Ohio demographics of industrial Democratic areas losing voters, while suburban areas are gaining GOP voters are not unique to Ohio. They are indicative of the entire Midwest. One only needs to look at the tremendous loss of population in Detroit. The city has lost 250,000 residents just from 2000-2010. It is now smaller than Columbus (Hartline, 2012).

People are leaving. You see the word "interstate" and you should know that the land that was cleared for those freeways came through the heart of the black community, just as it does in most cities. You see the words urban renewal, and since the introduction of that program a number of leaders from that time said that urban renewal really meant "negro removal."

Detroit? Not everybody is sold on Roehmer's decision to use that city has a "case study." Check out the following:

> Urban renewal, a term often associated with revitalization of decaying neighborhoods, was employed on a massive scale in Detroit during the 1950s and left a mark of still dubious distinction. Interstates carved up the city in the name of progress but its then unforeseen after effects would linger on like a ghostly apparition. Finally there was the Eisenhower recession of the late 1950s which shuttered many a Detroit factory, giving additional impetus to those seeking to bolt to the fledgling suburbs or leave the state altogether (Stahl, 2009).

The writer says that urban renewal in Detroit "left a mark of still dubious distinction." Again, this is most disingenuous. Let's look at the trail of problems that urban renewal's failure created: freeways relocating residents, housing being torn down leaving huge lots that attracted vermin, empty houses that even to this day are being used for drug sales, and when you add all these up, you come up with collective frustration from the residents who, in 1967, decided to riot and make a statement. The riot was instigated by a police bust gone bad at a club called "The Blind Pig," but the people knew what they were going to do to make a statement against the way their community had been raped. And the fact is that the riot – which Roemer could not have anticipated, but should have – was so intense that the city never really fully recovered.

Exodus to the suburbs by white folks meant that, as is the case, the city services would follow. That left black people abandoned and this paved the way for the riot that would take place 20 years later. That means that for twenty years, this city that the writer decided to "highlight" went through hell. So the question is: where was the social conscience, the social concern and commitment, *then?*

The process of setting in motion the rape of Detroit is described in urban planning terms in the following paragraph:

> The Housing Act of 1954 extended the federal assistance to include neighborhood conservation and rehabilitation programs as well as complete clearance and rebuilding. Under the new title of Urban Renewal, the federal government offers two-thirds federal

> aid for public improvements in non-clearance areas as it bad
> offered previously for clearance programs. Because Detroit bad
> carried on an extensive city planning program through the decade
> of the 194O's, it was uniquely prepared to assist in showing the
> kinds of housing need which exist in this city and to participate in
> the formulative phases of the programs (Roemer, 1958)

The federal government was the source of the funding. That means that someone at the city level in Detroit submitted a proposal and requested funding. In that proposal these planners promised they were going to improve the lives of the people and in doing so, make sure that they were "socially" responsible for what took place. These are similar to the proposals that are submitted today as part of the Community Development Block Grant (CDBG) program. And as was the case in the 1950s, there was apparently very little oversight, and an undeserved belief that "the city planners said it so it must be right."

Urban renewal was about "clearance," and that meant tearing down old houses (many of them could have been saved) and vacant lots. It was known as "slum clearance," and the specifics were just as outlandish as the following excerpt makes clear:

> Following World War II, and continuing into the early 1970s,
> "urban renewal" referred primarily to public efforts to
> revitalize aging and decaying inner cities, although some
> suburban communities undertook such projects as well.
> Including massive demolition, slum clearance, and
> rehabilitation, urban renewal proceeded initially from local
> and state legislation, which in Illinois included the
> Neighborhood Redevelopment Corporation Act of 1941
> (amended in 1953), the Blighted Areas Redevelopment Act
> of 1947, the Relocation Act of 1947, and the Urban
> Community Conservation Act of 1953. The earliest emphasis
> was placed on slum clearance or "redevelopment," which
> was followed by a focused effort to conserve threatened but
> not yet deteriorated neighborhoods (Hirsch, 2005).

Few people apparently ever asked who was responsible for the "decay" that was taking place "in the cities" in the first place? When white immigrants came in they apparently trashed the housing and basically created the slums. When black people began heading north, the white folks moved away and left the houses to us. It was when we came north and settled into these areas that the concern about "renewal" and "redevelopment" started getting bandied about.

I believe that this was an "experiment." Some white man got an idea to "clean up the negro slums." That is what they were calling them then, make no mistake about it. They weren't just slums just like North Omaha is not just a "community" – it's a black community. So you have white people sitting around a table deciding what to do about "the negro slums." And this is what they came up with: massive demolition, slum clearance, rehabilitation. Where is the construction? Rehabbing a house means to work on the structure that already exists. Where is the "renewal"? What we see is destruction and Band-Aid approaches. The only people who benefited from urban renewal were the developers and the coffers of the cities that were given that free money.

Keeping in mind that much of this was taking place behind the backs of the people who lived in these "slums," some of the money was used to provide mega-structures for whites who didn't even live in that area. As Roemer writes,

> Detroit, for example, had started condemnation of the Gratiot Redevelopment Site in 1947, two years before there was a federal assistance program for such projects as authorized in 1949. Similarly, Detroit appointed a Neighborhood Conservation and Improved Housing Committee in 1953. A year in advance of federal assistance for that phase of the program (Roemer, 1958)

Even without the money Detroit was in the process of dealing with "neighborhoods" and "improved housing." But these are euphemisms once again, essentially neighborhood conservation results in the same thing as urban renewal would: tearing it up, getting rid of the residents and "conserving the area" so that whites could return and be closer to the jobs downtown. The concept of "improved housing" more than likely used the same demolition approach that urban renewal used. They were working in this area and along came a grant that would assist them, and the city of Detroit, gradually growing blacker and blacker, became more of a "social experiment" than anything else.

The "planning" continues:

> In the preparation of its Master Plan. Detroit bas developed a land use plan showing areas best suited to industry, commercial use, and of course living areas, and the thoroughfares and expressways needed to interconnect these other activities. The living areas consist of 155 elementary school districts to which we have perhaps arbitrarily attached the designation neighborhoods, and 16 senior high school districts designated in our Master Plan as communities." (Roemer, 1958)

The "development of the land use plan" is what planners do and again, it's done on location and when it comes to land use, location and race become inextricably bound. They even color code their maps, and it wouldn't surprise me if the dark colors represent the areas where low-income and black people reside. Of course, they can't say that so planners have developed little buzz words that they use to keep from being charged with stratification or racism. They use terms like "blighted area," "at-risk residents" or "urban core" to identify the areas that lay people recognize as the ghetto or *el barrio*. This has been going on for a long time and the people in the planning department are a key to maintaining racial and residential segregation because they are the ones who set it up, they maintain it and then when it comes to raising free money from the government, they lie about it and promise to "clean things up." But it never gets done.

The fix was in. It has always been about the land and the control of that land. Mark Twain once said, "Buy land. They're not making it anymore." Someone has been listening because all over the nation, white people are buying up land in black communities. You've seen the signs in the major cities: "we buy old homes." You've seen the vacant lots being bought up by outside interests. When it was reported in 1978 that there were some 2,500 usable vacant lots in North Omaha, white boys from Nevada came into the area and swooped on them. In Dallas, the lots are apparent as are the dilapidated homes. When I asked City Councilwoman Carolyn Davis why the houses weren't being renovated, she said that "developers are holding on to them." (By the way, city councilpersons, along with developers, are in on the fix along with the planners)

In the case of Detroit, Roemer wrote in 1958 that,

> At the present time there are about 550,000 dwelling units in Detroit; 100,- 000 in structures built at least fifty years ago, and 300,000 built during World War 1 and the 192O's. A few of the older homes are still maintained in good condition, but most of them are now worn out and ready to be torn down. It is estimated that eight thousand acres of the city s residential areas need to be cleared and completely rebuilt. This amounts to *7.7* per cent of all dwelling units in the city (Roemer, 1958)

Notice how when it comes to citing total numbers of housing and dwelling units, there are raw numbers; but when it comes down to how many will be torn down, you run into vague generalities like, "a few of the older homes," "most of them are worn out." Then when it comes down to the all-powerful land question, again we go back to raw numbers with the number of acres and the percentage of dwelling units. This is by design: to keep the number to be destroyed "open" because they will employ discretion when it comes to that total number. They will tear down housing just to be tearing it down, salvageable or not. That is what happened in Omaha, Nebraska to the point where the planning director, Charlie

Hill, said many years later, "maybe we were too quick to tear down all that housing."

These planners and developers work together to create a funnel situation, directing the poor and minority to certain parts of the city through steering and redlining. Then, once they congregate in an area through segregation, those in power try to make it appear as if they didn't know what was going on. Take, for example, the following statements:

> Not all such areas can, however, be considered as suitable for residential rebuilding. Some have been blighted by their proximity to heavy industry, railroads, and other factors which make them unsuitable as residential areas. Thus Detroit's program proposes that 4,300 acres be rebuilt as residential neighborhoods and 3,000 acres as industrial districts, and that other dilapidated areas be used for recreational and commercial purposes. The process of clearing an area and rebuilding it in accordance with an over-all plan, an integral part of the Master Plan, is called Redevelopment (Roemer, 1958).

If the process is about "redevelopment" in the late 1950s, then explain why destruction continues to be the order of the day in the 21st century. In fact, in 2011, GQ magazine provided a brief history of the "redevelopment" that had taken place:

> In 1950, with nearly 2 million people living within its boundaries, Detroit was the fifth-largest city in America. Over a forty-year period, the auto industry had boomed in a way that changed the country, and Detroit's population more than sextupled. *But starting in the '50s, the city fell into decline. Factories closed. Jobs vanished.* In the wake of the 1967 riots, race relations *collapsed and the city became increasingly segregated.* By 1980 the population had dwindled to 1.2 million (Kahn, 2011 – emphasis added).

As is the case with Omaha, "the riots" get the blame for the decline of the central city. Few people every describe the racist conditions that led to the formation of the ghetto in the first place, the discriminatory maltreatment that led to the frustration that was inevitably vented during those riots (three riots in Omaha, and the major one in 1967 in Detroit).

In the preceding paragraph note that the beginning is the fifties – the same period that Roemer is describing as a period of "social planning." This was the beginning, and the product was the culmination of how white folks, in general, felt about the black community, in general. And this is the way it was in most major metropolitan areas.

Here is the excuse that the planners – who aided and abetted in the crimes against the black community of Detroit and elsewhere – use to explain the rape of these areas:

> With far fewer Detroiters to shelter, many of the city's houses were orphaned, threatening the existence and safety of everything around them. Blight metastasized across town, leaving much of the housing stock better suited for crackheads and squatters than for legitimate investors, possible gentrifiers, or working-class families with any remaining desire to stay. Today only 700,000 souls call Detroit home, and nearly a fourth of the city's houses—a number approaching 72,000 units—are empty (Kahn, 2011).

Look how what happened is described: the city's houses were "orphaned" because there were "fewer Detroiters to shelter." What it should say is, *"because of the greed of city planners, the segregation of the community got so out of control that white people, fearing a black backlash, abandoned the central city. As a result, city services followed them leading to further abandonment of the area of the city that needed help the most. This state of affairs, set in motion by city planners, led to the decimation of the city of Detroit."* This would be a lot closer to the truth than the drivel that appears in the preceding excerpt.

The blight didn't "metastasize across town" on its own. The source of the cancerous blight originated with the neglect of city planners. They saw it growing and did little or nothing. Then, instead of performing surgery that would isolate the blight and then eliminate it, they decided to perform "experimental surgery" at the expense of those who had the cancer! Their experiment failed, the cancer spread throughout the entire "body" of the city, and now, as outlined earlier, the onetime mega-city of Detroit is now about the size of the city of Columbus, Ohio.

Even in trying to transfer the blame, the words of city planners and their apologists like Roemer still clearly show incorrect perceptions of the black community and an almost childlike understanding of the nature and extent of the issues of urban life. For instance, Roemer writes,

> Over half of the city's dwellings may be called middle-aged. These homes, built during and after World War I but before the depression, form a circle of fifty-five neighborhoods within the city just beyond the inner core of dilapidation. Some of the middle-aged part of the city now begins to look a little neglected and run down. These homes today are unattractive to many families who are looking for modern city living. They are built generally on narrow lots. Because the neighborhoods did not nave the protection

of a zoning ordinance, scattered stores and factories became
intermingled with homes (Roemer, 1958)

When people who are supposed to be experts begin talking and writing about "maybe," "perhaps" and "almost" – terms like that – then you know they are lying or trying to present an image that is distorted or biased. Either the dwellings are middle-aged or not, and if they know that, then they should not only have the number that are middle-aged, but they should have the areas where the middle-aged housing is located.

The fact of the matter is, most of the homes in the United States were built before 1950, and they are in great shape. There was little, if any, cutting of corners, using half-assed materials and inferior supplies the way there is now. Those old homes were built to last. The planners know that, which is why they cannot be definite about the state of that housing. Statements like, *Some of the middle-aged part of the city now begins to look a little neglected and run down. These homes today are unattractive to many families who are looking for modern city living. They are built generally on narrow lots.*" How many is "some"? Is it most, a large number, or a few? What is "beginning to look a little neglected and run down?" Is there a standard for "looking" a certain way? In order for a house to be defined as neglected or run down, shouldn't there be some kind of check list, or do they just do drive-byes and say, "that one's no good"?

Most people just don't give a damn and they don't read between the lines of what these planners say or write. And the planners know that and don't expect to be challenged on such vague and inane statements. So when Roemer writes that, "These homes today are unattractive to many families who are looking for modern city living. They are built generally on narrow lots," what does that mean? Does the size of the lot have an impact on house quality? Who are these families that the homes look "unattractive" to and if so, what is their criteria? What is "modern city living" as it relates to attractiveness and sellability? None of these issues are addressed because the planners, the so-called experts, don't have the answers themselves. And what answers they are able to glean point the finger directly at their departments, their ideas, their blueprints and their master plans.

What is the fault of planners is then left up to the opinion of people who read these kinds of articles, but as the following passage shows, the onus should be placed squarely on the backs of the city planning department and the real estate developers:

As the city grew, whole neighborhoods were built up solidly
without playgrounds, parks, or other open areas for the recreational
needs of the people living in them. The neighborhoods now lie
across the flow of traffic between downtown Detroit and the newer

> suburbs. As a consequence, many former Detroiters in search of
> better homes and neighborhoods have moved far out into the
> suburbs (Roemer, 1958)

Disrespect and hatred for a current crop of people extends on to the children of those people. This explains why communities would be built without playgrounds or recreational outlets. First, there was the hatred of the white ethnics who came in. Then when they left, another group in a long line of ethnic succession came in. At no time did those in power respect the rights of children to be able to play and have fun. Those in power simply did not care, but they knew that children and others who lack recreational outlets will turn to "deviant" forms of activity to entertain themselves.

And that is how you get the desired results: people of color trapped in the urban core and white people heading to suburbia where the wide open spaces, larger houses, wider driveways, wider streets, greenery and colorful landscapes, await them.

Recall earlier when I wrote about how the housing stock that was built before the 1950s was built by people who truly cared about the condition of the housing? It appears that Roemer also understands this to be the case:

> However, since most of the houses were built under a strong
> building code they are solid, substantial buildings and can be
> modernized to be made as attractive as many newer homes. These
> middle-aged neighborhoods also have very great advantages of
> having schools, churches … and community buildings already
> built, and being convenient to downtown, to the Cultural Center,
> and to places of employment. Many people prefer the convenience
> and savings in travel time of living near the heart of the city. To
> restore and modernize these fifty-five middle- aged neighborhoods
> for modern city living is the goal of the Neighborhood
> Conservation Program (Roemer, 1958).

Earlier I established that there was no stated criteria on what constituted a house that was neglected or one that was designated to be torn down. Now here we see a case where older housing is given credit for being solid. This means that even the ones that reached the stage of being dilapidated or "old" still had prospects: as long as the foundations were good, these houses could have been upgraded and renovated. How many of these wonderful old homes bit the dust and were victimized by the wrecking ball before people like Roemer and other urban planners finally realized that many of these houses were salvageable?

This is all about convenience for white people. Just as is the case in Milwaukee and Omaha where the bulk of jobs are downtown, white folks begin to tire of long commute times. They want the expediency of getting to work fast and getting back home fast. That means relocating to the central city once the "negroes" have been relocated and displaced. Look at what Roemer writes above as he talks about these homes "being convenient to downtown … and to places of employment." He adds that, "Many people prefer the convenience and savings in travel time of living near the heart of the city."

Some cities also add the advantage of the central city being near some type of waterfront: a river, a large lake and so on. That is the case in Omaha (Missouri River), Milwaukee (Lake Michigan) and across Dallas which has so many rivers and lakes. What happens is that developers come in with plans to align those water fronts with condominiums priced beyond what middle-income people can afford. So what you have is a "community of interest" surrounding these waterfronts and creating (gated) communities to keep the "riff-raff" out.

In talking of relocation, which is what all this urban renewal stuff is about, Roemer makes a prediction that is accurate, but still falls way short:

> The acute social problem resulting from Urban Renewal and other
> civic improvement programs is that of relocating displaced
> families, small businesses, and industrial firms.
> The scope of Detroit's relocation is stupendous. It would be a
> conservative prediction, I think, to say that within the next twenty
> years some 25,000 families will be displaced by civic projects.
> Some of these, of course, would be rehoused in redevelopment
> areas when completed (Roemer, 1958)

Before you begin referring to these kinds of urban plans as "civic improvement programs" you have to take into consideration the effect, the impact and the production value of such programs. Just because it came into existence and got funding doesn't mean it was an "improvement" program. The main question is: based on the implementation of this program, was Detroit "improved"? The answer is "no." Was North Omaha improved as a result of urban renewal money? The answer is "no." Was Milwaukee improved as a result of federal funding for urban renewal? No. So that's three cities right there. Once is an accident, twice is a coincidence and three times is a trend. Therefore we can establish that, by design, these urban renewal projects achieved their goal: to destroy, disrupt and divide black communities, relocate black residents, and pave the way for the "return" of whites who can then be close to their jobs, close to the riverfront and downtown leisure, and in some cases, as is the case with Omaha, Nebraska, be closer to the major airport.

Roemer writes that it would be a conservative prediction to say that in 20 years (meaning 1978 since he wrote this article in 1958) that "some 25,000 families will be displaced by civic projects." He was way off. Detroit gradually deteriorated and now ten times that number has left the city since 2000.

Beware of words like "redevelopment" in the titles of organizations that claim to be about helping the neighborhoods, the community or some part of the community that may not be as politically sophisticated as other sections. It is a double entendre: redevelopment means that at one time, it was developed and now it is going to be developed again. This is one definition. In my view it means that the type of development that is taking place in a certain area of the city does not meet the standards, goals or vision of the people at City Hall. Therefore, it must be "redeveloped" in the image and interests of those who, for the most part, do not live in that part of the city.

Roemer asserts:

> The Citizens' Redevelopment Corporation, a nonprofit corporation
> made up of civic leaders in a variety of fields, was set up by the
> city to negotiate redevelopment of the area. Mr. Walter Reuther, as
> spokesman for the corporation, outlined the objectives as follows:
> 1. The neighborhood should be so designed that it would appeal to
> professional and clerical workers in the central business area as
> good city living close to their work (Roemer, 1958)

Walter Reuther was a white man who worked to improve the status of the unions and as a result of that, committed himself to smoothing over any issues of racism that might exist. Let's look at these objectives and analyze them within the context in which they were proposed and then see if they translate into today's current venue of urban planning.

The first objective is about proximity to downtown and the jobs therein. Since I would venture that most blacks worked in the auto industry, blue collar jobs and the like, this message is for the white folks who want to return to the area to cut down on commute time to and from work.

The second objective offers that,

> 2. The neighborhood should contain a variety of dwelling types
> and sizes to appeal to a range of income groups — there should be
> high buildings and low buildings, large units and small units, low
> rents and high rents (Roemer, 1958)

This is more of an ideal than it is a sane objective to be actualized. The size of buildings is based on the function of those buildings, and it is not a wise idea to mix residential types: apartment buildings and single-family units on the same street can present problems. How? On one side of the street you have renters and on the other side you have people who own their homes. Reliable studies clearly show that renters, because they have no vested interest in their properties, are usually less committed to the neighborhood than those who are buying their homes.

The third objective from the 1950s recommends that,

> 3. Public housing and private housing should be integrated through the neighborhood.

This is not only idealistic, but outright foolish. It is an indicator that Reuther was more of an optimist than the other members of his racial group. This is a call for class integration and housing approaches don't allow for this. The idea of mixing public and private housing is almost as abominable to the elites in power as the mixing of the races. If you mix the housing, you mix the people and if you mix the people, that screws up the demographic statistics that are needed to qualify the area as "low income," "at-risk" or some other label that will, in turn, generate federal money!

The fourth objective is that (4). There should be biracial occupancy. See objective three.

Reuther and his friends close out by stating that, "The likelihood of attaining all these objectives is a good question for the sociologist to answer." Among other things, I am a sociologist – a former doctoral students and instructor of the subject. But it doesn't take a sociologist to understand what is taking place in Detroit today because it is rooted in the foundation that was set during the days of Walter Reuther and the Detroit planning department. Malcolm X said it best: "Of all our studies, history is best qualified to reward our research."

Only when the plans have been formed, the objectives put together, the goals established and the vision agreed upon by the elites do the masses get the opportunity to become involved. They get to respond to what has been done or rubber stamp the lies that these "experts" tell them. That is why many years later, they find that the only thing that they contributed to the planning was their physical presence.

Here is how the urban planner would describe such a relationship:

> Finally, there are a number of social problems inherent in Detroit's Neighborhood Conservation Program, which will affect one-third of the city and nearly 300,000 homes. Residents of the fifty-five neighborhoods concerned must give active support to the program if it is to be successful. They must organize as block and neighborhood conference groups; they must work together on minor improvement projects; they must take pride in the appearance of their homes and make necessary repairs and

renovation. Most of these neighborhoods are biracial (Roemer, 1958)

Now, with the framework and foundation established, all of a sudden this "Neighborhood Conservation Program" – named and established by the power elite of the city – is the responsibility of the grass roots masses. It becomes their responsibility to organize conference groups, work together on projects, fix up their homes, make repairs and renovations.

Here is the problem I have: why is it always the poor and minority who are expected to volunteer? Why do those who have least continue to be told that they must "get involved" in a program or project without any compensation? Granted, it is their community that they are living in, but the program that revolves around that community was created by PAID individuals who used taxpayer dollars and free grant money! As more people began to understand how unfair this was, and began to tire of being treated like children by being told by outsiders that they "must" do this and "must" do that, the program began to understandably, deteriorate.

More objectives are established, and these are aimed at the planner:

> In conservation areas the planner in his work must set his sights toward the achievement of the following objectives: 1. Provide for adequate playgrounds and recreational areas, including expansion of existing ones if necessary (Roemer, 1958)

This is a good suggestion, but again it hails back to the fact that these planners knew that such playgrounds and recreational areas were needed long ago. Why were they not included?

The second objective calls that the planners, *"Provide for adequate school facilities of acceptable standards."* My research of urban planning as it relates to schools means that what is proposed here as an objective is not realistic.

To begin with, a proposal for a new school goes before a Planning Commission of some type. The meeting is usually inclusive of public input. Prior to that the money for the schools is usually raised through a bond proposal that is placed on a ballot. Once that is done and the planning meeting takes place, the Board puts out bids for an architect, and provide that architect with the square footage of the school, the location, and so on.

This should be beyond the purview of planners and, for the most part, it is. They know nothing of school specifications and can only deal with the zoning issues, the size of the lot and related land issues.

The third objective for planners is to, "revise the street pattern to discourage through traffic." This is an area that should include citizen input and, for the most part, is one that should also include a consideration of crosswalks. Reliable studies have shown that,

> All age and gender groups agreed that crosswalks, speed bumps, better timing of traffic lights, and more stop signs would increase pedestrian safety in the Black community. In addition, most groups agreed that pedestrians' knowledge regarding pedestrian safety laws (e.g., jaywalking) is lacking. The groups also agreed that pedestrians are more inclined to put themselves at risk, as opposed to drivers putting them at risk (National Highway Traffic Safety Administration, 2003)

This is one area that the community's residents should be spearheading. Because of the low regard for residents of the black community, planning departments, aided and abetted by the local Department of Public Works, intentionally allow crosswalk stripes to fade, stop signs to get knocked down and not replaced, sidewalks to deteriorate, and a host of other pedestrian-related violations. It is only when someone is hurt, a lawsuit against the city is threatened or worse, that they then come into the area with their trucks and make a visible presence to dupe the residents into thinking that they "care."

The fourth objective for the planner is to, "eliminate undesirable, nonconforming structures." This is where a specific example of what they are talking about would be appropriate. Otherwise, as far as I'm concerned, there are statues of white men fighting wars, carrying swords and standing around looking stupid in almost every community in this country. In my view these are "non-conforming structures" because while those soldiers and "heroes" were fighting for this nation's freedom, their people were holding us in various states of bondage and servitude.

The fifth objective suggests that planners, "Eliminate dilapidated dwellings." Well based on what I've provided us with in this "counter-document," it is clear that this is one area that city planners not only have a great deal of experience at doing, but seem to actually love the idea. They love it so much that, by their own admission, they've torn down structure that could have probably been saved! A better objective would be to form some kind of "building evaluation committee" made up of planners and local residents to tour, inspect and then discuss which buildings/houses/structures could and should be saved and which ones should be torn down.

Objective six to planners suggests that they, "Encourage owners to improve and properly maintain property structures." This should be a matter of law and, since the 1950s, it is a matter of law in most cities. If you own a house you are obligated to maintain it or see to it that those renting from you are in charge of maintaining it. In today's world, there are housing associations that will inspect the property to see that fences are within code and the lawn is mode. So in this area of maintaining property structures by these absentee landlords in most cases, one might argue that a modicum of progress has been made.

With the six objectives out of the way, one can tell that the Roemer article was written at a time when it was believed that urban renewal programs would have a long life – which they did not. Every adaptation or modification of the program, including name changes, always ended with black and poor people getting short shrift while developers made millions and city planning departments continued to isolate, neglect, manipulate and exploit (based on whatever the situation called for) the low-income communities in their cities.

Roemer's conclusion appears below:

> As the Urban Renewal Program matures and gains experience, much of the policy must be reformulated. Social economists on the staff of the City Plan Commission have been laying the organizational groundwork of the Neighborhood Conservation Program for three years, yet each stage of progress brings new social problems. Other projects, too, will make new and unforeseen demands. Our objective is to plan not only the city beautiful, but the city economically and socially healthful (Roemer, 1958).

Unless he is talking about "trial and error," the first sentence is a sophistic one. It should read, "in order for the Urban Renewal program to mature and gain experience, much of the policy must be reformulated." You don't accept the fact that it is immature and lacking in experience and then continue on, unabated. But that is the attitude that these planners have when it comes to black communities; they feel that if they make a mistake, so what? Who is going to care? What are they (black people) going to do?

Then come predictions that are rooted in nothing more than wishful thinking, where Roemer writes, "other projects, too, will make new and unforeseen demands. Our objective is to plan not only the city beautiful, but the city economically and socially healthful."

Notice that when we move beyond the neighborhood, beyond the community and start talking about "the city," all of a sudden these incredibly descriptive ideals begin to blossom: "city beautiful," "city economically and socially healthful." This goes beyond the scope of what the article was about, which was essentially urban renewal, and urban renewal is relegated to a particular area of the city, the area that needs the most help. Urban renewal is about slum clearance. So then where does he get off talking about the "city beautiful"? At no other time are blacks considered a part of the city – unless you're talking about tax time.

CONCLUSION

In this paper I hope to have made it clear, through reasoning and careful analysis, that urban planners are largely responsible for the segregated state of affairs that permeates the American landscape. I hope to show that behind the actions of the urban planner is the same attitude that exists on the part of others who have power and who have a "bone to pick," real or imagined, with black people and the communities that we are relegated to. I have critiqued and commented those attitudes which shape the thinking behind the types of articles that served as the basis for policy which, in turn, led to the thinking of many of today's city and neighborhood planners.

This paper, utilizing critical race theory, offered up explanations of planning as well as "white privilege." As I wrote earlier, if you look around communities across America and then visit the planning departments, the lily-whiteness of these departments makes it clear that what is produced has nothing to do with having a social conscience that includes people of color. How, I ask, are you going to sit around a meeting table with all white people (and maybe one or two scared minorities who won't speak up, lest they lose their jobs) and map out a strategy that is going to help black people? The arrogance that such an approach embodies is the epitome of what "white privilege" is all about.

This paper is aimed at arming the powerless with information so that they will no longer be hoodwinked and bamboozled by those in power.

REFERENCES

Bell, D. (1970, Spring). Quo warranto? -- Notes on the governance of universities in the 1970s. *The Public Interest*, 19.

Bell, D. (1994). *Confronting authority: Reflections of an ardent proteste*r. Boston, Mass.: Beacon Books.

Cutler, D., and E. L. Glaeser. (1999). Are ghettos good or bad? *Quarterly Journal of Economic Research*.

Cutler, D, E. L. Glaeser, and J. Vigdor. (1999). The rise and decline of the American ghetto. *Journal of Political Economy*.

Fogelon, R. M. (2005). *Bourgeois nightmares: Suburbia 1870–1930*. New Haven, Connecticut: Yale University Press.

Hartline, D. (2012, October 7). The data and demographics that detail why Romney will defeat Obama in Ohio. *Free Republic*. Retrieved from www.freerepublic.com/focus/f-gop/2941662/posts.

Hirsch, A.R. (2005). Urban renewal. Encyclopedia of Chicago. Retrieved from www.encyclopedia.chicagohistory.org/pages/1295.html

Kahn, H. (2011, May). Destroying Detroit (In order to save it). *GQ*.

Ladson-Billings, G.J. (1999). Preparing teachers for diverse student populations: A critical race theory perspective. *Review of Research in Education*, 24.

Ladson-Billings, G.J. (2000, May/June). Fighting for our lives: Preparing teachers to teach African students. *Journal of Teacher Education*, 51.

Ladson-Billings, G.J. (1996, Autumn). 'Your blues ain't like mine': Keeping issues of race and racism on the multicultural agenda. *Theory into Practice*, 35.

Ladson-Billings, G.J. (1995, Fall). Toward a critical race theory of education. *Teachers College Record*, 97.

Ladson-Billings, G.J. (1990). Blurring the borders: Voices of African liberatory pedagogy in the United States and Canada. *Journal of Education*, 172.

Lynn, Marvin. (1999, January) Toward a critical race pedagogy: A research note. *Urban Education*, 33.

McIntosh, P., (1988) White privilege: Unpacking the invisible knapsack. Retrieved June 28, 2004 from http://www.utoronto.ca/acc/events/peggy1.htm.

National Highway Traffic Safety Administration (2003, December 4). Highway safety in black/African-American communities: Issues and strategies. Retrieved from www.nhtsa.gov/people/injury/research/blafamercommissues/index.html

Peavy, Liz. (2000, March). I can see clearly now: The Kuona process – a teaching strategy for liberation. *Urban Education*, 35.

Roemer, A.A. (1958, Winter). A city planner views the social aspeects of urban renewal. *Alpha Kappa Deltan.*

Rothwell, J. & Massey, D.S. (2009, April 9). The Effect of Density Zoning on Racial Segregation in U.S. Urban. *Urban Affairs Review*, 44.

Stahl, K. (2009). The great rebellion: A socio-economic analysis of the 1967 Detroit riot. Self-published. www.detroits-great-rebellion.com/The-Road-to-67-html

Tate, W.F. (1997). Critical Race Theory and education: History, theory and implications. *Review of Research in Education*, 22. pp. 195-247

Constitutional and Legal Issues of Urban Planning and Land Use Control:
An Urban Geography Analysis

<u>INTRODUCTION</u>

<u>THE ISSUE OF ZONING AND "TAKING"</u>

While the information on billboard regulations (p. 288) and historic preservation laws and the relationship of both of these subjects to planning was insightful, I was particularly interested in zoning, the police power and the legal rulings which governed these two important forms of land use control. I am further interested in the issue of land use control when the variable of "race" becomes a part of the equation.

> The framers of the U.S. Constitution in 1787 could scarcely have
> foreseen that the United States would eventually be a "nation of
> cities", in the phrase of historian Sam Bass Warner (1966) (p. 252)

The framers of the Constitution, as we now know, were members of the elite, and were white and male. Based upon that fact alone, one can hardly question how "inclusive" they were when they were "foreseeing" what they believed America would become. One thing was for sure; they held slaves and, for the most part, believed that those individuals were inferior. So it matters little about what they produce because we know that the mind dictates actions. If one believes that the races should be separate – and these men surely believed that – then the institutions, policies and procedures produced by these men will reinforce that belief. That's the way it was with the Founding Fathers, and that's the way it appears to be today with city administrations, planning departments and planners themselves – especially as those "plans" relate to how land will be used.

Moving on,

> Procedural due process "centers not so much on what is done but
> on how it has been done" … Substantive due process … concerns
> the purpose of the government action, while the taking issue
> considers it economic impact (p. 253)

As it relates to substantive due process, the judge declared a scathing indictment of zoning based on substantive due process and equal protection grounds when he said, in part, "In the last analysis, the result to be accomplished is to classify the population and segregate them according to their income or situation in life." (p. 262)

The article claims that, "If this opinion had been upheld by the U.S. Supreme Court, the face of metropolitan America might look rather different today. However it was reversed" (p. 262) How might it look different? Is America not, indeed, residentially and racially segregated?

America is already segregated by income and "situation in life," and that is the case despite a plethora of civil rights laws, housing decisions, rules and regulations prohibiting steering, redlining and blockbusting and remains the case whether the governing administration is liberal, moderate or conservative. Again, the issue of "race" is one that should be discussed more when it comes to land use planning because, as W.E.B. DuBois wrote, "the problem of the 20th Century is the problem of the color line." And this remains true even in this, the 21st Century.

The land use article continues by claiming:

> The most enduring issue confronting zoning and other land use
> regulation is the "taking issue" – to what extent can regulations
> reduce the value of private property without compensation to the
> owner? (p. 258)

This is only an "issue" when the person whose land is being taken is minority, low income or politically unsophisticated. The taking of land of those considered "different" is a long-time American tradition which began with the taking of land from the members of the indigenous population. From that point on, the taking of land was a matter of who had the most money, the most guns, the most power. This was the case prior to "regulations" and now, in a more technologically astute America, remains the case if the person is not aware, does not have good legal representation and depending on how badly the government wants the land. With the advent of Eminent Domain, those in power still have the right to take land whenever they want to, and need only show that it serves "the public good" – meaning the well-being of those in the majority.

> Where private property is deliberately taken for a public use or
> purpose, as for streets, parks or schools, the public authority
> clearly must pay the private owner "just compensation." This
> means fair market value as established by a jury (p. 259).

"Just compensation" according to prices and estimates put together by individuals who intentionally devalue the land in certain areas of the city. That is why those in power flex their muscles in these areas. Freeways are rammed through poor areas and "developments" are forced into these areas because the land is cheap based on real estate values. If the area is black, the land is said to be worth less than in an area that is white and suburban. How can this be? Land is land. But since this is the case, "fair and just compensation" means more to the suburbanite than to the central city resident, even though both may be homeowners.

Put another way,

> On the other hand, zoning necessarily reduces some property
> values by limiting the range of choice and manner in which the
> property may be developed and utilized. Should such reduction in
> the value of some property for the benefit of others be
> compensable? (p. 259)

This is but one form of property value reduction. What about the reductions based on race of the people who live in that area? It exists all over America, from the largest cities to the middle sized cities, anywhere where there exists a "pocket of poverty."

The police power and zoning, then, do not work the same in all parts of the city. They are not applied the same or ruled in the same in courts of law. Poor people do not receive the same kind of justice as those who have money, and there are hundreds, if not thousands, of studies which show that this is the case. America is based on the ceaseless pursuit of profit, and this extends into the area of real estate and, as a result, into the minds and habits of those who are planners and who assist in making planning decisions.

ZONING AND THE LAND QUESTION

The issue of zoning is one which is controversial when the variable of "race" is interjected. The article stated, "Zoning is a tool in the hands of governmental bodies which enables them to more efficiently meet the demands of evolving and growing communities … Zoning provisions may not be used … to avoid the increased responsibilities and economic burdens which time and natural growth invariably bring" (p. 275)

> The early period of zoning was marked by a paradox concerning aesthetics. On the one hand, the basic terms of Euclidian zoning – segregation of uses, minimum lot size, setbacks, and so forth – are inherently aesthetic in nature. They embody the aesthetic of the turn-of-the-century garden suburb: single-family detached homes with spacious, landscaped from yards set back evenly from the street with nonresidential activities banished from the area (p. 285).

My point regarding the significance of race is even echoed by the author when he cites the case of *Southern Burlington County NAACP v. Township of Mount Laurel 336 A.2d 713, 1975*, and it figures that the NAACP would be involved and bring the issue of race into play. If they didn't do it, the planners certainly would not have. At any rate, it was found that Mount Laurel wanted to control growth by accepting a certain kind of population (white folks) and that "through its zoning ordinances has exhibited economic discrimination in that the poor have been deprived of adequate housing, and has used federal, state, county, and local finances and resources solely for the betterment of middle- and upper-income persons" (p. 277).

And, "the opinion explicitly raises FOR PERHAPS THE FIRST TIME the constitutional issue as to "whose general welfare must be served or not violated in the field of land use regulation" (p. 277). We should remember the words of

Justice William O. Douglas when he wrote what I consider to be a racist definition of aesthetic in planning:

> The concept of the public welfare is broad and inclusive … The values it represents are spiritual as well as physical, aesthetic as well as monetary. It is within the power of the legislature to determine that the community should be beautiful as well as healthy, spacious as well as clean, well-balanced as well as carefully patrolled … If those who govern the District of Columbia decide that the Nation's Capitol should be beautiful as well as sanitary there is nothing in the Fifth Amendment that stands in the way (75S.Ct.at 102-103).

All communities should be spacious and beautiful and sanitary, should they not? Therefore, by delineating above about the legislature having the power "to determine" that the community should be those things, it is clear that some communities should, and some communities should not. If this was not the case, then every community would look the same, have the same access to services and be provided with the same resources. But are they? No. And whose fault is it? It is the fault of the legislatures who allocate money and the cities who take money earmarked for poor areas and spend it developing suburbs and exurbs and downtowns.

The Mount Laurel case opened up the issue of discrimination and race and some good things came out of it, including making every municipality provide lower cost housing opportunities for its resident poor, and the formation of a special panel of judges and using affirmative action to provide low-cost housing (p. 279). The Mount Laurel case also led to the establishment of a Council on Affordable Housing and provided a mediation and review process.

Zoning and the issue of "reason" are sometimes difficult to understand. It is explained as follows:

> "Reasonableness" is thus often used as a surrogate for "constitutionality." Although it may beg the questions, reasonableness has provided a convenient rubric for courts to resolve zoning challenges. The inquiry takes the following form: Is the ordinance reasonably related to a valid purpose of the police power and does it reserve for the owner some reasonable way to use the property (although not necessarily the most profitable one)? (p. 255)

What is "valid" for those in power is, in far too many cases, "invalid" to those who are being imposed upon. The majority rules and although minorities are said to have rights, those rights are overridden when it comes to the police power. The concept of "reasonableness" is based upon what those in the majority view as being valid and how the majority benefits from the way the property is used. This is why freeways continue to go through poor and minority communities, destroying entire subcultures. North Omaha is but one example of how the police power and how the rights of suburbanites and their need to expedite the trip from the Eppley Airfield to West Omaha was deemed more "reasonable" than the rights of the poor and the number of low-income housing units that were destroyed to make way for the interstate.

It all appears arbitrary to me. The article claims,

> After nearly four decades of national experience with zoning, Haar
> … reported: "For the most part, however, zoning has preceded
> planning in the communities which now provide for the latter
> activity, and indeed, nearly one-half of the cities with
> comprehensive zoning ordinances have not adopted master plans at
> all … (p. 257)

In my view, zoning IS planning; it plans for business and residences to combine when it is in the best interests of the community. It is a combination of what the residents want and what is best for their kids. But then when "others" move in, zoning is used to segregate and alienate. Planners then come into the picture, not to do the right thing and undo the wrong that was committed – but to justify and strengthen those wrongs! This partially explains the following excerpt:

> Bettman argued that modern urban development was producing
> unprecedented problems of congestion and inefficiency. He argued
> that orderliness of land usage pursuant to a master plan is a proper
> use of the police power (p. 263)

Modern urban development is as racist as the people who abused the white ethnics coming into the cities. Following the compartmentalization of those people, and watching while the sewers backed up and health problems killed many of them, the modern urban development then allowed the newly arriving blacks to experience the same congestion and health problems. "Orderliness of land use," at least in my view, was reserved for the well-to-do and later, for those whites who were fleeing the inner cities to head for the suburbs.

In the case of *Nollan v. California Coastal Commission 107S.Ct. 3141, 1987*, " … a restriction on a rebuilding permit for an oceanfront home that required the owners to allow the public an easement to walk along the dry sand (private) portion of the beach in front of their home. This was consistent with similar restrictions placed on new and rebuilt shorefront by the Commission to promote public access along beaches…"(p. 265)

The court ruled that if California wanted an easement across the Nollans' property, then the state must pay for it. This case "thus reflected a long-standing doctrine that the police power may properly be used to prevent public harm but not to confer public benefits without compensation" (p. 265). But just the fact that there was an "assumption" that this could become law shows the arrogance and subtle underhandedness of zoning administrators and planners. For a less politically sophisticated community in a less desirable social and geographic setting, such one-sided laws would perhaps not be stifled by the courts.

In *Lucas v. South Carolina Coastal Council 112 S.Ct.2886, 1992,* the issue of fair compensation for the taking of land was addressed and while a trial court agreed and awarded Lucas $1.2 million for his beach front property, The South Carolina Supreme Court reversed the trial court, holding the permit denial to be a valid application of the police power … (p. 266).

Zoning supports those who have the money to afford good legal defense. But what about the poor and how does zoning operate when the variable of "race" comes into play? In my view, all three types of zoning cited on page 270 have the potential for being racist when the variable of "race" comes into play.

For instance, exclusionary zoning is "the use of zoning to deter construction of homes or siting of mobile homes for moderate-income families or members of racial or other minorities." Recently in the Omaha World Herald, there was an article in the August 4, 2000 issue of the paper under the headline, "Judge Says Town Has Racist Zoning." It appears that in Sunnyvale, Texas, "A federal judge has ruled that leaders in the predominantly white Dallas suburb have been shutting out minorities and the poor for 50 years through illegal zoning laws." Continuing:

> Sunnyvale Mayor Jim Phaup said the city may appeal the
> ruling. He disputed Bachmeyer's allegation that the city of
> about 3,000 was formed to exclude minorities. "It's all about
> open spaces and country fields. It has nothing to do with
> discriminatory practices," Phaup says (Omaha World Herald,
> p. 11).

It has to do with white racism and that is evidenced by the following excerpt:

> Reggie Smith, a plaintiff in the lawsuit, said his construction
> company tried unsuccessfully in 1988 to build affordable homes
> and apartments in Sunnyvale. He said he overheard racial slurs
> during public meetings regarding his application. Urban experts
> say regulating for size or square footage of homes is exclusionary

> because it drives up the cost of a home. But few such zoning
> practices have been challenged in federal court , said David Rusk,
> a former Albuquerque mayor and author of a book examining the
> social costs of exclusionary zoning (Omaha World Herald, p. 11).

I'm not concerned about the racial slurs that Smith claims he heard at the meetings. Since he didn't bother to address them or deal with them, then he is just another "quiet nigger" in my book.

But my concern is that the article talks of "urban experts" who talk of regulating the size or square footage of homes being exclusionary. Why can't "planners" do it? Why WON'T planners do it? Why does it take a former mayor to write a book on "exclusionary zoning"? I'll tell you why: because of the "politics" involved in planning, that's why. The Planning Department serves the existing political order or lives off of the government dole through funding from the office of Housing and Urban Development. Those planners see racist actions, ordinances, variances and proposals before them every day, but they don't act unless the action is in accord with the existing power structure.

Frederick Law Olmstead, the man who built New York's Central Park, faced it in his day, and it's still going on. Without the "urban experts" around – people like Douglass Massey and Nancy Denton (who co-wrote "American Apartheid"), Peter Suzuki (the director of UNOs Urban Studies program) and the like – the urban planners would be running amok on poor communities and doing the racist bidding of whatever the power structure dictates.

In regard to Fiscal zoning, it is defined on page 270 of the urban planning article as, "the use of zoning to minimize local property taxes by encouraging revenue generating activities such as shopping centers and industrial parks while discouraging revenue-demanding uses such as lower-cost homes for families with children (regardless of race)."

This is exactly what is happening in North Omaha right now. Placing an industrial park in an area where businesses are nil and where people are poor. Why? To keep the property taxes elsewhere, down. At the same time, lower-cost homes are torn down to pave the way for the North Freeway, and expensive homes such as those being built by Michael Maroney in his "Concord Townhomes" project, are being given preferential treatment. Why? To attract yuppies and others who have the financial power back into the central city, near downtown where the real jobs are. Commute time gets cut down, the area is "re-taken" by the whites who fled in the 1960s and blacks are relocated to the northwestern sector of the area.

Finally, NIMBY, which stands for "not in my back yard." This form of zoning and other legal means are used to "resist the location of unwanted uses, facilities, or activities within the municipality (such as regional incinerators or toxic waste disposal sites, prisons, mental health facilities, oil refineries, public housing).

But NIMBY is good for some and bad for others. After all, where are those toxic waste disposal sites, garbage dumps, packing houses, prisons and public housing placed? Either in a rural area or in or near a central city. For the most part the rural areas get the prisons because politicians want those areas to have jobs.

In addition, the prison population is considered and counted as part of the congressional district, although the prisoners cannot vote. Meanwhile, the central cities get the toxic disposal sites, such as ASARCO (right near North Omaha in the downtown area) and even now it is discovered that there is toxic land on the site that was formerly Druid Hill Elementary School. "Not in my back yard," for the most part, has come to mean "put it in the low-income area" and poison THOSE people, not our suburban kids.

Finally in 1986 the assumption for the responsibility for housing policy diluted the impact of the courts and placed the power in the hands of state legislatures. According to one scholar, the courts were ill-suited and inappropriate forums to resolve technical housing issues (p. 280). Not just the technical issues – the social ones as well.

Not that the legislatures are doing any better. Look at the Nebraska situation: is North Omaha faring any better just because the legislature exists? North Omaha looks worse NOW than it did twenty years ago. So the courts might be out of touch and may be ill-suited, but the same can be said about the legislature when it comes to the black community. After all, the abuse of HUD monies by the city of Omaha had to be approved by the state HUD office, and the legislators had to know about the projects that were being prioritized and the amount of money allocated to the state.

The "essence of the issue is which public is implied in constitutional protection of the "general welfare" – the strictly local public, or the larger publics of the region, state, nation or globe?" (p. 270) I have a feeling that the 'public' being defined is not based on geographic size, but on numbers and race. In this context, "general welfare" comes to mean the welfare of the "general public," the majority of people. This comes to mean the white majority here in America. This is seen in why freeways don't go through suburban housing districts, why toxic waste is stored in low-income areas, why low-income housing is placed in low-income areas creating economic re-segregation and why racial segregation continues to exist in America. The "general public" means the white majority, pure and simple.

In the sub-chapter of "Urban Housing for the Poor," evidence of racism and concern for the "general welfare" of the public becomes most evident:

> While housing activists labored to open the suburbs to affordable
> housing, existing stocks of older housing in the central cities
> continued to decline During the 1950s and 1960s, efforts to save or
> replace urban housing followed two general approaches: public
> housing and urban renewal. Both involved a partnership of federal
> funding and technical guidance with local administration. Both
> approaches were to be challenged as ineffective and
> counterproductive (p. 281).

If they were "challenged as ineffective and counterproductive" then they must have been ineffective and counterproductive, right? Why can't the author bring himself to say that? Those of us who are minority who watched as housing went down and was not replaced, KNOW well that urban renewal basically meant, "Negro removal."

HOUSING PROGRAMS AND THE CENTRAL CITY

Secondly, if the approaches of public housing and urban renewal did not work, then whose fault is that and why were the programs continually re-funded? Why does it take five or ten years for the government to "find out" that something is "failing" in the central city? The answer is because the people who make up the government – local, state or national – do not live in these central city areas for the most part. They live OUTSIDE of the area and once they leave their jobs, they really don't care how the plan goes. After all, jobs are being created and the economy is expanding, and that means votes. But the people who are supposed to benefit are being "experimented on" with these approaches and if it works, fine but if it doesn't work, those in power don't really have to worry about facing any repercussions.

The mistakes are made because those coming up with these ideas don't really care about the end result. Then, when the failure does take place, scholars and urban planners come along to "intellectually explain away" what took place. A case in point appears in the following passage:

> Congress established the Slum Clearance Program for replacement
> of tenements with publicly owned housing projects … Many
> public housing units were uninhabitable by the mid-1960s due to
> inappropriate design, isolated location, occupancy policies, and
> lack of upkeep (p. 281).

This is what happened in Omaha when Aulden Aust, the former director of city planning, decided to destroy hundreds of houses in North Omaha, claiming that they were paving the way for Urban Renewal. Later, he would say that this was a mistake, that those houses could have been renovated. But what do we have: a mistake made at the expense of people who are not politically sophisticated, who are poor and who are minority. So what if a mistake is made? Does anybody care enough to punish the government for destroying black lives?

How can a program that includes housing units which were not designed appropriately, that were built in isolated locations (far from jobs and community), contained discriminatory occupancy policies and lacked upkeep from those hired to do just that, how can a program like this go unpunished? How can the formulators continue to find jobs as urban planners? How can history downplay the destruction and devastation that blacks and other minorities had to face while these "programs" came and failed? Who speaks for the poor?

For example, take St. Louis:

> The infamous Pruitt-Igoe Project in St. Louis, for example, consisted of 43 eleven-story buildings. By 1970, 26 of these were boarded up, and in 1972 all were demolished by the city's housing authority (p. 282).

What about the insanity that took place in and around the Robert Taylor Homes and the Cabrini-Green Housing projects in Chicago? What about the failures of high rises all over the nation and people being burned up in them? Elevators failing? Taken over by gangs? A major waste of taxpayers' money because someone wanted to "experiment." They figured that by going up in the air (building multi-story buildings) they could build more units and use less actual land. There are no high-rise projects in white suburban communities. Even the high rise hotels have zoning limits placed on them. So once again we have different levels of priority and concern based upon the income and the race of the resident population.

Race not a factor? It becomes clear when those in the suburbs and those with political power want to concentrate and segregated people based upon race. The following excerpt bears out this allegation:

> Aside from poor design, a fundamental objection of civil rights advocates to federal public housing policy was the practice of locating most projects (except elderly housing) in black ghetto areas, thus reinforcing patterns of racial segregation since most occupants were nonwhite. In a suit filed by the NAACP, the federal district court of Chicago held that this practice violated the Fourteenth Amendment and ordered new public housing to be scattered in small clusters throughout the city (p. 282).

Why did it take "civil rights" advocates to expose a problem that was created by urban planners and "experts"? Why did it take civil rights activists to see that those in power were "re-segregating" the American social landscape? The answer is clear and it shows that once the variable of "race" is interjected into the "plan," the same rules and regulations which apply to the "general population" and for the "general welfare" usually don't apply for any number of reasons. We need only look at the issue of land use, as we are doing now, to see that this allegation has historical precedent and continues on to this day.

How else to explain the resistance to "scattered-site housing" by these Omaha suburbanites? Where is the scattered site housing going, for the most part? Right into North Omaha. There are some sites elsewhere in Omaha, but the white community groups got the city to change the design and the locations and basically turned the low-income houses into condos of sorts. But this was the exception, not the rule. One need only attend a city council meeting when the issue of low-income housing arises to see residents coming out and using the myth of "lowered property values." Laurenti debunked that lie more than three decades ago. It only continues to exist because those in the suburbs continue to want segregation from people who are different.

Why does it take community activists and civil rights advocates to point out this racialist issues? Part of the answer can be found in the following paragraph:

> The record of federal involvement in housing for the poor,
> however, has generally been shameful in comparison with the
> many forms of federal subsidy to the habitability of middle- and
> upper-class suburbs (p. 282).

In the vernacular of the ghetto, "different strokes for different folks." And while the preceding excerpt makes it appears as if the dichotomy is based on housing for the poor versus middle and upper-class suburbs, the issue is really centered on the people who make up these two areas. When stripped of its pomp and ceremony, the issue is low income versus well-to-do, minority versus non-minority.

And since the issue was one of race, for the most part, it only stands to reason that racism would be an integral part of the process – keeping minorities down and out of the way. Urban Renewal was but one example of that:

> The federal Urban Renewal Program was also widely discredited.
> Under the Housing Acts of 1949 and 1954, urban renewal funded
> local authorities to plan, acquire, clear and redevelop designated
> areas of "urban blight." With the approval of the U.S. Supreme
> Court in Berman v. Parker in 1954 … the program cleared

> thousands of acres of inner-city tenements and displaced tens of
> thousands of low-income households and small businesses. Aside
> from the areas rebuilt with public facilities such as schools and
> parks, most urban renewal land was sold at a subsidized price to
> private redevelopers to be reused according to the urban renewal
> plan (pp. 282-283).

The private developers benefited, the city that received the money benefited, many people were employed as part of the program (more non-minorities than minorities, no doubt) and the program was a feather in the cap of whomever claimed to be about "helping the poor." But even the most conservative planner has to admit that major displacement of populations took place, and poor people lost their homes and their livelihoods in the name of "progress" that never really took place.

Now, in retrospect, everybody wants to be a moralist or a critic:

> Urban renewal was attacked from several standpoints. Housing
> advocates complained that poor people displaced by the projects
> could not afford the new units built the same sites and were given
> little help in finding alternative housing … Also, there was no
> compensation by urban renewal authorities to displaced tenants
> and small businesses … In response to these criticisms, the Federal
> Uniform Relocation Assistance Act of 1970 authorized grants and
> relocation assistance to households and businesses by federally
> funded projects (p. 283).

At first there was no compensation to those who were relocated or displaced. But the fact of the matter is, even with the advent of the Federal Uniform Relocation Assistant Act of 1970 which gave out some grants and "relocation assistance," these funds were inadequate and the "assistance" was short-term: one-time only. So if you had a home that was paid for and you were relocated to an apartment, $10,000 was not only an underpayment for your home, but it would only last so long now that you are a renter, not an owner. And the "assistance" came in the form of "advice" and "referrals," not cash. In other words, most of those who were displaced ended up doing WORSE than they were doing before the government came in and took their homes and moved them away from an area where they had grown to feel comfortable.

The problems didn't only impact upon the hard-core slum dwellers, either:

> Others criticized the disruption of ethnically diverse urban
> neighborhoods and their replacement by sterile, unsafe high-rise
> development (p. 283).

Moving on,

> In 1965, Congress created the Department of Housing and Urban Development (HUD) as recommended by President Johnson's Task Force on Metropolitan and Urban Problems to serve as an umbrella for federal housing programs … In 1966, the Demonstration Cities and Metropolitan Development Act of 1966 launched the "Model Cities" program, which sought to upgrade community facilities, jobs and social programs in some 150 cities (p. 283).

Levy (2000) reminds us that, "In 1966, while its influence with Congress was still great, the Johnson administration had pushed through the Model Cities Program. Building upon long-established public housing and urban renewal efforts, Model Cities attempted to integrate physical redevelopment of inner city neighborhoods with a wide range of social services and job opportunities" (p. 100). Model Cities failed just as other programs before it had failed. But were the people fired? Were they banned from ever practicing their trades as planners, engineers or theorists? No. Who suffered? The very people that were in need of help and the very communities that already had more than their fair share of problems.

And, " although administered by the Department of Housing and Urban Development rather than OEO, Model Cities reflected the growing appreciation of the urban character of the nation's poor population and was generally perceived as part of the War on Poverty" (ibid.,) But the end result remained the same.

> *The vast concrete headquarters of HUD and the Department of Transportation, which occupy adjacent sites of former urban renewal land in the southwest quadrant of Washington, D.C., are monuments to this brief by exuberant era of domestic concern (sadly overshadowed by the other war, in Vietnam) (p. 284).*

Finally, it was noted that, "Nationally, more than 1000 local historic preservation laws were in effect as of the mid-1980s" (p. 290). So while there is concern about the aging housing stock and the historical character of the city, there is not an equal amount of concern expressed about the minorities and low-income people who live in many of the areas which have the historic landmark designation!

CONCLUSION

REFERENCES

Levy, John M. (2003). **Contemporary Urban Planning**. Englewood Cliffs, New Jersey: Prentice-Hall.

MINORITY CITIZEN PARTICIPATION IN THE OMAHA CITY PLANNING, DESIGN AND COMMUNITY DEVELOPMENT PROCESS:

An Analysis of Selective Application, Discriminatory Treatment and a Conspiracy to Systematically Impoverish an African-American Community in Omaha, Nebraska

ABSTRACT

This black paper, part of a book on the history of North Omaha that I will be completing some time later this year, will pose the question and then seek to provide answers and solutions as to why there is such a dearth of minority (black) participation in the community development and planning processes in Omaha, Nebraska. Even when the issues involve minority communities themselves, there is little evidence that there was input from the residents of those communities. This study will consist of content analysis, several interviews and some secondary analysis of archival data as the primary methodological approaches. At the end of the paper, a number of proposals and suggestions are advanced that will change the attitudes and atmosphere surrounding the incorporation of minorities into the community development and planning processes, resulting in a more collective and representative effort and product.

---Matthew C. Stelly

.I. INTRODUCTION

This paper was originally written for a student taking a class in an area college that was supposed to be credible. Just the fact that this paper is of such high quality should have alerted the teacher to the fact that the student, a virtual idiot, could not have penned it. But since I've been writing graduate papers for students all over the country since 1980, I know for a fact that the people in the classroom either don't give a shit or are as dumb as a bag full of hammers.

Whatever the case, this paper has been upgraded from its earlier version so that the people reading it will better understand the nature and scope of the errors they are committing in the name of "community development." Without citizen participation and input, the city of Omaha is in direct violation of every grant that it applies for. In an effort to cover up this omission, they quickly put together bullshit, fly-by-night community groups, neighborhood associations and construct multi-million dollar "community engagement centers," all gauged for maintaining white control of the city, fostering more racial and residential segregation, and maintaining the status quo, consisting mainly of a good ol' boys network, silly blonde white women and a few token negroes who are given keys that don't fit anything.

Context of the Problem

This paper offers that there has historically been a dearth of minority participation in the community development/planning processes in Omaha and while there have been some informal (grass roots) examples of such issues being defined, illuminated and eventually addressed, the fact still remains that at the formal level – the levels that involve huge expenditures of money and as a result, represent the potential for minority involvement, the possible creation of jobs and more importantly, fair and equitable citizen input – there is a glaring lack of such participation.

This paper further posits that increased minority citizen participation in the community development/planning process can lead to better structure, enhanced management and a more far-reaching and positive product when it comes to bringing about important physical and social changes.

Progress takes place every day, but it is clear that one person's progress can be another person's setback. Goss (2001) wrote that, "to succeed, public agencies have to want to do so … While relationships between government agencies and civil society are becoming healthier, there is still little or no understanding about how to structure and manage them" (p. 62). As Alan Barr remarks, user and community participation is a central concern of recent social policy and it seems to hold out the only real options for positive social development (Barr, 2000: p. 55).

Arnstein (1969) correctly wrote that, "citizen participation is a categorical term for citizen power. It is the redistribution of power that enables the have-not citizens, presently excluded from the political and economic processes, to be deliberately included in the future. It is a strategy by which the have-nots join in determining how information is shared, goals and policies are set, tax resources are allocated, programs are operated, and benefits like contracts and patronize are parceled out. In short, it is the means by which they can induce significant social reform which enables them to share in the benefits of the affluent society" (p. 217).

Purpose of the Study

This paper is being written from the perspective of someone who adopts the community developer approach to addressing urban issues and urban planning. The community development perspective is one that works to engage and organize community-based organizations in the process of development by employing a grass-roots or what Ouchi (1981) referred to as "bottoms up" approach. By empowering the masses of people and educating them, the final result is not only more representative of the needs of the people, but also more reflective of the views of all entities and approaches involved in decision-making.

What one publication had to say about bringing "color" to the international intellectual table surely rings true, in a micro level sense, when it comes to what Omaha could do, how it would benefit, and what the increase in minority involvement in the community development process could have the potential to mean:

> … [I]t is through the exchange of knowledge, research and ideas that we begin to exchange hostility and ignorance for our understanding and insight. Because as … citizens we learn that in being separated and isolated by our geographical and scholastic boundaries none of us gets a holistic picture of our true humanity, but together we create a mosaic that exemplifies our collective and individual human value and worth. It is through this exchange of ideas that we create feasts instead of famines, discover cures for diseases, wane off wars and … educate our communities and empower our disadvantaged. As scholars and people of color, our voices need to be heard, and once there they can begin to illuminate the voices of the forgotten and raise issues that have traditionally been ignored (Black Issues in Higher Education, 2003: p. 74).

With all this in mind, the core purpose of this study is to provide ideas and approaches that will increase the ranks of African-Americans (minorities) within the realm of community development/urban planning.

Background of the Study

Informally, blacks have been a part of planning even before it was an issue of "urban planning." One of the first neighborhood associations in the city was the Ideal Improvement Club, a community group that lobbied and wrote letters to city hall regarding improvements in and around North Omaha. Along with the Omaha Monitor, the city's first African-American newspaper, black involvement in the planning process consisted of editorials and articles about what was needed in the black community, most of these issues involving sidewalks, safety, lighting and a major issue that was resolved, the paving of 24th Street.

As a matter of formality, the City of Omaha Planning Department itself has employed very few blacks up to and until 1975 when it received its first Community Development Block Grant. While there have been a smattering of blacks employed by the Planning Department, most input that involved major decisions, decisions that centered around the economic development efforts involving North Omaha (the city's African-American community), were largely raised, defined and then addressed by Caucasian planners and other department members.

Another prong of formality is the formation of associations and agencies that specialized in working with the city (and being funded by it) to address the urban planning issues of the area. These include the now defunct Urban Development Business Corporation and the United Contractors Association of Nebraska; a 1980s organization that was an adjunct to the city, North Omaha Community Development, and Omaha Economic Development Association, perhaps the most successful of such groups.

Other related issues that will be briefly explored will be agencies such as the Omaha Housing Authority and New Community Development, two groups that have taken a more focused (housing) route to addressing community development and planning issues. .

Research Question

The essential research question being posed here is "why has there historically been a glaring lack of African-American participation in the urban planning and community development processes in Omaha, Nebraska?

Limitations

The limitations of this study begin with the obvious lack of content-related information on the planning process in Omaha as that process relates to African-American input. While there are some studies, put together by the Omaha Planning

Department, that addressed Latino involvement, much of the information gathered for this study was acquired from newspaper articles, some reference papers provided to me by former members of the Planning Department, interviews with those who worked closely with the City on community development projects, as well as discussions with local political, civic and religious leaders who had recollections of what few African-Americans played a formal and/or informal role in the urban planning/community development process.

Another limitation of the study is that it would have been interesting to have had more time to distinguish between "formal" and "informal" participation on the part of African-Americans as it related to the urban planning/community development process. While this paper mentions or alludes to actions taken by at least one proactive neighborhood association (the Ideal Improvement Club) and while it is documented that editorials in African-American newspapers pricked the conscience of and motivated community persons to organize and address some of the issues permeating the North Omaha urban core during the 1930 and more recently, there still appears to be much more information on and evidence regarding other issues spearheaded by African-Americans (e.g., the maintenance and use of the Burdette baseball field, the lobbying for the first YMCA and Boys Club, and other issues regarding street repair and appropriate lighting in the urban core area).

A third limitation is a definition of "shortage" when it comes to the low numbers who have been involved in or with the Planning Department. Omaha's seemingly low numbers might be high if compared to other cities of comparable size. It would be interesting to conduct a comparison and survey comparing Omaha with citizens of similar size and to compare and contrast the numbers and, more importantly, the roles of African-Americans in the community development/urban planning capacities of these various cities.

Finally, it is difficult to assess what the intentions of people are. It cannot be said that there is a conspiracy against blacks or that all actions are rooted in racism of racial discrimination. What is attempted in this thesis is to view the numbers of minorities involved, the actions of those in power and what has or has not taken place in terms of minority input into community development decisions that have been made. Therefore a limitation might be that the culture of racial exclusion in Omaha served as a basis for decisions made by planners in terms of their views of minority or African-American input (e.g., peer pressure, social concerns about the qualifications of blacks, accepted stereotypes regarding black attitudes or mentality, etc.).

<u>Significance of the Study</u>

The significance of this study is that if the enclosed proposals and suggestions are adopted, the City of Omaha Planning Department, the Omaha Economic Development Corporation, and anyone interested in becoming more involved in the planning and community development process, would benefit. The contents of this thesis have the potential to bring about a change in the current state of affairs that exists in Omaha, where few minorities are a part of the urban planning process, even when this process and the development that it spawns takes place in the minority community.

Rather than project or predict what "could be" if minorities were allowed to become more involved in this process, I have extracted some notes from a field research assignment that was provided last year. This was an assignment that opened my eyes to the historical greatness of that area of the city known as "North Omaha," "the near Northside," and of course, as "the urban core," "the ghetto" and "the inner city." Because of this information, this thesis adds to the section on the "significance" of what is being proposed, *evidence* of what once existed and took place. This evidence hinges upon and revolves around the North Omaha community during its heyday, a time when this writer views what took place as a prototype of "informal planning" and development by African-Americans, for African-Americans.

North Omaha, and 24th Street in particular, has always been near or at the bottom of the priority list when it came to the provision of public services. Such was the case when it came to lighting in the area and concerns, expressed by residents, that the 24th and Lake Street area was too dimly lit. But this did not stop the community from banding together and doing what had to be done to bring about important changes related to planning and community development.

For example, as far back as May of 1940, it took major prompting from the black community and the Omaha Star to get Mayor Dan B. Butler to admit that, "There is need for better lighting on North 24th Street" (Omaha Star, 1940: 1). In fact, the mayor made a big deal out of it and opted to include a parade as part of the May 17th event, which would lead to the pushing of a button that, in turn, would turn on the lights at exactly 8:15 on that Friday evening. According to the Omaha Star,

> Business places on North Twenty-fourth street who (sic) have
> already shown a cooperative spirit in this celebration are:
> Edholm Sherman Laundry, Duffy Pharmacy, J.D. Lewis
> Mortuary, United Cab, Johnson Drug, Ideal Bottling Co., Royal
> Cleaners, Donovan Bros., Federal Market, Tuchman Bros.,
> Emerson Saratoga Laundry, Crosstown Bar, Champion,
> Chemical Products co., J. Spigal, E.E. Café, Bordy Clothing,

Reliable Clothing Co., Freidman and Ralph Taylor (Omaha Star,
1940: 1).

Back then it was called, "The Deuce." Ms. Fannie Claxton, one of the first women to ever teach in the Omaha Public Schools, was kind enough to share some of the names of some of the businesses with me during an interview at my father's church, Prince of Peace Baptist Church, several months ago for a Field Research course that I was participating in. During that interview, she said,

> I remember that Singleton's sold crawdads, and we called him,
> "The Crawdad Man." There was Hayes Hardware, and Joe
> Lynch owned the tailor shop at 24th and Clark Street. Cliff
> Robbins was the first owner of the Fair Deal Café and later on he
> sold it to Charlie Hill. There was the Green Lantern and Walter
> Dean owned the Fish Grotto at 22nd and Lake Street. The Johnny
> Davis Grocery Store was at 26th and Seward, but later on moved
> to 26th and Franklin. We had McCallister's Ice Cream and there
> was Mary's Chicken Hut at 30th and Miami (F. Claxton, personal
> communication, September 16, 2005

When asked about larger businesses such as hotels, Henry Mason, another interviewee during the same aforementioned Field Research course, seemed to remember the businesses as if it were yesterday:

> There was Speck's Hotel at 16th and Cuming Street, and the
> Calhoun Hotel at 24th and Lake. The Johnny Walker Hotel was at
> 25th and Charles and the Washington Hotel was at 24th and
> Parker (H. Mason, personal communication, September 4, 2005).

According to a December 1, 1991 article by George Smith, an *Omaha World Herald* staff writer, "Black in the early Sixties the area known as the Near North Side bustled with business and prosperity. Grocery stores, shops, nightclubs, restaurants, and many beautiful well-kept homes. The intersection of 24th and Lake Street was the center and meeting place for Omaha's black culture, many great jazz players appeared there" (p. 1)

Again, according to Henry Mason, the 24th and Lake Street area was alive in the traditional sense, but it was the underground economy that kept it going. "We had all night gambling shacks, all night buffets and people sold alcohol until the wee hours," he said. Mr. Mason said that it was this kind of life that kept much of what was going on in the legitimate African-American business world, afloat (H. Mason, personal communication, September 4, 2005).

"There was the Lee Von Hotel at 2212 Seward which also offered rooms by the day or by the week," Mason said. He added that the hotels were not the kind that catered only to regular patrons. "They were rooms where the men folk up here from the South could stay while they worked at the packing houses over on the south side." But he added that, "they were also places where the prostitutes could bring their johns and engage in business on that end." Such activity was lucrative in those days, because black men had jobs and their families were hundreds of miles away in places like Mississippi, Arkansas, Alabama and Tennessee. Mason himself, hails from Memphis (H. Mason, personal communication, September 4, 2005).

Mason also said that, "As if there were not enough barber shops, two black men named Costello and Cook moved in about 1928 and added their names to the list. Their shop was a popular one, and was located at 802 South 13th Street, a haircut was 35 cents and a shave was 15 cents (H. Mason, personal communication, September 5, 2005).

If it was a sit-down meal you wanted, there was the Lunch Stand at 24th and Blondo, "for good service and big eats." Or how about the La France Café, which offered "real down home cooking," and was owned by James Griffin and located at 2526 Lake Street? Then there was Cothrane's Café, located at 1406 North 24th Street. There was the Chicago Restaurant, formerly Chinaman Sam's Place, that opened in 1928 from 6am until midnight. The new proprietors, Mr. and Mrs. Benjamin F. Burton, promised the lowest prices at the 107 South 14th Street location.

Myers Funeral Home, which was founded in 1921 and is considered to be the oldest surviving black business in the entire state of Nebraska. By 1927, advertisements were appearing in the Monitor, along with a picture of W.L. Myers, with the slogan, "Endeavoring at all times to meet the demand economically as well as scientifically."

By 1928, Central Chevrolet Company began advertising in the Omaha Monitor, meaning that the company saw potential in the black car buyer. Central Chevrolet, located at 2036 Farnam Street, featured Chevys, Fords, Buicks and a carmaker known as the Jewett. The ad made it clear that, "These cars have all been reconditioned and are sold with an O.K. that counts." Bloom Auto, 2204 Farnam offered both used cars and special terms, including 1825 Flint Sedan, the 1923 Jordan Brougham, the 1928 Essex Coach to name but a few.

North Omaha Star advertising manager Charlene Spencer said that her knowledge of the area and the businesses is "greater than most because my grandmother and mother talk about the good old days all the time." She recalled that Jim Bell had one of the first night clubs in Omaha. According to Spencer,

> Jim Bell's Club Harlem was located a few yards from Omaha's
> legendary North Twenty-Fourth and Lake Streets, the main
> corner of Omaha's black stem, the hub of the Near North Side, as
> Omaha's black ghetto was known. The Club Harlem had a full
> line of chorus girls, a twelve-piece orchestra, and imported top-
> grade comedians, singers, emcees, and other acts for their floor
> shows. The club catered to all races and was frequented by a
> sizable percentage of rich whites from Omaha's Dundee section
> (C. Spencer, personal communication, September 27, 2005).

Archie's Lounge, 3136 Lake Street, was dubbed as "Omaha's Finest Jazz Spot," and again billed as the place where you could find "live music." The location has a great history itself. Archie's Lounge was originally Johnny Owens' place, and then it changed to Club Lido. After that, it became Mr. G's; when it was Club Lido and Mr. G's, business was brisk because it was located across the street from the Hilltop housing projects and stayed open and packed most of the time. When Shirley Jordan purchased it, she renamed it "The Backstreet Lounge," and it made money and continues to make money from a regular, more upscale clientele. The projects that were formerly across the street have since been demolished and the owners of the property, Salem Baptist Church, are not happy about a lounge being located on a block where they own several properties. To be continued (C. Spencer, personal communication, September 27, 2005).

Another well-known night spot was the Dreamland Ballroom, located at 24th and Grant Streets. Acts from all over the nation came through Omaha, including Little Johnny Taylor and Roland Mitchell's Orchestra, who both appeared there on the night of Friday June 13, 1964. Taylor's major hit at the time was "Part Time Love," and he sang his new hit, "Since I Found a New Love." On December 17, 1965, the Bobby Bland Revue came to town.

The "clubs" were very popular in the 1960s and 1970s, and boasted their own buildings and, of course, memberships to key people who paid for inclusion and then got special concessions and consideration. Claiming to be "Omaha's Most Talked About Club," the Midwest Athletic Club was located near 17th and Wirt Streets. With Willie Mitchell as president, the Midwest Athletic Club was founded in 1938. After it was torn down in the 1970s, a mansion was built on the site and has since been occupied by a number of well-to-do blacks.

The Off-Beat Supper Club, located in the heart of the black community, on "The Deuce" (2410 Lake Street) was a place where, on Tuesday and Thursday nights, you would be able to attend such features as the Teen-Age Jamboree Show and Dance, which sometimes would feature Mike Lewis and his King Bees.

This is all being shared to make it clear that despite being the poorest of the poor, despite being locked out of the formal planning process and denied political representation until the advent of district elections in the middle 1970s, North Omaha's African-American community engaged in a form of "informal planning" that led to the creation of businesses, the maintenance of those businesses and had a lifestyle that attracted people from all over the nation. This then, represents the basis for the "significance" of this thesis. While certainly not comparable to the west Omaha suburbs, the southwest Omaha mansions or the Regency area, it is clear that there have always been people who have ideas and energy that can lead to planning that can benefit everyone.

The significance of this study, then, is to show that the potential and hard work, not to mention the legacy and tradition, all existed in Omaha at the grass roots (informal) levels. One might argue that during North Omaha's halcyon days, there was a great deal of hard work, commitment and emphasis on self-reliance in terms of support for businesses, churches and individuals. This "informal" dimension of community development has always existed, but it is the formal approach – approaches emanating primarily from the City of Omaha Planning Department – that have power and resources to bring about profound social and geo-physical change, but which omit or neglect the input of the very people who are in the majority in the North Omaha area.

II. CITIZEN PARTICIPATION: A LITERATURE REVIEW

America and the American dream are built on the assumption that every citizen has an equal opportunity to succeed. Unfortunately, all too many Americans face the stark reality that those who begin life in poverty will end life in poverty. African Americans living in concentrated pockets of poverty or segregated communities in urban America are a special source of concern (Massey & Denton 1992; Fong, 1994; Gramlich, Laren, & Sealand, 1992). Several studies point to the importance of involving those who live directly in certain areas in the planning process and that their bonds of community and social networks can be used to bring about socioeconomic improvements (Glaser, Parker, & Li, 2003; Kelly, 1977).

The concept of involving citizens and making participation a requirement has long been a part of a number of pieces of federal legislation. The Urban Affairs Department at the Virginia Tech University (1999), working on conjunction with the American Institute of Certified Planners, has created a list or timeline of such participatory requirements, and these range from Senate Document 97 (1962), the Economic Opportunity Act (1964), The Model Cities legislation (1966) and the 1972 Federal Water Pollution Control Act to the Housing and Community Development Act of 1975 and the Sunshine Act of 1977, all understood the importance of getting citizens involved in issues that would impact upon their communities (pp. 1-2).

As opposed to older structuralist conceptions, recent theorizing of the so-called "advocacy planning" or for that matter, issues such as the "interactive state" (O'Donovan, 2000) explicitly foreground power as constructed within and through relationships between actors and widens the concept of 'governance' beyond that of government to involve a range of people and groups as a number of levels. While citizen participation is bottoms up, it is also clear that the issue involves group interactions between a number of levels of bureaucracy and between different groups from different parts of any given community.

A feeling of vested interest is a key part of involving minorities in the community development process. Glaser, et. al. (2003) found that allegiance to neighborhood and community represents important centripetal forces that are essential to community development efforts, and although attachment to neighborhood and community are generally important regardless of race, they are particularly important to low-income African-American communities (pp. 546-547). And involvement in the planning process, from the very outset was cited by Bass & Applegate (2001) as a venture that worked to perfection in Sonora, California.

Bound to any discussion of community development and minority inclusion has to be the issue of social capital. Henderson (2001), quoting Allan, offers that, "The concept of social capital provides us with a language for both legitimizing and promoting the significance of the social resources that a society, community or group can harness for its own development" (p. 31). It is the loss of social capital, argues its creator Robert Putnam, that has led to what he calls "the steady decline of participation in American life" (Wallis, et. al., 1998: p. 254). Putnam's use of social capital treats it as a basic element in building a civil society. It is community development then, with emphasis on making those with less social capital more involved, that can lead to long-term growth on a physical, cultural, economic and, of course, social, basis.

Creating social capital or expanding on it can be a time-consuming process. This is perhaps why some view the idea of community development as being essentially one of incremental work, beginning with smaller units such as neighborhoods, and then moving and expanding from there (Henderson, 2003; Taylor, 2003). It is agreed by most that it is the neighborhood, as a unit, to which most people can relate and which contains a solid group of informal networks and groups (Henderson, 2003).

When it comes to community development, several articles point out the class and cultural differences that exist between those who are involved in such development and design. For instance, in writing about the active living movement and low-income areas, Day (2006) wrote that the movement focused much attention on the design attributes of middle-class, especially suburban, environments that may limit opportunities for everyday physical activity (p. 309). Similarly, development approaches that are not inclusive and are class-based or biased may not lead to the kinds of improvements that are in the best interests of local residents in any given area.

When it comes to increasing involvement in public service, Brown (2002) suggested that the expressed needs and opinions of the local people be taken into count as a precondition (p. 74).

Henderson (2003) offers that community cohesion and social inclusion policies have major implications for community development, especially for the work it does at the neighborhood level. He identifies key policy areas where group inclusion in the community development process can be particularly important: planning and development, provision for young people, crime reduction and policing, design and livability of the public realm, and methods of frontline service delivery (p. 38).

When it comes to impediments to citizen participation, de Viggiani, Jones and Naidoo (2004) found that one significant barrier to increasing minority and black participation in community horticulture was that of funding. Without funding, it was found, it was difficult for projects to engage in proactive outreach work or to network with local community groups and associations, and further meant that they were unable to reach marginalized or socially excluded groups (p. 98).

What is needed is a wider agenda for participation and inclusion or, as Goss (2001) wrote, a situation where community developers will begin, "to see the possibility .. of a local network of governance which does not simply presume the rules of inclusion, or of decision-making, but which enable them to be actively negotiated" (p. 61).

III. METHODOLOGY

The methodology employed is multi-faced, but primarily the use of secondary analysis of archival data. Articles on citizen participation were gleaned, and discussions took place with several members of the minority community. Background information was acquired regarding the role of blacks in both informal and formal aspects of community development and planning. Because of the process that was selected, there are no qualitative methodological issues to describe (e.g., sample population, the design of the instrument, survey instrument, etc.).

IV. MINORITIES IN THE COMMUNITY DEVELOPMENT PROCESS: OMAHA OVERVIEW

The importance of diversity in the process of community development is seen in what is produced by such efforts. In writing about downtown areas, for instance, Rypkena (2003) made the following observation:

> Downtown's strength is not homogeneity with everywhere else; the strength of downtown is its differentiation form anywhere else. Differentiated downtowns mean diverse downtowns. But that diversity must not only be encouraged between downtowns but celebrated within downtowns … In part, diversity, too, is related to globalization. We live in a world where there are far more Brown, Yellow, and Black people than White, where there are more Hindus, more Buddhists, and more Muslims than non-Hispanic Christians … Over the next 50 years, 97% of all the world's net population growth will be in Asia, Africa, and Latin America (Rypkena, 2003: p. 13).

Diversity in the community development process is reaping positive dividends on the global level because it makes sense on even the most basic of philosophical levels.

As it was concluded in a paper on urban planning and globalization a few semesters back,

> Just because urban planners know about daily life, they may feel that they can deal with planning issues and problems. They know about certain aspects of development and that is important. But we can't just hand all of the planning over to them because they don't always have the bigger picture. Different parts of the world have different issues, and as these three cities show, those issues differ based on caste, class, race, politics, and geography (Smartt, 2006: p. 15).

Inclusion of minorities, increasing the numbers of people of color in the community development process, is not only fair but it is sensible. The world is becoming more diverse and the global village is becoming one large interchangeable part. To be ethnocentric or bigoted (or exclusionary) with such a reality looming is not only counter-productive but could possibly be self-destructive. The more viewpoints and input there is in any given project or activity, the more inclusive the end result will be and the more people will be satisfied.

Godschalk (2004) provides an operational definition of what the new urbanism is all about when he defines it as, "an urban design movement committed to re-establishing the relationship between the art of a building and the making of community, through citizen based participatory planning and design" (p. 5). As importantly, developers have to recognize that a key component of the physical design is oftentimes the cultural, ethnic and racial diversity of a given area. Day (2006) documents that when it comes to designs of urban settings in the U.S., many of them "continue to be occupied disproportionately by poor people and people of color" while Allen & Turner (1989) write that, "In the U.S., urban areas are typically more diverse than exurban and rural areas" (p. 524).

Omaha has been involved in community development as far back as one can remember. And if one researches the topic, it is clear that today's Omaha By Design and Destination Midtown projects are updated extensions of the early days of Omaha, when parks and recreation were a priority. As one source documents:

> City planners allowed land for parks and Omaha became known for its outdoor recreational areas. Names like Elmwood, Hanscom, Riverview, Kountze, Mandan, Miller, Fontenelle, Hummel, and Levi Carter showed green on the city's maps. As early as the 1920s, Omaha was third nationally in per capital park area. The city also boasted the third largest corn and livestock markets, was fourth nationally in home ownership, and second in per capita telephone use. The county's population grew by more than fifty percent that decade, with new Asian and Hispanic immigrants adding to the mix (Reilly, et. al., 2004: p. 60).

The community development process is somewhat complicated because the concept is defined differently based upon what area of the city ones seems to be concentrating on. However, for the sake of this paper, the community development process in Omaha has been divided into three phases: (1) Planning, self-reliance and segregation; (2) Phase 2: Planning, North Omahans and Federal Intervention and (3) Contemporary community development and minority input

Phase 1: Planning, Self-Reliance and Segregation

In terms of the 1930s, Moore (1971) writes that, "Omaha blacks as a whole still remained out of the mainstream of economic life during the thirties and failed to share fully in the recovery brought about by World War II" (p. 13). But that didn't stop them from organizing and working for economic unity.

Although there has historically been a dearth of minority involvement in the community development/planning process in Omaha in recent years, such was not always the case. Depending upon your definition of what constitutes "community development," African-Americans expressed an interest and involvement in improving and developing their community and parts of it even as far back as the early 1900s. That involvement could be seen in efforts that might be viewed as formal (letter writing to government officials, petition drives and actual hands-on activity) as well as informal (editorials and articles in local newspapers, fundraising efforts aimed at addressing minority community needs, etc.).

It would therefore be impossible to discuss black involvement in the community development/planning process without first discussing the concept of advocacy planning and the role that such planning, whether formally executed or informally undertaken, has played in the activities and attitudes of North Omaha residents and the Omaha black community.

Stieglitz (1999) writes that, "Human beings are born different: we are different in both physical appearance and social/cultural identity. This holds true for individuals, as well as for groups and communities. The concept of differentiation, which is the starting point of advocacy planning, is therefore central to planning. As originally defined … advocacy planning referred to the defense of excluded interests" (p. 57).

In a context where residential segregation is the norm, it is clear that those who are segregated represent the "excluded interests" that are alluded to in the definition provided above. As a result, those interests can be defended either formally (lobbying, working through governmental entities) or informally (protesting, picketing, newspaper editorials, etc.). Those involved in advocacy planning, according to Davidoff (1996) should adhere to very high values in order to serve disadvantaged communities" (p. 307).

But the disadvantaged should play a key role because, if they do not, then all you have is paternalistic control. Guinier & Torres (2002) suggest that, "the dominant approach to representation in the United States today seems to worship at the shrine of synecdoche, ignoring the complexity of the representational relationship in a multiracial democracy. Democracy is supposed to bring the people into the arena of public decision-making as participants, not as spectators" (p. 21).

Early among these efforts were the works of the Ideal Improvement Club. This organization, one of the first of many self-help groups that sprang up in Omaha's black community in the mid-1950s, addressed a number of community development issues that were germane to a segregated African-American community during that time.

For example, in January of 1960, 24th Street finally got paved by the city. The Ideal Improvement Club, behind the tireless work of North Omahans A.R. Goodlet and Mrs. Anita Hayes, met with City Public Works Director George Fisher and pointed out that the street had railroad tracks and slippery brick pavement and was in need of repair. The Omaha Star of January 15, 1960 outlined how important the actions of these two people had been:

> The railway tracks have been a traffic hazard for a long time and have hampered smooth traffic flow from North Omaha to South Omaha. Mr. [George] Fisher's [City Public Works Director] … announcement is a direct result of the activity of the Ideal Improvement Club … They were persistent even when it appeared that the Department would rather have done work in other sections of the city. The Ideal Improvement Club pointed out that 24th Street is the only street that runs completely from North to South Omaha … The community owes Mr. Goodlet and his group their thanks for efforts in persuading the city fathers to give a little attention to this area also (Omaha Star, 1960: 1).

On the heels of this major breakthrough came the paving of Lake Street, which in turn, prompted a major "thank you" from Sam J. Cornelius, then the Executive Secretary of the Near North Branch of the YMCA. In a letter dated May 27th but reprinted in the Omaha Star on June 12th, Cornelius wrote,

> Ideal Improvement Club
> c/o: A.R. Goodlet, President
> 2815 Binney
> Omaha, Nebraska
>
> Dear Mr. Goodlet:
> Congratulations to the Ideal Improvement Club on its outstanding efforts in getting Lake Street paved.
> This kind of leadership and cooperation among the citizens in this city make one proud to be living here in Omaha.
> The work of the Ideal Improvement Club in this community is certainly worthy of outstanding recognition. Your leadership as president is, without a doubt, the kind of leadership that today's time demands.
> Sincerely,
> Samuel J. Cornelius
> Executive Secretary

Less formal activities aimed at improving the community were also a part of the North Omaha thrust. Among these were editorials in one of the first African-American newspapers to serve the area, the Omaha Star.

The early editions of the Omaha Star newspaper carried a recurring college on the editorial page called "The Roving Reporter." This was no fluff piece; the questions that were asked were hard core questions and addressed the kinds of community development issues that are still issues of concern in central cities today. For example, in August 20, 1938 issue, the question posed was, "Do you think North Twenty-Fourth Street is properly lighted as compared to other neighborhood business sections of the city?

This question goes directly to the issue of "place framing," which is what Deborah Martin (2003) outlines in an article titled, "Place-Making: Constituting a Neighborhood for Organizing and Activism." A point where I agree with Martin is where she outlines how space – that is, the setting, geographic location, and sociospatial context of a neighborhood – influences the formation of collective identities and activist agendas (p. 731).

This is how the North Omaha community – the ghetto – gave form and function to a number of organizations and efforts that met the needs of the people of various time periods. In this case, the answers to the questions posed by the Roving Reporter provided an idea as to what was going on in the minds of ghetto residents and shows that we did not childishly sit around waiting for the white man to come around and give us ideas.

In regard to the lighting issue, James "Jimmy" Jewell, then the owner of Tuxedo Billiard Parlor, answered, "I think we are slighted as far as lighting facilities are concerned, North 24th Street from Cuming to Lake is not only poorly lighted (sic), but is the last area to be lighted (sic) and the first to have the lights turned off."

In the same response section of the editorial page of the Omaha Star, Mr. R. Taylor of the Lux Barber Shop said, "I feel we need quite a bit of improvement. It would add a great deal to our business as well as to the appearance of North Twenty-Fourth Street." In the same publication, Mr. J.H. Anderson of Climax Cleaners replied, "That is the first thing I noticed when I came to Omaha – the poor lighting system on North Twenty-fourth street, and I think something ought to be done to improve this condition."

Today, as neighborhood associations around the city apply for and receive grant money for Neighborhood Watches, garbage cleanup and other minor details, inner city neighborhood groups like the Ideal Improvement Club in the 1920s and today's own Highlander, Wirt-Binney-Spencer, and Triple One neighborhood groups deal with inner city issues, which include violence and crime. And again, our ideas as far back as 1928 generated questions and answers that are now being put into effect by those who live OUTSIDE of the area.

Want proof? The August 27, 1928 edition of the Omaha Star's "Roving Reporter" question was, "What is the best means of eliminating the congregation of boys around our business establishments?" Here are some of the answers.

Mr. A.B. Wright of 2872 Maple said, "What we need to eliminate this congregating is adequate amusements for our young people, like the whites – in the form of swimming pools, playgrounds, tennis courts, and a first class YMCA and YWCA. We are taxed the same sin most instances more than the white people and should have the same consideration for our young people in return for our taxes." Miss Annie Franklin of 3026 "R" Street said, "In order to keep the boys from hanging around business establishments I would suggest more activities at the Recreational centers and nearby parks should be erected." Mr. C.B. Mayo of 2422 Lake Street replied, "I don't think resorting to law enforcement would e right, because these boys have to have some place to meet, but there should be some adequate form of clean amusements, like playgrounds, and a YMCA to occupy their time."

These ideas are the seeds of community development efforts that are formalized today by the likes of Omaha Economic Development Corporation, New Community Development and the now-defunct North Omaha Community Development. While the area was being neglected by the City Planning Department, urban core residents knew what had to be done, were aware of their rights as taxpayers and apparently lived by that old religious belief that, "an idle mind is the devil's workshop."

Because of segregation, the tendency during the early days of settlement in North Omaha was for blacks to look inward first before relying on "the system" to address its needs. This was undoubtedly a practice fomented during their days in the South, where segregation and discrimination were even more concentrated, and where the threat of death often loomed and was directed at any individual or group that dared to approach the establishment or requested help. Such activity, in that region of the nation and during that time period, was viewed all too often as an act of black aggression, audacity or as "getting uppity."

As a result of such thinking and tendencies, when it was time to construct a YMCA for black youth, it was the "Roving Reporter" section of the Omaha Star that once again provided the reasoning by posing the question, in the September 3, 1938 edition of the Omaha Star, "What do you think is an appropriate time to stat campaigning for a Y.W.C.A.?

To back up the need for the YWCA (or, more than likely, a YMCA), the Omaha Star published an editorial on the same page as the "Roving Reporter." The editorial, titled, "Omaha Needs A Y.M.C.A., had the following viewpoint to share:

Omaha, with its 16,000 Negroes, has not kept pace with similar cities of its size throughout the country in that it has failed to recognize the need of (sic) a Y.M.C.A., an institution in which the four cardinal principles of character may be imparted to the men of tomorrow.

Following up the opinions as related by nine of Omaha's influential citizenry in the columns of the Roving Reporter in the edition of September 3rd, The Omaha Star also feels that there is a need for a YMCA in our great city. Such an institution would help to keep our boys off the streets and from congregating in front of and blocking the sidewalks leading to the entrances of our business paces on Twenty-Fourth Street. It would be a means of elevating their minds to higher ideals. It would draw them closer to church. It would be a means of developing more healthy bodies. All in all, it would develop real manhood in our boys.

It is being suggested that a committee of men who are interested in the welfare of our boys be formed; invite some outstanding Negro National Y.M.C.A representative to come to our city for the purpose of surveying the field and making recommendations for the organization of the work.

Informal approaches at community development continued well into the 1960s. In December of 1963, Douglas Stewart became the Executive Director of the Urban League. In February of 1964, he wrote a series of essays to the Omaha Star titled, "An Overview of the Socio-Economic Conditions of Omaha Non-White People." Stewart wrote, in part, Following is the text of those essays:

"Ye shall speak the truth and it will make you free."

Since December, 1963, I have been a resident of Omaha and Executive Director of the Omaha Urban League.

During this brief period I have talked to many citizens of Omaha, both Negro and Caucasian, about the problems of the minority group community in our city. On numerous occasions, too many for comfort, I have been told there are no problems faced by the non-white population in Omaha. This reply was rather disturbing to me as a recent arrival because visual observation of the Negro ghetto, commonly referred to in Omaha as the Near Northside, told me different.

In many respects, seeing is believing. It was therefore necessary for me to do a little research and fact finding to determine the true situation because I am truly convinced that the first and basic aspect of problem solving is to recognize and admit that a problem exists.

On March 7th, a sequel to the preceding article appeared. Stewart explained,

> The previous [article] … was made, not in an apologetic manner, but more explanatory because the Urban League as an agency does not engage in direct action such as picketing or boycotts. We believe as an agency that racial problems in a community are manifested in many ways and at many levels, and therefore, a multiplicity of techniques and approaches are required to successfully cope with them. No single organization can profess to have a monopoly in this field or to have all the answers as to methodology.

Stewart added,

> The Urban League movement is committed to use of such methods as research, conferences, public education and community organization. However, we have no quarrel with efforts under responsible leadership using acceptable methods and seeking the same ultimate goals of a free, democratic and healthy society as does the Urban League … At the same time it must be recognized that certain stubborn problem situations historically have not responded to Urban League methodology. Some of these, however, have been successfully dealt with by litigation, boycotts, sit-ins, picketing, etc. … In essence, we have been faced with and are currently facing tumult, social upheaval, fermentation, and perhaps there will be profound social change (Stewart, 1964: 1).

There is little doubt that African-Americans in Omaha lobbied and advocated for community development on both a formal and an informal level. Because of the lack of a minority presence in City Hall, particularly in the City Planning Department, the informal approaches to community development and planning were essentially the only tools that African-Americans had to work with.

Phase 2: Planning, North Omahans and Federal Intervention

Although the following chronology is admittedly cursory, it provides some semblance of evidence that Omaha has been involved in the community development process on a formal basis for several decades and has worked with local, county and Federal entities to expand the community and improve it. This paper will briefly address urban renewal and the Community Development Block Grant Program. In addition, several organizations that were spawned in response to the need for community development, the United Contractors Association of

Nebraska, the Omaha Economic Development Corporation and, more recently, New Community Development, will also be discussed.

Much of the issues revolving around or involving "planning" in North Omaha had to do with housing and population density. The pleas by Northside political and civic leadership for "open housing" was the major controversy during the late 1960s through the 1970s. Even after winning this victory, the city of Omaha remained segregated through what the Urban League of Nebraska in 1978 concluded was a systematic combination of redlining and steering of black citizens seeking housing (Urban League of Nebraska, 1978: pp. 31-32).

The coming of federal programs to Omaha did little to address the issue of housing. The following overview provides some context which lays the basis for establishing the role of the City of Omaha Planning Department in the gradual decline of North and why this thesis is calling for more minority (African-American) inclusion in the community development and urban planning processes.

Minorities and Urban Renewal

In 1961, in the middle of a controversy surrounding urban renewal in North Omaha, the Omaha Star offered neither praise nor disapproval but asked only that "Negroes be treated fairly under the bill." The newspaper also referred to a study by the NAACP that said that the majority of the population uprooted by urban renewal projects were black people. In addition, the newspaper said that less than 2 percent of the new homes built during the 1950s were available to black people and called for a non-discrimination clause in any redevelopment project (Omaha Star, 1961: 1).

In 1963, one month before President John F. Kennedy was assassinated, "the question of fair housing replaced urban renewal as the hot topic in the Dworak administration. At a time when the federal government showed an increase in housing discrimination, civil rights demonstrations marched on City Hall. And,

> In late October 1963, two weeks after the City Council allocated money for a housing discrimination study which Washington added as a requirement of the Community Renewal Program, the Reverends Rudolph McNair and Kelsey Jones, both Negroes, led a civil rights protest inside the Council chambers. The demonstrators organized by the Citizens Coordinating Committee for Civil Liberties, sang and carried signs that denounced racial discrimination before the Councilmen … (Stevens, 1981: 120).

The protesters were arrested but the next day Reverend McNair challenged the entire black population of Omaha, then about 30,000 in number, to attend the next City Council meeting in a silent protest. Two thousand black people showed up in and around City Hall during the first half hour of the Council meeting, and, as Stevens documents, "the quiet demonstration ended without incident, and the police arrested no one" (1981: 120-121).

By analyzing the housing problems in North Omaha, we find that: (1) Blacks have historically been confined to that area of the city; (2) the housing in that area is inferior; (3) the demolition-to-construction ratio means even less housing here in 2001, since there have been few housing starts in North Omaha since 1980; (4) the housing starts that do exist are being constructed for individuals who are middle and upper income, not for the low-income residents of North Omaha; (5) the stigma attached to the area because it is predominantly black, perpetuates the racist inclinations of whites and the poor race relations which continue to persist.

If the housing stock can be controlled, so can the people who need it. Omaha has learned this lesson well, and used every trick in the book to keep from providing decent housing for inner city residents.

For example in 1964, the Omaha Star reported the following back-and-forth debate on the issue of housing:

> Four sources of "contradictory information" to that of a random
> sample of housing in an area bounded by Sixteenth, Thirteenth,
> Cuming and Grace Streets made by the Urban Renewal and
> Permits and Inspections Departments will be given to the City
> Council Tuesday afternoon. The city's survey said that only one of
> 130 living dwellings inspected was overcrowded … (p. 1).

But Urban League Director Douglas E. Stewart "indicated to the Council during that same time (1964) that he had statistics that showed that the 1960 U.S. census asserted that 17 percent of the housing in the census tracts covered in the survey are overcrowded. Stewart noted that he had factual information which refuted other claims of the survey" (Omaha Star 1964: 1). An article from the Omaha Star, dated September 18, 1964, reports on Stewart's presentation and clearly shows the relationship of health concerns and housing as it relates to North Omaha:

> At Tuesday's Council session, the Urban League recommended
> that: the city of Omaha intensify its program of enforcing the
> minimum dwelling standards ordinance in the blighted areas of
> our city with the objectives of improving and rehabilitating
> property wherever it is economically feasible and the
> demolishment (sic) of that property which cannot be made fit for
> human habitation."

> Pointing out that "nowhere are men of good will more indelibly
> indicated than in the slums of our city,' Douglas Stewart, Urban
> League executive director declared: "I am angry and ashamed of
> man's inhumanity, his cruelty and his indifference to the
> suffering of human beings who are his fellow citizens – That we
> should permit, much less subject, citizens to live in hovels and
> hell holes such as Hogarth depicted two centuries ago is
> unworthy of this great city"

"Informal planning approaches," as this thesis declares them, continued in the form of protests and on-going pressure on city government.
As evidence of how little has changed since those days in the early 1960s to the present when it comes down to the issue of population density and conflict in and around the black community of Omaha, one need only glean a report entitled, "Social Problems, Disease and Substandard Housing," submitted to Mayor Dworak January, 1963 by the Social Planning Unit of the United Community Services. And what that report said in 1963 still applies to North Omaha today, some 38 years later:

> The report noted that the incidence of disease, anti-social behavior,
> social maladjustment and economic dependency occurred with
> greater frequency in areas of substandard housing. Stewart related
> that the report contained the following cautions when drawing
> conclusions from the data contained therein: a) the sheer density of
> population affects the occurrence of social and health problems; b)
> the community's attitude and discrimination affects where and how
> minority groups live; c) Job security and income affects, to some
> extent, the type of housing available to individuals and families; d)
> The cultural background of people living in the neighborhood
> affects, to some degree, its rate of deterioration" (Omaha Star,
> 1964: 1).

The lack of black input into these important issues that were impacting upon North Omaha created a "fear" of any program that was supposed to "help the Negro." The residents, for the most part, had been promised that things would get better, and had been reading about the changes that were taking place in major cities elsewhere in the country. So even though Omaha's black community was passive in many ways, it continued to voice opposition to urban renewal coming to the River City. As Stevens posited,

> By 1970, a majority of the vocal black leaders voiced strong
> opposition to urban renewal. They did not believe that the
> government leaders would seek the advice of blacks during the

planning of projects. Urban renewal, they contended, would force
Negroes out of their homes without giving them a voice in where
they would be rehoused. Lawrence McVoy, a board member of
Greater Omaha Community Action and a former president of the
Omaha NAACP, said the city "has never accepted the participation
of the poor, even in welfare programs" (Stevens, 1981: 140).

In a 1971 book titled, *Odyssey: Journey Through Black America.* long-time
Omaha dentist Earle Person made this observation:

> When the whites put together their downtown area, their slogan
> was: "Can do." We [blacks in Omaha] saw that the slogan for the
> Near North Side was: "Won't do." The prime movers just say,
> "Well, we'll try a few little things, form a committee, call in an
> outside research organization, make a study." And they do survey
> after survey after survey, and all of them get stuck away in some
> file … (Selby & Selby, 1971: 290).

This is why exclusion did so much harm to the long-range well-being of
North Omahans, not only in terms of social and political, but also in terms of
psychologically. Being constantly denied and ignored, as other parts of the city
developed, sent a clear message to the minority and poor: their inclusion simply
was not wanted.

This is why the words of Guinier & Torres (2002) ring so true when they
posit, "Participation is not solely a means to gain a specific benefit; it is also a
means of understanding our own position. Different ideas energize the process and
challenge us to rethink our own truths" (p. 22). A key section of this thesis
provides examples of what could take place in and around North Omaha when the
residents there exercised their rights as citizens and implemented their ideas. Such
an approach was never really given its due consideration by the powers that be.

In sum, many of the federal programs of the 1960s and so on were knee-jerk
reactions to riots and turmoil and were applied by throwing huge amounts of
money at "minority problems." Now, some five decades after those efforts, it is
clear that many of them destroyed more housing (and as a result, livelihoods) in
central cities of America than they saved. Increased minority input into the process
(not just token jobs as part of a federal hiring and appeasement campaign) might
have enabled that money to be better spent.

1975: CDBG Comes to Omaha

Omaha got involved in the program in 1976; the following year the Community Development Block Grant funding was made even more enticing with the advent of another program, as described by Levy (2000) on page 173:

> In 1977 Congress expanded the scope of community development efforts somewhat by providing additional funds intended specifically for local economic development. These funds were provided under the Urban Development Action Grant (UDAG) program. Communities that met certain criteria for poverty, age of housing stock, unemployment, and slowness of employment growth were eligible for grants.

As several individuals informed me during the writing of this paper, the City of Omaha has received more than $150 million in CDBG funds since 1975. These were monies generated by the poverty of North Omaha, and monies that were, once received, steered into other areas of the city including such non-necessities as Eugene Leahy Park downtown, skywalks, skyscrapers and west Omaha expansion into the exurbs.

The arrival of the Community Development Block Grant program did pave the way for some minority input. It was in 1975 that the Omaha Economic Development Corporation became formalized under the program and, with the assistance of then Planning Department director Martin Shukert, OEDC director Al Goodwin was able to secure several major housing contracts and in subsequent years, was included in the annual allocation as a developer for projects that primarily impacted the area known as the near North Side.

Several other organizations, along with OEDC, existed prior to 1975, but survived primarily through small allocations from the Mayor's office. Among these development groups were the Urban Business Development Corporation and the short-lived Inner City Development Group.

The arrival of the Community Development Block Grant program also gave rise to involvement of the Urban League of Nebraska in the planning process. Small grants were allocated to the League, although the projects were not directly related to community development. The League was provided with some funding for voter registration, education and information workshops, and then director George Dean, beginning in 1977, began working with the City Planning Department on issues related to public housing subsidies, including energy assistance, weatherization and housing renovations. Beginning in 1980, Greater Omaha Community Action joined this role, although the source of its funding was the Community Service Block Grant, which was awarded by the State, not the City.

The "development project" that Marty Shukert said was going to be "the catalyst for commercial redevelopment in the area" (King, 1981: 6), the Blue Lion Center, did very little and is now owned by the City of Omaha. In fact in February 1984 it was NOCD that had to retain the services of P.J. Morgan Company to "manage" the Blue Lion Center. A group called Local Initiatives Support Corporation, Omaha Committee, gave $50, 000 to NOCD to pay for P.J. Morgan's services as the leasing agent and, get this, to "train NOCD staff so it eventually can manage the center on its own."

The September 16, 1983 edition of the Omaha World Herald reported the following:

> North Omaha Community Development Inc., project developer
> of the Blue Lion Center, has received assistance from the
> National Center for Neighborhood Enterprise and the National
> Association for Neighborhoods, both based in Washington, D.C.
> Over the last eight months, representatives of the two national
> groups have made several visits to Omaha, said Carl Christian,
> NOCD executive director … The National Association of
> Neighborhoods' goal in providing technical assistance is to
> promote neighborhood based service delivery for community
> organizations such as NOCD, Christian said … Christian said
> NOCD will enter into a contract with the City of Omaha to
> maintain landscaping, lighting and parking areas around the Blue
> Lion Center on city-owned property. The National Association
> of Neighborhoods also is providing technical assistance to
> NOCD personnel in the area of horticulture.

In January of 1985, when North Omaha Community Development was slowly being eased out of any association with the city because of the alleged mismanagement of its books, Carl Christian told the *Omaha World Herald* that the organization, "wants to continue to move toward self-sufficiency and less dependence on federal grants" (Omaha World Herald, 1985). But by that time it was too late to talk about being "self-sufficient:" the writing was already on the wall. Is it any wonder it failed?

In February of 1988, a *World-Herald* article asserted that, "a plan to move a north Omaha police unit into the Blue Lion Center doesn't mean the city is converting the building to government offices, Mayor [Bernie] Simon said Thursday. "We see the Blue Lion as being the keystone to 24th and Lake Streets," the mayor said. "A keystone means that it won't be all government offices." In December of 2003, businesses in the Blue Lion were evicted and the building is now mostly the City-run offices of Workforce Development.

But the lack of minority input meant that the CDBG funds were going to be spent in a way that the City felt was best. But by 1980, although by that time the city has received more than $20 million in CDBG funds, North Omaha continued to deteriorate.

Even a politician as conservative as then City Councilman Tim Rouse was able to describe – and in this case also sum up – what had taken place in and around North Omaha in a 1980 Omaha World Herald editorial. In that editorial, Rouse, who alleged that the Veys administration has neglected blacks in Northeast Omaha, said that the black neighborhood in Northeast Omaha needs more than an equal amount of effort because of 20 to 30 years of neglect (Omaha World Herald, 1980: 4).

The City of Omaha has received more than $150 million in Community Development Block Grant funds since the first award in 1975. And yet when talking to North Omaha residents and those involved in community development, most will admit that the area known as North Omaha, the target area for such grants, is now less developed than it was in 1975, thirty-one years ago. The inclusion of more minorities, at least the opinions and views of more minorities when it came to the community development process and the expenditures of the CDBG grants, might have led to more expansive development in and around the target area.

Phase 3: Contemporary Planning and Minority Input

By "contemporary planning," there is no base year for such a definition. What is meant is simply those efforts that took place both during the advent of Community Development Block Grant allocations and primarily during the beginning of the mayorship of Mike Boyle, which began in 1980. Many sang the praises of the new mayor following a tight-fisted and contentious mayorship of Al Veys, the enabling of minorities did come into fruition – to a degree. While African-Americans such as Eddie Staton and Jeff Ross and Ruth Jackson, along with several others, were given department head status, the Planning Department basically remained all white, with the exception of a few minorities who were hired using the CDBG grant and the long-time Black face, Ken Johnson.

Even when minority inclusion existed in appearance, many wonder if such inclusion was ever taken seriously or if it was window dressing to appease a doubting and rapidly deteriorating community. Many of these concerns, based on informal discussions with community people, several civic leaders and a host of ministers who have been in Omaha for decades, seemed to center around a group called North Omaha Community Development. In fact, after hearing stories about what this organization intended to do and what was actually done, the story itself served as the nugget for an idea which led to the subject of this thesis.

North Omaha Community Development

Though created for the purpose of serving as a liaison between north Omaha neighborhoods and the City of Omaha, in retrospect it appears that North Omaha Community Development, as Senator Chambers alleged, was nothing more than "an adjunct to the city" (Chambers, 1982).

Garnett saw the writing in the wall and, during his frequent meetings with various mayors, he learned, no doubt, about their plans to invade the black community by pushing the indigenous population further and further northwest. A World-Herald editorial, titled "Skyline Over North Omaha Brightens," continued to promise jobs and "development" to the area by using vague terms like "appears," and "should" so as not to make an actual promise that would have to be fulfilled:

> Last August, it was noted editorially that there was a surge of activity to revitalize Omaha's North Side … Omaha also appears finally ready to get on with building the extension of the North Freeway and the Arthur C. Storz Expressway to Eppley Airfield. This should offer the better transportation needed to provide development and jobs in the area. As the New Year begins the skies over North Omaha do, indeed, look brighter for 1981 and the years to follow (Omaha World Herald, 1981: 4).

But despite the promises, the coming and going of Model Cities and Urban Renewal, and the arrival of Community Development Block Grants, the Planning Department of the City of Omaha continued to offer claims of improving the area, but the improvements were a long time in coming. The shortage of low-income housing, despite the fact that housing was being condemned and destroyed at an alarming rate, continued to point to the contradictory activities of the urban planners who refused to listen to what African-American civic leaders had to say.

In an article titled, "Jobs, Housing Remain Problems: Future Still Shaky for Many Blacks," Flanery and Brown (1986) interviewed local and national housing experts who assess the Omaha situation most accurately:

> A shortage of housing for blacks and other low-income people will worsen, said Robert Armstrong, executive director of the Omaha Housing Authority. "We'll do what's we can to expand our housing stock, but we won't come close to solving our housing problems," he said. Armstrong said the housing problem won't be resolved until unemployment among blacks is sharply reduced. Until that happens, he said, "We're sitting on a keg of dynamite that could explode any time" (p. 14).

In addition to issues of housing was the adjoining issue of the lack of jobs which, in turn, was the key to being able to afford a decent place to live. The issue was always about blacks taking care of themselves and this meant supporting a family by having a job. The experts and the planners who were in decision making positions had to be aware of that. And the fact that these realities were ignored is one reason why during the riots of 1966, and again in 1968 and '69, Omaha blacks who were looting and throwing bottles and bricks were also chanting, "jobs, jobs, jobs."

Recall from the "significance of this study" section of this thesis that the periods when North Omaha was at its best, the halcyon days of the black community, were days when black males and females were employed, when families were stable as a result of those jobs, and when black self-determination, through the support of black and other inner city businesses, could be realized. Those in power saw that and went about impacting upon each of these variables and today, in the year 2001, the Black community fares worse than it did in the 40s and 50s.

It is therefore only inevitable that those who live in the area would adopt some sense of hopelessness when they continue to see their situation deteriorating. In fact, as recently as 1991, long-time North Omaha activist and scholar Dr. Rodney Wead, showed a similar lack of confidence in the future when, during an interview with the Omaha World Herald, he said,

> So "forgotten" is the area that "it should be demolished, said Rodney Wead, an assistant professor of black studies at the University of Nebraska at Omaha and an associate professor at Creighton University. "I think we should raze every property in the area with the exception of Kellom Knolls Apartments, the Kellom Valley Shops and the new housing project at 24th and Grace Street and the historical landmarks at lake and 24th," said Wead, 56. As a child, Wead lived in the Logan Fontenelle housing project in the area for nine years. "I am tired of us putting Band-Aids on huge wounds," he said. "It would be cost-effective … We could start over" (Smith, 1991: 1).

The "study area" discussed by Blair (1992) in the following excerpt is the same as the traditional Black community of which I am writing and, as a result, his observations are fundamentally correct:

> …the study area has lost a significant number of housing units in the 20 years since 1970, a decrease of 14.4 percent. The lost units number in the thousands. The State of Black Omaha, 1984 also noted a large drop in the number of housing units from 1970 to

> 1980 in the Black community, and this is likely, in part, because of
> the construction of the North Freeway during this time period …
> (p. 27).

All this is mentioned because much it took place on NOCD's watch. It appeared that even though NOCD was focused on organizing neighborhoods in and around the North Omaha area, NOCD's role as far as consultation with the mayor and the Planning Department was negligible. Once on the City payroll perhaps it was not in the organization's best interests to voice major concerns such as the need for improve sewers, lighting and roads in and around North Omaha.

But the essential complaint about North Omaha Community Development appears to be its role in the acquisition and then subsequent loss of the Blue Lion Center.

The Blue Lion Center was "given" to NOCD as a way to continue its funding for salaries and operating expenses. The logic was that NOCD would be the manager of the Blue Lion, rent out offices and space to various organizations and that rent money would serve as a basis for operating expenses for the organization. But in a classic example of minority inclusion without proper training or experience, the NOCD staff mis-managed the Center, and could not maintain existing tenants and, in fact, had to evict a number of them once the rents on the Blue Lion were raised to meet NOCD expenses.

Finally, after continued efforts to bring in new tenants but failing, NOCD defaulted on the building. The City had to intercede and purchase the building back, which is the current status of the property, which is now filled primarily with City related offices, mainly The Department of Workforce Development. After losing the Blue Lion, North Omaha Community Development's name was further besmirched because of public charges that funds were mis-managed and money was owed to the City as a result.

Omaha By Design

According to Omaha By Design Director Connie Spelman, the Omaha By Design plan had been in the works for some time. She made it clear during our interview that it started in January 2002. My earlier belief that Daub set the groundwork was immediately refuted by Ms. Spelman. One article documented that the plan was officially adopted by the city in December of 2004 (Kotok, 2006). But as far back as January of 2004, businessmen paved the way, as Kotok (2004) wrote:

> [Kiewit Chairman Ken] … Stinson and two other corporate
> leaders – First National Chairman Bruce Lauritzen and World-

herald Publisher John Gottschalk – are financing and raising the $800,000 to develop standards to dress up the city, an effort called Omaha By Design. The executives' involvement served notice to the development community that it should take Omaha By Design seriously.

And,

The idea of improving the looks of Omaha has been building for years. "The wakeup call" came in late 2002, Stinson said. That was when the first plan surfaced to transform Avaya, Inc.'s sprawling front lawn along L Street between 120th and 132nd Streets into an unadorned parking lot outside three huge plain-front retailers. Stinson said development in Omaha is "not all bad, haphazard and abysmal … But we could do a lot better" (Kotok, 2004).

It had been presumed that there was a link between Omaha By Design and the Destination Midtown concept that is geared toward that area of the city. However, when asked what prompted all the attention on the midtown area, Spelman claimed that, "There is not more importance placed on Midtown. Midtown is treated like every other area in Omaha" (Spelman, 2006).

As the topic of Omaha By Design was researched, there were a number of people who had never heard of it and, among Blacks, a number of people who felt it was another plan that had nothing to do with North Omaha.

According to one source,

Thirty year as ago the redevelopment of downtown Omaha began with a dream to "Return to the River." The Gene Leahy Mall was the first step in realizing the dream and a major catalyst for the development of the ConAgra Campus and the Heartland of America Park. The dream expanded to the riverfront and then, in six short years a transformation occurred with two billion dollars of investment in the Riverfront and downtown Omaha – the First National Bank Tower, Qwest Center Omaha, Holland Performing Arts Center, Gallup University, the National Park Service District Office … (Omaha By Design, 2006: p. 3).

All of this was the prelude for Omaha By Design. The vision was rooted in a three parts: "Green Omaha, Civic Omaha and Neighborhood Omaha. Each is critical to the overall goal of creating a vibrant, functional and appealing community for both businesses and individuals" (Omaha By Design, 2006: p. 2).

In reference to the Tourism Bureau and its relationship with Omaha By Design, Spelman told me, "The tourism bureau has a link on our site, and they reciprocate by having our link on their site." She said that the management of the Tourism Bureau would be under Ms. Markel's auspices and that the role tourism and promotions plays in our organization is very important. It's our heartbeat. It brings people into the city and allows them to view our public spaces (Spelman, 2006).

With more minority input, Omaha By Design could be more inclusive in its production, especially since a key part of Omaha By Design is the midtown area of the city, one that is already being addressed with the "Destination Midtown" project, a project that is headed by an African-American female, Tawana Black. But the key is that Omaha By Design is a chance to show that the "design" is an inclusive one and not one that caters to the existing segregated state of the city.

Frank Brown as Urban Planner

Frank Brown is the City Councilman who represents District 2, that area of the city where the majority of the city's African-Americans reside. He is not an urban planner or a community developer. But upon being elected and realizing that his area was the fastest deteriorating sector of the city, Brown worked closely with the City Planning Department to usher in some physical changes to the African-American community, especially in the heart of the area, 24th and Lake Streets. Before continuing on, Brown's role in a group called D2NC and the role of Inner City Neighborhood Councils will be briefly addressed, as these issues provide a basis for understanding this Councilman's role in the community development, economic revitalization and urban planning efforts taking place in and around North Omaha.

Full Circle: the D2NC and Inner City Neighborhood Councils

The recent commitment to "super neighborhood groups" outlined in 2006 by Mayor Mike Fahey, beginning with the Benson, Alliance, actually got its start with a creation by City Councilman Frank Brown and the advent of the District 2 Neighborhood Coalition – D2NC.

The District 2 Neighborhood Coalition came about in 2000 when Frank Brown wanted an organization that would bring together North Omahans in an organized fashion. Although the organization got off the ground, not much was done in terms of concrete programs after Brown turned it over to others to run it. In 2004, new elections ushered in an entirely new board, although then Neighborhood Center of Greater Omaha assistant director resigned after some conflicts with then

Center director Deidre Andrews. Selected to lead the organization was Dell Gines, who had served as the former director of the Omaha Small Business Network.

Today the D2NC defines itself as the umbrella organization for all of the neighborhood associations in the North Omaha, and states that its mission is to organize and advocate on behalf of the local neighborhoods in the North Omaha community and build strong communities, safe communities, and wealthy communities. It would be a temporary pillar, at best.

The literature lists "four pillars" that support the mission of the organization. They are: (1) *To economically empower* North Omaha neighborhoods through actively working with the city, economic developers and with local businesses to create economic opportunities and jobs in our North Omaha community; (2) *To socially empower* North Omaha neighborhoods through developing strong neighborhood associations that control and police their local blocks and neighborhoods; (3) *To politically empower* North Omaha Neighborhoods through grassroots organizing our community and working with politicians, police, and social agencies to insure our voice is heard when decisions are made that affect our neighborhoods, and (4) *To physically empower* North Omaha Neighborhoods through the aid in creating neighborhood watch groups, and other programs.

With D2NC plodding along, Brown then went about the business of working with Planning Director Robert Peters to bring some immediate and highly visible changes to the core of North Omaha. These changes include the construction of a Family Housing Advisory Services building on the southwest corner of 24th and Lake Streets, an upgrading of the Omaha Technical Business incubator on the northeast corner, and the introduction of the Preston Love Arts and Humanities Jazz Museum on the northwest corner. These projects, along with renovation of the Strehlow Apartments and the re-naming of them after State Senator Ernie Chambers (Chambers Court), enabled Brown to earn his stripes as an innovator and a community developer.

Some have argued that much of what Brown has engineered is cosmetic, in terms of not creating job or generating a tax base. But the fact still remains that Brown, as an African-American, has shown what he can do by being involved in the community development/urban planning process, the subject and focus of this thesis. Again, it is a clear example of the initiative and energy of a person of color who, if "allowed" to be a player in community development, can bring about positive changes that are inclusive and which give the appearance that the City of Omaha does, indeed, care about the African-American community and truly wants to bring a halt to the deterioration.

Informal planning successes and the work of Councilman Brown, then, make it clear that increasing the numbers of African-Americans in the planning and community development processes is a "win-win" situation for everyone.

V. GETTING MINORITIES INVOLVED IN COMMUNITY DEVELOPMENT

As stated above, involving minorities in the community development and planning processes reaps benefits that benefit everyone. Still as yet, there is undoubtedly a shortage of minority involvement in the community development/planning process in Omaha, just as there is across the nation. Why is this the case?

Generally speaking, even before distinguishing in regard to the issue of race, is the fractionalization of people, in general. A publication called *Green Spaces* (2004) offers up the following referendum:

> The signs are that we are moving away from the notion of
> society, with communities becoming fragmented and individuals
> more reclusive. But community spirit is not dead. People regret
> they are living increasingly isolated live in buildings, and silently
> crave opportunities to go outside and meet once more as a
> community (p. 20).

The preceding paragraph explains what is needed and what could be used to bridge gaps while, at the same time, increasing the ranks and percentages of minorities and blacks involved in the community development process.

Research unveils a model and a generic way to explain how minorities have been excluded from the community development process. Arnstein's Ladder of Citizen Participation is an excellent way to visualize how minorities have been excluded and then, even after token inclusion, have had a negligible impact on the community development process.

While the graphic of the Arnstein chart itself is attached to the appendices of this paper, one can easily glean the various levels of citizen participation. While the top rungs of the ladder are designated as "degrees of power (consisting of citizen control, delegated power and partnership), it becomes clear that when it comes to these areas, minorities have been largely excluded.

Following the turbulent 1960s when blacks and other minorities began to demand more inclusion and more say in what is taking place in their communities, strategies were used to allow "a few into the ranks." According to the Arnstein chart, this area is known as "degrees of tokenism," and consists of placation, consultation and informing.

As far as can be gleaned, this is an area that Omaha continues to utilize when it comes to minorities. There is a smattering of minority input into the community development process, but failed attempts like North Omaha Community Development awakened a number of people in the area about how the city placated leadership by creating what Chambers (1982) referred to as "an adjunct to the city." While NOCD did a great deal of informing and consultation, little of it led to anything that really energized North Omaha. Even when the city opted to turn the Blue Lion Center over to the group so that NOCD could use the rents from the building for revenue, the group was so disorganized that it failed. The City eventually bought the building back and it is now the site of the Workforce Development program.

The lower part of the ladder of citizen participation consists of the area that Arnstein refers to as "non-participation." These two areas – therapy and manipulation – describe where minorities and blacks were at prior to the 1960s. According to Arnstein, "the aim is to cure or educate the participants" (Arnstein, 1969: 217). This is the kind of paternalism that black people endured during the pre-1960s and community development, if any was aimed at the area at all, was imposed on the masses of people and there was little or no input from those who were to be affected.

Sometimes the reason for that input being requested was due to an incorrect perception of skills and potential contributions. Chait & Seip (1999) assert that calls for broad inclusiveness too often assume community participants come on equal footing. In reality, while they contribute their life skills, experiences and crucial knowledge about their neighborhoods, they are often disadvantaged in terms of access to resources, time, technical skills and knowledge of government practices and terminology.

In addition to the oftentimes exclusionary realities of American society, there are a number of economic factors which might even serve as greater reasons for why there is such low minority involvement in the community development decisions that impact upon their lives. Castells (1993) has identified three distinct socioeconomic transformations that reflect on the economy which, in turn, impacts negative upon African Americans and black communities. These are (1) knowledge as growth in the economy, (2) shifts in industries, and (3) the emergence of a marginalized labor force (pp. 111-112).

The new knowledge base and hi-tech seems to leave segregated groups behind, and this creates a "digital divide" that has been extensively written about. Since "knowledge is power," it stands to reason that those who lack it will be left behind when it comes to input on what to do in the area of community development. Likewise, the shifts in industries can impact negatively on minority life because most blacks were involved in the manufacturing segment and once those factories closed or relocated, the jobs were gone. With the foundries and meatpacking jobs gone, any prospects for an economic base were destroyed. Latinos faced a similar concern when the packing houses closed in South Omaha.

Finally, the emergence of a marginalized labor force is a direct result of the previous two factors. In addition to those factors, marginalization is maintained because of inadequate education and poverty conditions. Community development and involvement in it means something different to people who are out fighting to put food on the table or a roof over their heads; survival and bread-and-butter issues take precedence over infrastructure, street development and other community development type issues.

<u>Proposals To Increase Minority Participation in Community Development</u>

Increasing the numbers of minorities in any discipline or activity is always a matter of attitude. The question that has to be asked is, "are these intentions sincere?" Sometimes minorities are wanted for reasons that are other than legitimate (to fill a quota, to appease a ruling, to temporarily comply with a law, etc.), and the records are replete with examples of tokenism of this kind.

EXPANDING THE SCOPE OF TRADITIONAL PLANNING

Traditional planning, like most other disciplines in American society, starts off as being a domain for non-minorities because it is an area where the power to transform geographic areas is paramount. To date in Omaha, few blacks have been a part of that formal decision-making, although black protest did usher in the need for those in power to render some concessions and for "community development" type agencies to be created and subsequently funded through Federal dollars and, in some cases in other cities, actually becoming a part of the city's organizational structure.
Qadeer (1997) wrote that, "Multiculturalism necessitates broadening the scope of pluralism in planning" (481). In addition,

> Multiculturalism as a public philosophy acknowledges racial and
> cultural differences in a society and encourages their sustenance
> and expression … This philosophy envisages the society as a
> mosaic of beliefs, practices … To fulfill these requirements, the
> first step is to eliminate … discrimination on the one hand, and
> cultural biases in the use of land, the housing market, and the
> provision of urban services on the other hand (pp. 482-483).

The fact of the matter is that the scope and procedures of citizen involvement in the planning process have to be modified to accommodate multicultural practices, approaches and beliefs. The day of "whites only" may be gone, but when it comes to community development, there is still a visible lack of inclusion of the views and perspectives of minorities. As a result, increasing numbers in an area like community development can only serve to help everyone involved, because when areas of the city are improved based on decisions that are made by concerned individuals from different areas, the entire city benefits from that improvement.

Simply put, Omaha has to grow up. Dana Markel of the City of Omaha's Convention and Visitor's Bureau (which is now a part of the Chamber of Commerce) expressed her concerns that when minority tourist conventions are held and Omaha sends a representative, that rep is usually a white person. She felt that this made Omaha appear to be racially exclusive and she hoped this image would change. As a result, the Convention Bureau has since hired two African-Americans to work in that department.

The same has to take place for planners, an area that actually has more options. Minority input can be contracted, it can become an entity within planning, or existing agencies such as the Urban League of Nebraska or the Omaha Opportunities Industrialization Center could have their expertise on the North Omaha area utilized. Omaha has never hired a black person who had specific planning experience. The highest ranking black in the department carries the title, "Economic Development Manager," and is not mentioned when projects, such as the ones engineered by Councilman Brown, are brought to the fore by the media and civic leaders.

EMPHASIS ON VALUE OF MINORITY INPUT

Anderson (2006) tackled an issue of recruiting underrepresented individuals into careers in agriculture. While this might sound very different than working to increase minority numbers in community development, the fact is that both concerns are very similar. The fact is that minority numbers are increasing all over the world and the United States (Cohen, 2001: 88-89), and it behooves everyone in all spheres of activity to begin understanding the need for minority input and representation. One point made by Anderson that is most telling is that minorities become more active when the experience is meaningful (p. 12).

The same applies for the area of community development, where minorities must believe that their input has some short- and long-term value and will positively impact upon the communities in which they live and beyond. Others have also seen the need to increase minority representation in the quest to create a more diverse community in various areas of activity (Abraham, 2006; Gunter, 2004).

The fact is, getting minorities involved in the community development process and emphasizing and showing appreciation for the value of their input gives them a feeling of having a vested interest in their own destiny. Glaser, et. al. (2003) concluded that the viability of local government-sponsored community development initiatives when it comes to poor ethnic enclaves hinges on the perceptions of residents and further, "if residents view the enclave in which they live as their 'community of choice,' they will be more likely to join with local government to co-produce community improvements" (p. 547).

In a nutshell, the issue of minority inclusion into the community development process is an issue of empowerment and enabling those who are to be impacted to have a more active voice in the decisions that influence their futures.

COMMUNITY DEVELOPMENT BLOCK GRANT WEEK

Although this is an event that is already being celebrated, this proposal is for it to be taken more seriously here in Omaha and, as a part of that serious event, perhaps include some of the "emphasis on the value of minority input" that was proposed in the previous suggestion. One issue that is of concern is that from year to year, there is no consistency in terms of when the event is to be publicly acknowledged.

For example, in 2004, it was announced that the dates were April 12-18th; in 2005, the dates were March 28 through April 1st. Most recently, in 2006, the dates were April 17-23, 2006 and the celebration was known as National Community Development Week. It was defined thusly:

> CDBG Week is a perfect time to demonstrate and showcase the many ways in which CDBG funded activities significantly improve the quality of life in communities and, most importantly, the lives of the lower-income residents. It is the backbone of virtually all community development throughout the nation. The goal of National Community Development Week is to encourage those who benefit from the Community Development Block Grant (CDBG) program to communicate with their congressional representatives, and their locally elected officials of its important role in their lives (Housing and Urban Development, 2005)

Community Development Block Grant week could become a joint arrangement between the City of Omaha Planning Department, the University of Nebraska at Omaha Urban Studies Department and an inner city agency such as the Urban League off Nebraska, the Omaha Economic Development Corporation, New Community Development or Family Housing Advisory Services. For that matter, even the UNO Neighborhood Center of Greater Omaha could become actively involved with planning of events and using that site as a place where a seminar, forum or mini-conference could be held dealing with the specific issue of increasing minority inclusion in the community development and urban planning processes.

MINORITY INPUT DEVELOPMENT CONFERENCE(S)

In piggy-backing on the previous proposal, the creation of an annual Minority Input Development Conference might go a long way toward expanding the numbers of people of color who become more involved in the community development/urban planning process. Many of the other suggestions offered up in this thesis could also be a part of this important conference, one that could present the opportunity for North Omaha African-Americans and south Omaha's Latino communities to come together with the city fathers to plan and work toward creating scholarships, internships and other opportunities to get people of color more involved in the community development process.

COMMUNITY BENEFITS AGREEMENTS

Involving people, in general, and minorities, in particular, in the community development process might be an approach related to what Engquist (2006) and others have called "community benefits agreements" or CBAs (p. 1). As used in New York, for instance, "Most CBAs involve builders pledging to create open space; use union labor; set hiring quotas for women, minorities and local residents … "(p. 21). But is it possible that these CBAs, as they relate to involving more minorities, could also be used to promote more African-American/minority inclusion in the community development process?

PARTICIPATION ALLOTMENTS

For example, instead of setting hiring quotas (which are illegal anyway), why not set what could be called "participation allotments"? These would be based on zip code, not just race. But in Omaha, because of residential segregation, representatives on a given committee or those assigned to a project would be assigned representing low-income areas versus suburbs. It is clear, for instance, that 68107 is where most of the city's Hispanics reside, and most people know that 68111, 68110 and 68104 are areas where the majority of the city's blacks can be found. The use of community benefits agreements then, would be relevant, culturally-inclusive and a boon to each area of the city.

THE NEW PUBLIC SERVICE APPROACH

Another suggestion, ideology or approach that might be employed could lie in what Denhardt and Denhardt (2000) refer to as, "The New Public Service.

In a nutshell, these are: (1) Serve, rather than steer, meaning that government becomes another player, albeit an important play in the process of moving society in one direction or another, and their role becomes more along the lines of service delivery as opposed to control; (2) The public interest is the aim, not the by-product, meaning that not only is widespread public dialogue and deliberation central, but government as a role not only as a facilitator, but has a moral obligation to assure solutions that are generated through such processes are fully consistently with norms of justice and fairness"; (3) Think strategically, act democratically, meaning that the key is to join all parties together in the process of carrying out programs that will move in the desired direction, performing this function by ensuring that government is open and accessible, that it is responsive and that it operates to serve citizens and create opportunities for citizenship; (4) Serve citizens, not customers – in other words, people acting as citizens must demonstrate their concern for the larger community, their commitment to matters that go beyond sort-term interests, and their willingness to assume personal responsibility for what happens in their neighborhoods and the community; the New Public Service seeks to encourage more and more people to fulfill their responsibilities as citizens and for government to be especially sensitive to the voice of citizens"; (5) Accountability isn't simple, meaning that while the old public administration and the New Public Management both tend to oversimplify the issue, it is the role of public administrators to make conflicts and parameters known, "so that these realities become a part of the process of discourse. Doing so not only makes for realistic solutions, it builds citizenship and accountability"; (6) Value people, not just productivity, which means shared leadership, collaboration, and empowerment become the norm both inside and outside the organization"; (7) Value citizenship and public service above entrepreneurship. This final tenet means that the "New Public Service "suggests that public administrators must not only share power, work through people, and broker solutions, they must reconceptualize their role in the governance process as responsible participants, not entrepreneur (Denhardt & Denhardt, 2000: pp. 554-557).
. Yet another way to get minorities involved in the process is by using intermediaries, of what Smith and Blanc (1997) refer to as "smugglers." As they define this role,

> The smuggler in society is one who aids socially deprived groups
> and others who need help in expressing themselves in order to be
> heard and to make known their rights (p. 300).

Because of the long-time exclusion of minority input into the community development process, any "smugglers" that might come to the fore will also be viewed with disdain. That is why in this paper it is postulated that the key to increasing minority numbers begins with an attitude, one that is rooted in the belief that minority inclusion will be respected and valued and not be seen as incidental or tokenistic.

Brown (2002), in discussing involvement in public service in his pathfinder communities, offered four suggestions that could surely also be used as part of a drive to increase minority involvement in community development: (1) consultation and awareness-raising with local residents or service users; (2) developing community capacity and infrastructure; (3) community involvement in management of ... [its] projects; (4) widening participation (p. 75).

The preceding describes what is needed in the community development process – it has to become more inclusive. The days of external imposition on communities has to come to an end because it creates frustration and, in the long run, various forms of aggression. Those young people who are rebelling in the low-income areas of Omaha are doing so because of frustration. These young people see how powerless and voiceless their parents are and seek to lash out against a system that will not listen. The sooner Omaha sees this and responds to it by opening up its minds and community development programs to minorities, the sooner young people (and their parents) will feel that they have a vested interest in the future of the city as a whole.

CITIZEN PANELS

Along these lines, another approach that could be utilized to increase minority involvement in the community development process revolves around what Jones and Jones (2002) refer to as "participatory consultation techniques, "citizen panels" and "citizen juries." In sum,

> Citizens' panels ... are promoted as helping to extend local
> democracy through involving citizens in the planning and design f
> services and other policy options ... A typical panel consists of
> about 1,000 people, carefully selected to represent, statistically, the
> area profile. ... The citizens' jury is an interesting example that
> tries to combine the merits of all the different approaches. Juries
> are not only seen as an efficient way of gathering the public's

> views on public services, they are also seen as participatory,
> playing a role in democratic renewal. Through participation in a
> jury it is suggested that people will be more aware of their role as
> citizens. A citizens' jury involves a group of members of the public
> – usually about 15, selected through some random process –
> engaging intensively with an issue over several days (pp. 60 & 61).

These panels sound rather large at first. But while researching for this paper, I came across several instances where "blue ribbon panels" and "task forces" and the like were formed to address specific issues. In one case the issue was riot prevention, and in another it was to address open housing violations. These huge committees, one formed as recently as 1994 under then Mayor Hal Daub, include all these people who then issue small reports that are never read or acted upon. This should not be the case when the subject is community development and minority inclusion. The citizen jury might be a good way to begin and, from that jury, a larger list of citizens could be chosen and their names placed in a "Community Development Inclusion Vita Bank" that could be relied upon when major decisions are to be formulated and/or decided upon.

A final point that must be remembered is that although most of those involved want to truly see increased minority involvement in the community development process, the situation that exists is not one that can rely solely upon existing models or approaches. Although there are fitting paradigms that can fit in meeting the need (some of them addressed and proposed herein), the dire need of the minority community calls for unique and direct approaches.

Summing the cultural differences and dire need up best is Zaferatos (1998) who briefly discussed issues of planning, community development, and the plight of another minority group – the American Indian:

> The variables affecting the development of American Indian
> reservation communities are the most complex found in
> American planning. These variables result from a long history
> of political and cultural subjugation, forced subdivision and the
> subsequent sale reservation lands to non-Indians, jurisdictional
> encroachment by non-tribal governments, and marginal
> reservation economies (p. 395).

These are realities and fundamental historical facts that also plague the African-American communities of America and the North Omaha community, in particular. As a result, cultural concerns are as important for today's planning and inclusion of blacks is as important as anything that has been done or will be done to address the needs of those trapped on the reservations.

A multicultural approach to involving minorities in the community development process can work. Lee (2004) describes the work that was done by the East Bay Asian Development Corporation and how that organization, based in predominantly black Oakland, California, was still as yet able to involve diverse segments of the population in its efforts, not only in terms of board membership but also in regard to actually hiring low income people from different segments of the community (pp. 163-169).

It is clear that the EBADC started with understanding the situation they were in. They realized that they were operating in a set of conditions where there was a diversity of people and interests. While not deviating from their goal, they were able to meet their goals and even expand because of the inclusion of members of different groups. This approach, combined with the citizen's jury/citizens panels outlined earlier, could be instituted in Omaha and go a long way toward enhancing and expanding existing and future community development activities.

CAPACITY-BUILDING

Then there is the issue of capacity building and the role that it can play in incorporating more minorities into the community development process (Henderson, 2003; Brown, 2002). This can range from support for existing partnerships, provision of community buildings as a base for organizing and new technology to joint training programs and, of course, additional funding. It can even include business franchising, which not only offers jobs and opportunities, but also develops a sense of self for the entire area (Smith, 1999: pp. 35-38).

Capacity building should not be imposed "from on high" as might have been done in the past or has the Arnstein Ladder of Citizen Participation implies. It appears that capacity building should be a two-way street: as the internal, cultural and awareness capacities of the grass roots masses are enhanced and included, the capacity of those who are empowered to make decisions are also enhanced on a moral and cultural level. Both sides learn more about the other and as a result, the end result is going to be one that builds on the capacities of both sides and improves the final product, whatever that might be.

The "capacity" that is built then, is two way and mutual, with both sides benefiting. This unity addresses community development issues on a variety of levels, and especially issues involving public space. Since the issue of community development is one addressing what to do with public space, the input from a group of people will not only be more inclusive and make the final result more representative, but also trump individual tastes or designers looking to garner awards or pad their resumes. One article outlines the situation nicely:

> So many public spaces are still being designed and built which
> do not fully support user needs and so never fulfill their potential
> to enhance *people's experience of the public realm* ...It is not
> that there is a lack of skilled designers – there are lots of award-
> winning public spaces ... But even these highly regarded spaces,
> for which the designers or managers have often received acclaim
> from their profession, can be rejected by potential users (Green
> Places, 2004: 20—emphasis original).

The fact is, "If a 'good design is one that supports users' needs, then we need to consult people about those needs" (Green Places, 2004: p. 21).

In describing the successes of the community reinvestment movement (a bank-driven form of community development), Dreier (2003) wrote,

> A new political majority must be built around identifying and
> building on concerns that unite those who live in central cities
> with residents of suburbs and between groups that do community
> organizing and labor unions ... Half of American's voters live in
> the suburbs of our metropolitan areas ... their interests must be
> joined to the interests of those who live in central cities ... (p.
> 353).

Ultimately, if minorities are ever going to become more involved in the community development process, it is going to come down to communication and on-going, sincere interaction between all the "players" involved. As Harris (2003) has observed,

> In order to feel secure about where we live, and be informed
> about options and opportunities, we need connections to others.
> Those connections are strengthened by trust, which itself is
> reasserted by informal interaction in a 'neutral' context – in the
> street, in shops, parks and other public and civic spaces. If
> communication is severely constrained, it is not just conviviality
> that may diminish. Where necessary information is not
> accessible, or social networks do not flourish, people can easily
> become excluded and their communities can atrophy (p. 6).

Finally, what Taylor (2000) wrote about neighborhoods and the need for managers to be retrained, which surely applies to planners and community developers as well, is most germane as he writes, "Neighborhood management needs catalysts and sustainers. Capacity building will involve major organizational development programs – not just piecemeal provision or even inspiring social entrepreneurs" (p. 42).

Ultimately, it is about the coming together of different forces that is going to make more black inclusion in the community development process work for everyone. To an extent, it is much the same as the way that Hardy (2001) discusses public and private partnerships:

> The notion of public-private partnership is almost a cliché these days. Yet it is fundamentally important: You can't operate a city without public institutions, and those are in place because of private interests. Cities have a public realm and a private realm, and how these come together defines life in the city. At the most basic level, streets are public and the buildings that front them are usually private, and it is the interface between the two that makes a city work (p. 16).

Simply put, we need each other. Chat & Seip (1999) remind us that our "winner take all" society values individual achievement and material wealth above collaboration and collective endeavor. As schoolchildren, we are taught to compete and protect our self-interest; as adults, our waning interest in political engagement has wakened our ability to identify ourselves as members of a broader community.

HUMAN CAPITAL DEVELOPMENT/BUSINESS INVESTMENT

In addition to capacity building, there is also a need to view minority participation in the realm of community development as an issue of human capital. Generally speaking, human capital is about the power of human potential. More specifically, according to Hawkins (2005), "human capital development is the augmentation of an individual's capacity to successfully enter the workforce. This augmentation may take the form of enhanced skills, experiences and knowledge, or improvements in personality, reputation and appearance … In some cases it even includes talent development" (p. 38).

Again, different "talents" are developed by and for different people. What those in power need is increased awareness and understanding of those that they have traditionally ignored or overlooked. What those at the bottom of the socioeconomic ladder need is an opportunity to have input into those decisions that impact upon their destinies. The talents of both sides are beneficial to those on the other side and in the final analysis, human capital is expanded.

When it comes to increasing minority involvement in community development, corporations, agencies, universities and other institutions can also do their fair share.

Fannie Mae, for example, has a number of programs where they not only work to increase minority home ownership, but also seek to involve more minorities in the community development process. Although the primary thrust is housing, there is little doubt that this is an advocacy approach as it relates to the provision of financial support to nonprofit housing groups that, in turn, empower individuals and inform them about their role and commitment to the areas where the housing is located. This advocacy approach to community development through housing includes education, outreach and working to shape public policy (Roach, 2002: p. 22).

The creation of entities like the Brooklyn-based Community Capital Bank (CCB) is another way to increase minority involvement in the community development process. By lending money to minority and women entrepreneurs, a niche that larger banks may ignore, the outreach of entities like this and the training and education that goes along with it makes important contributions to developing communities and urging minorities to become more actively involved in the process (Rasmusson, 2002: p. 17).

Such an approach also includes assisting entrepreneurs with writing their business plans and getting funding for those plans. This is akin to Omaha's own Small Business Network, located at 24th and Lake Streets, which serves as an incubator for small business. But this incubator does not do the community development work and have the role of working with people to view their role as developers the way that the CCB in New York does. Perhaps if the OSBN worked more closely with the Urban Studies Department at UNO and the City of Omaha Planning Department (which funds it), it could tie its loans and incubator roles to long-term commitments to North Omaha in terms of on-going individual and group development.

INVOLVEMENT OF HIGHER EDUCATION

Educational institutions can do their bit as well. Wooten (1982) offered up the suggestion that a carefully designed program of consumer education could address the problems of consumer importance in the housing market and the meager levels of citizen participation in planning.

The College of Public Affairs and Community Service of the University of Nebraska at Omaha has long been on the cutting edge of involving itself in projects that impact upon Omaha's black community. In addition to sponsoring the Neighborhood Center of Greater Omaha, CPACS has also helped to produce a number of reports in conjunction with the Urban League of Nebraska. All of this, in addition to the training, education and certifications provided through the Urban Studies, Social Work, Criminal Justice and Public Administration programs, work together to provide information and resources that can be used to involve more minorities in community development.

UNO is not alone. Colleges and universities all over the country are collaborating with residents, government and organizations to work in various urban and ethnic neighborhoods (Black Issues in Higher Education, 2002: 31). And if universities can recruit and increase minority enrollment and involvement in a wide range of disciplines (e.g., teacher education, sciences, law, business – then the same can be done in the arena of community development (Bennett, 2002: pp. 21-29).

Higher education can create new courses, at the undergraduate and graduate levels, that more closely focus on community development, revitalization and urban planning. Although the Urban Studies degree is a good one and is very informative as it exists, I am learning more about Urban Planning from the research assignments and having gleaned a number of graduate catalogues, I am most intrigued about transportation, city design, urban law and zoning codes and other issues that go far beyond what is being offered now. As a part of an urban planning course at the undergraduate and graduate level, specialization in areas such as housing, block grant allocations and community revitalization would teach young people the importance of becoming more actively involved in the areas that they came from.

Along similar lines as the proposal offered above, the creation of what could be called "Community Development Internships" could be offered at the graduate level and these individuals would learn the importance of working in metro areas and inner cities with actual on-the-job training and first-hand experience. Through these internships, younger people would be inspired to become more involved in working with community leaders, community organizations and with area City Planning Departments. The experiences that they would gain from this involvement would surely carry over into their career aspirations and interests after they graduate. That would and could include wanting to become more involved in issues like community development and urban planning.

INVOLVEMENT OF THE AFRICAN-AMERICAN CHURCH

Another proposal being offered in this paper is that the black church become more actively involved in the training of blacks in the area of community work and that it work to stress how important it is to contribute to the development of the community. Nebraska has a total of 118 predominantly black churches, and 116 of these are located in Omaha. Omaha has a total of 458 churches, so black churches account for 25% of all churches in this city, where blacks are allegedly but 13% of the population (McCord, 1991: 53). One study showed how pastor-level factors positively affected the successful recruitment and implementation of community-based health programs in Black churches (Markens, et. al., 2002: pp. 805-810). If that can take place in a city like Los Angeles, surely a small area like North Omaha with so many black religious institutions can inspire more black involvement in community development programs.

The economic side of community development is important (and is oftentimes referred to as "economic development") could range from offering new franchise opportunities for an area to expanding diversity efforts in businesses that can then reach out to new markets, which includes low income sectors of the community (Smith, 1999; DuPont, 1999; Lamar, 2000). What would be more in line with "saving souls" that teaching the value of work to congregation members by engaging in franchise opportunities and starting up businesses in an impoverished area of the city ("As a man thinketh, so is he").

<u>What Black Organizations and Leadership Can Do</u>

While researching this paper and writing papers in other courses in pursuit of the degree, it became apparent to me that black organizations in North Omaha have a similar tendency; that is, the tendency to appoint or hire directors or presidents of various organizations and then proceed to allow these individuals near free-reign and lifetime employment.

During this tenure, these "leaders" are not retained based on accomplishments or merit but indeed, simply because they have balanced a budget or organized successful fundraising campaigns or annual dinners. If not that, then they are in office so long that board members retain them based on superficial reasons: the individual goes to the "right" church, has a link to individuals who actually have power and influence and therefore should stay in power to that these networks can generate future funding; or because the person is "nice" and therefore not offensive to white sensibilities.

The result of such "loyalty" to these individuals is that it promotes what could be called "singularity of leadership." These individuals remain in office so long that they become the know-all, think-all for the group. In addition, these individuals make the major mistake of not training any young person who can maintain the organization long after they are gone.

I found this to be true in the case of the Great Plains Black History Museum (Ms. Calloway is in bad health and has some mental concerns); the Malcolm X Memorial Foundation (whose founder, Rowena Moore co-founded and then horded since the property that the Malcolm X Birth site was one is property that she owned) which now, following Ms. Moore's demise, flounders because of untrained leaders; the Omaha Star newspaper, which now flounders under someone with a dearth of journalistic background (Dr. Marguerita Washington) and who has no plan to train or mentor a successor, even though she is nearing 70 years of age;

Al Goodwin, the former director at the Omaha Economic Development Corporation stepped down after decades and then, instead of bringing on a younger person who was mentored, essentially handed the reins over to a clone, Michael Maroney of the very-similar New Community Development Corporation.

Even Nebraska State Senator Ernie Chambers, who represents the Northside's 2nd District, falls prey to the lack of a protégé or heir apparent to pick up where he left off. Chambers, who has served in the Legislature for over 35 years, even boasts on his evening talk show that, "There will never be anyone else like me representing District 11." And the reason for that is that not only he refuse to train or mentor future black leaders, but that his district has changed demographically because of the North Freeway, the demolition of the Hilltop Projects and other urban renewal realities. But like Calloway, Moore and Goodwin, Chambers is also guilty of not mentoring or preparing someone young to pick up the mantle once the individual "leader" is gone.

These facts, in my view, serve as a foundation and core reason why there is also a dearth in community development and urban planning initiatives at the City, County and State levels. Minorities are not being mentored or trained to accept leadership roles by blacks who have held these positions for long periods of time and have become elderly or burned out.

This goes directly to the issue of leadership, attitude and a key reason why there is a dearth of blacks in the community development/urban planning process. If the political leadership is doing its job, there should be black presence and/or input into all issues that impact upon the black community. And yet there are glaring gulfs in areas that affect North Omaha, with urban planning and community development being the most obvious one. Other than one or two names that dominate the subject area, there are few people in North Omaha who even understand what community development means, let alone who the people are who are charged with making it happen.

Minorities in general and African-Americans in particular can no longer sit and expect the Federal government to impose sanctions on city entities that discriminate or exclude them. Although citizen participation is required in almost every community development program or project that is Federally-funded, localities themselves are usually left with discretion in that area and end up doing, as Arnstein pointed out, as they please in terms of deciding between the degree and amount of control that is "allowed."

Although minority participation has increased in many instances, some might argue that the move from "non-participation" to that of "tokenism" is really tantamount to no progress at all. Today's strategy, as exhibited by the city of Omaha and other governmental community development entities, tends to lean toward the "placation" component that Arnstein wrote about and described as, " …

co-optation of hand-picked 'worthies' onto committees. It allows citizens to advise or plan ad infinitum but retains for power holders the right to judge the legitimacy or feasibility of the advice" (Arnstein, 1968: p. 222).

The fact is, African-American leaders are going to have to begin concerning themselves with the "partnership" dimension of the ladder of citizen participation. As defined, "Power is in fact redistributed through negotiation between citizens and power holders. Planning and decision-making responsibilities are shared, e.g., through joint committees" (Arnstein, 1969: pp. 222-223).

What appears to be the case is that leadership, particularly African-American leadership at the local level, is more concerned about or committed to "influence" more than it is to the need for power. Karenga (1993), makes the distinction that when it comes to the liberal strategy of most black leaders there is "a general confusion on influence with power, i.e., personal persuasion with structural capacity" (p. 331).

This may be the key reason for the lack of black involvement in the community development process. By opting for influence, or those who are deemed most influential, leadership is deciding on who speaks for who based on appointments, titles, and statuses within the system. If those statuses and roles are of the token variety that Arnstein wrote about, then these individuals become tools of the system and, as such, may not have the best interests of the masses at heart.

Black leadership can no longer be smugly satisfied with being "a player" in the community development process. They are going to have to begin seeking leadership roles, seizing leadership opportunities and being in the vanguard when it comes to projects, not only in the central city, but anywhere in Omaha where there is a significant minority presence. From issues ranging from the planning process to the actual designs, or even the selection of the designers and developers, black leadership is going to have to seriously consider some of the proposals offered in this Capstone paper and then act accordingly.

SUMMARY & CONCLUSION

Community development is as much social as it is political, and involving minorities in the process of community development and planning is one that is going to call for more than just rhetoric regarding inclusion, but an attitude and a political commitment of sorts. Jones and Jones (2002) come close to what is needed when they discuss the issue of citizenship and democracy:

> … it is crucial to create a dialogue through open, public
> discussion, because citizenship is a quality that can only be
> realized in public. Dialogue and debate constitute a key process

> which identifies common interests and determines a policy
> outcome. Thus, the way in which the collective view, the
> content, has been developed is what gives the final outcome its
> authority. This perspective accords with the idea of politics put
> forward by Gramsci … who saw politics as 'production', in other
> words the way that groups and individuals shape developments
> within society (p. 58).

Shaping developments in society is one thing, but being inclusive in the process of shaping those developments is the issue and order of the day. Again, with the world becoming smaller because of hi-tech and with the global community becoming more of a reality, demographics are changing and the old racially exclusive ways of doing things will simply not work for the long-term. Admittedly, more people of color are being included in planning and development at the international levels, but most of those being included are people of color from other countries (e.g., India, China, Japan, etc.). Therefore, there is some color consciousness that is paying off when the opportunities present themselves.

Despite this, North Omaha has experienced several decades of gradual physical decline, and this has led to a kind of socio-psychological decline which may even now be seen with the spate of shootings that have plagued the area. While some want to blame parents, schools and even the police, the fact of the matter is that many blacks in North Omaha don't feel as if they are a part of the city, as if they don't even matter.

Although revitalization efforts have attempted to stabilize the area, most are devoid of having any benefit to the indigenous population. Instead, funded and directed by the daughter of one of the richest men in the world, development in North Omaha is aided and abetted by a city planning department that has failed North Omaha for the past 40 years.

At present gentrification is taking place because of the area's proximity to the Riverfront, which is now being rebuilt with businesses, night clubs and several condominium projects. North Omaha, in the meantime, is experiencing little growth although there are on-going spotty attempts at revitalization (e.g., Preston Love Jazz Museum, Family Housing Advisory Services building, the Jazz Park, etc.).

Because political leadership is elected on a district basis, those selected are usually alone; Frank Brown on the City Council is but one of seven, and Senator Ernie Chambers is but one of 49. Chris Rodgers of the Douglas County Board of Commissioners is one of 8. Such small numbers do not give the area much political clout, hence the reliance on an organized, informed grassroots base.

O'Hara writes about the two approaches mentioned urban revitalization of the type that is apparently taking place at the 24th and Lake Street area, and adds that,

> The accepted focus of urban development on improving a community's economic conditions has not only overlooked social and environmental effects, but also urban residents themselves. Development needs are generally defined by development "experts" rather than local residents. This is particularly true for low income urban areas whose residents are perceived as the (more or less deserving) recipients of welfare and charity but seldom as knowledgeable authorities of local economic, social, cultural and environmental conditions. Urban residents experience a twofold isolation: isolation from the economic successes of a growing economy benefiting those outside the urban setting, and isolation from the political decision making process affecting their own life context (1999, p. 1328-1329).

This "isolation" appears to describe what is taking place in Omaha when it comes to the lack of citizen input. As a result, the North Omaha area remains poor while others come in and do as they want in terms of urban revitalization, social sustainability and other efforts. Citizen participation has been ignored by the powers that be. And that is why back communities around the country continue to suffer, continue to deteriorate and languish while the downtowns, the suburbs and other areas of the city receive the benefit of the Community Development Block Grants and other Federal and state monies.

Were more minorities involved in planning process, perhaps more "ethnoburbs" would be the result. Li defined an ethnoburb as, " … suburban ethnic clusters of residential areas and business districts in large metropolitan areas'. They are multi-ethnic communities in which one ethnic group has a significant concentration … ethnoburbs undermine all of the assumptions of traditional invasion-succession models, and fundamental to this is that, unlike traditional inner-city enclaves, these concentrations are the results of their creator's economic strength, not of economic and social marginalization (Li, 1998).

These areas are also referred to as "enclave economies" (Cummings, 1999), and they serve to provide potential employment and business advantages to minorities and, more germane to this paper, the enclave theory has direct relevance for community development planners, especially those who design and implement minority procurement and incubation programs such as those addressed elsewhere in this paper (the Omaha Small Business Network and Brooklyn's CCB, to name but two). One study found that African-Americans conducting business within the traditional boundaries of sixty-three major cities were neither advantaged or harmed by the alleged protected markets associated with a segregated enclave economy (Cummings, 1999: p. 58).

The fact is, such an approach can nevertheless lead to community development by providing a solid tax base and jobs for those who reside in a previously ignored or underdeveloped area of the city (Cummings, 1999: pp. 50-61).

This is not a call for re-segregation or isolation, but a realization that community development must take into consideration the culture and values of the people in a given area of that city. Zaferatos (1998) is correct when he writes, in regard, to American communities that, "the definition of a tribe's community goals is an intrinsic process that reflects the distinct needs and social values of each tribal community … Many tribal nations share a common set of concerns derived from a collective past – they each strive for cultural survival, political independence, and economic betterment" (p. 409).

Community development should mean expansion of options for residents from all backgrounds. Residents, in turn, should be involved in deciding what those options are. But while taking into consideration the importance of minority inclusion in the process, all involved must understand the importance of unity. In "Renewing Cities and Suburbs," Wagner (2004) writes that with minority representation in suburbs on the rise, planners should be "designing togetherness," meaning that the human impulse to create communities could mean increased isolation of minority groups within larger urban areas and environments. She asserts that transcending the cultural and other barriers keeping the neighbors apart will require clear communication and cooperation and suggests that growing experiments in co-housing, eco-villages, and other schemes offer lessons for mainstream urban/suburban planners (p. 18). This undoubtedly also rings true for community developers.

The closer this thesis came to being completed, the more I realized that Urban Planning and community development are two areas that has been responsible for the segregation of various types of people over the centuries. This was done in conjunction with the political, social and economic structures that direct every single city, town, village and township in America. The more that was learned, the more interest was generated. How people can lay out entire cities and decide where communities will be, how they will be shaped and who will live where is truly fascinating. How the developers and planners construct "master plans" with very little community input is a reality that must come to an end. As Mier (1994) wrote,

> What is missing from the current debate over urban policy is any
> willingness to attack the urban problem a matter of racial and

> economic segregation. Liberals appeal for large-scale federal aid
> for social welfare and economic development programs in the
> inner cities. This is the Big Buck Strategy. Conservatives talk
> about inner city enterprise zones, public housing "perestroika"
> and "empowerment." This is the Big Bootstrap Strategy.

And here is the key:

> At heart Big Buckers and Big Bootstrappers are selling the same
> idea: quarantine "them" in inner city ghettos and barrios away
> from "us" and help "them" build from within – with money or
> moral incentives. Both ideological camps believe that separate
> can be made equal, or at least equal enough to be tolerate (Mier,
> 1994).

Again, read the title of this production: "Minority Participation in the Omaha City Planning, Design and Community Development Process: An Analysis of Selective Application, Discriminatory Treatment and a Conspiracy to Systematically Impoverish an African-American Community." In other words, an intentional, long-term movement to maintain racial segregation while appearing to promote community engagement, diversity, multiculturalism and inclusion. This paper will expose these lies for the sheer and shallow facades that they truly are.

Therefore, it was not the intent or purpose of this black paper to argue the political merits of racial separatism or self-help. The purpose was to provide paradigms, procedures and proposals that would enable those in power to better understand that the system is better off by being more inclusive, stronger by allowing people of color to make contributions and have input into community development and planning decisions, and more stable when the population sees the diversity of the city represented in the process of decision making and the products of those decisions.

REFERENCES

Allen, J.P. & Turner, E. (1989). The most ethnically diverse places in the United States. *Urban Geography,* 10, (6).

Anderson, J.C. (2006, March/April). Insights for recruiting underrepresented individuals into careers in agriculture, food and natural resources. *The Agricultural Education Magazine,* 78, (5).

Arnstein, S.R. (1969). Ladder of public participation. *Journal of American Planning Association, 35,* (4).

Barr, A. (2000, Autumn). Involving the community in planning – the case of community care. *Scottish Journal of Community Work and Development,* 6. Bass, L. and Applegate, G. (2001, November). Come, let us reason together. *Public Management,* 83,(10).

Behr, K., & King, R. (2005, August). Continued citizen involvement proves effective. *Public Management, 87,* (7).

Bennett, C.I. (2002, March). Enhancing ethnic diversity at a Big Ten university through Project TEAM: A case study in teacher education. *Educational Researcher,* 31, (2).

Black Issues in Higher Education. (2002, December 19). Anchors in the community. 19, (22).

Black Issues in Higher Education, (2003, March 27). Bringing color to the international intellectual table. 20, (3).

Brain, D. (2006, Spring). Democracy and urban design: The transect as civic renewal. *Places,* 18, (1).

Brown, A.P. (2002). Public involvement in service improvement: The Working for Communities Programme. *Journal of Community Work and Development,* 1, (3).

Castells, M. (1993) European cities, the informational society, and the global economy. In R.T. Le Gates and F. Stout (Eds.) *The City Reader.* New York, New York: Routledge Publishing.

Chait, J.G. & Seip, M.E. (1999, Winter). Are we prepared to participate. *Places,* 12, (2).

Chambers, Ernie.(1982, January 20). "Chambers Responds to NOCD's Tyler." *The Omaha World Herald.*

Cohen, A. (2001, July/August). What if the US had a non-white majority? *World Link,* 14, (4).

Cummings, S. (1999, Winter). African-American entrepreneurship in the suburbs: Protected markets and enclave business development. *Journal of the American Planning Association,* 65, (1).

Dalstrom, Harl. (1988). *A.V. Sorenson and the New Omaha.* Omaha, Nebraska: Douglas County Historical Society: Lamplighter Press.
Daly, K.E. (2001, January/February). Urban design and the civic process. *Public Libraries.*

Davidoff, P. (1996). Advocacy and pluralism in planning. In S. Campbell & S. Fainstein (Eds.). *Readings in Planning Theory.* Malden, Massachusetts: Blackwell Publishing.

Day, K. (2006, Winter). Active living and social justice. *Journal of the American Planning Association,* 72, (1).

Denhardt, R.B., & Denhardt, J.V. (2000, November/December). The new public service: Serving rather than steering. *Public Administration Review,* 60, (6).

Dreier, P. (2003, Autumn). The future of community reinvestment: Challenges and opportunities in a changing environment. *Journal of the American Planning Association,* 69, (4).

DuPont, D.K. (1999, April 5). Minority markets offer diverse opportunities. *Hotel & Motel Management,* 214, (6).

Engquist, E. (2006, March 27-April 2). Developers' deal-making escalates. *Crain's New York Business,* 22, (13).

Fong, E. (1994). Residential proximity among racial groups in U.S. and Canadian neighborhoods. *Urban Affairs Quarterly,* 330, (2).

Fountaine, D. & Slagen, J. (2001, October). Strategic planning: Equally important for the smaller community. *Public Management.*
Ghose, I. (2005, April). The complexities of citizen participation through collaborative governance. *Space and Polity,* 9, (1).

Glaser, M.A., Lee, E., & Li, Hong. (2003, Fall). Community of choice or ghetto of last resort: Community development and the viability of an African-American Community. *The Review of Policy Research,* 20, (3).

Godschalk, D.R. (2004, Winter). Land use planning challenges: Coping with conflicts in visions of sustainable development and livable communities. *Journal of the American Planning Association*, 70, (1).

Gonzalez, Cindy. (1991, November 30). "Minister Faults North Omaha Plan." *The Omaha World Herald.*

--------------------. (1996, November 15). "New Vision Seen for Former Project Site." *The Omaha World Herald.*

Goodsell, Paul. (1990, January 25). "Feds Drop Hint: Scattered Sites Better Proposal." *The Omaha World Herald.*

Goss, S. (2001). *Making local governance work: Networks, relationships and the management of change.* Basingstoke Hampshire, England: Palgrave Macmillan.

Gramlich, E., Laren, D., & Sealand, N. (1992). Moving into and out of poor urban aeas. *Journal of Policy Studies,* 24, (6).

Green Places. (2004, May). Power to the people, 5.

Guinier, L. and Torres, G. (2002, February 18). The miner's canary. *The Nation,* 274, (6).

Gunter, H. (2004, July 19). Awareness, education key to recruitment efforts. *Hotel & Motel Management.*

Hardy, H. (2001, Fall). Public spaces: partnership, collaboration, reclaiming. *Places,* 14, (2).

Hare, Nathan. "Black Ecology." *The Black Scholar.* May 1970.

Harrison, Alferdteen. "Preface" in Alferdteen Harrison (Ed.) *Black Exodus.* Jackson, Mississippi: UP of Mississippi. 1991.

Harris, K. (2003). 'Keep your distance': Remote communication, face-to-face, and the nature of community. *Journal of Community Work and Development,* 1, (4).

Hawkins, C.V. (2005, Summer). Human capital development as an economic development strategy: The case of Workforce Plus. *Critical Planning.*

Henderson, P. (2003). The place of 'neighbourhood' in regeneration and social inclusion policies. *Journal of Community Work and Development,* 1, (4).

Henion, T.L. (1991, December 1). "Faces of Omaha." "Reactions to Park Plan Mixed in North Omaha." *The Omaha World Herald.*

Housing and Urban Development (2006). CDBG week. Retrieved on September 30, 2006 from http://www.hud.gov/offics/cpd/communitydevelopment/cdweek.cfm

Jones, J. and Jones, L. (2002). *Research and citizen participation. Journal of Community Work and Development,* 1, (3).

Karenga, M. (1993). Introduction to black studies. Los Angeles: University of Sankore Press.

Kelly, R.M. (1977). *Community control of economic development: The board of directors of community development corporations.* New York, New York: Praeger Publishers.

King, Larry. (1981, October 4). "Funds Question is Latest Hurdle for N. Freeway." *Omaha World Herald.*

Koebel, C.T. (2003, Autumn). Crossing the class and color lines: From public housing to white suburbia. *Journal of the American Planning Association,* 69, (4).

Kotok, C. David. "27 Years of Controversy Surround N. Freeway." *Omaha World Herald.* September 20, 1981.

Krajicek, David. (1980, October 22). "Speakers List Conditions for Freeway Support." *The Omaha World Herald.*

--------------------. (1980, February 6). "Road Plan Flailed by North Omahans." *The Omaha World Herald.*

Lamar, H. (2000, June). Building urban communities: Programs promote franchise ownership to develop inner-city areas. *Black Enterprise,* 11, (67).

Larsen, Lawrence H. and Barbara J. Cottrell. The Gate City: A History of Omaha (Vol. IV). No City. Pruett Publishing Company. 1982.

Lee, L.J. (2004). Being global locally. *Journal of Urban Affairs,* 26, (2).
Levy, J.M. (2000). Contemporary Urban Planning Upper Saddle River, New Jersey: Prentice Hall Publishers, 2000).

Li, W. (1998). Anatomy of a new ethnic settlement: The Chinese ethnoburb in Los Angeles. *Urban Studies,* 75.

Markens, S., Fox, S.A., Taub, B., & Gilbert, M.L. (2002, May). Role of black churches in health promotion programs: Lessons from the Los Angeles Mammography Promotion in Churches Program. *American Journal of Public Health,* 92, (5).

Massey, D. & Denton, N., (1992). American apartheid: Segregation and the making of the underclass. Cambridge, Massachusetts: Harvard University Press.

McCord, Julia. (1991, February 16). Black churches celebrate their role. *Omaha World Herald.*

Mier, Robert (1994, Spring). Some observations on race in planning [1]." *Journal of the American Planning Association,.* 60, (2).

National Housing Law Project, (2002, June). *False hope: A critical assessment of the HOPE VI public housing redevelopment program.* Oakland, California: National Housing Law Project
.

Nixon, N.L. (1979, August 17). *The Mexican American settlement of Omaha.* Report to the Omaha City Planning Department.

O'Donovan, O. (2000). Re-theorizing the interactive state: Reflections on a popular participatory initiative in Ireland. *Community Development Journal,* 35, (3).

O'hara, S.U. (1999). Community based urban development: A strategy for improving social sustainability. *International Journal of Social Economics,* 26, (10-11).

Omaha Star (1940, May 16).. "Urges Defense 'From Within'." May 16, 1940.

Omaha Star, The. . "Urban League Says OHA Director Doesn't Have Tenants' Best Interest." April 15, 1971.

------------------------. "Ideal Improvement Club Wins Victory." January 17, 1970.

----------------------. "Near Northsiders Ask City to Improve Services." August 4, 1967.

-------------------. "The Freeway Folly." October 8, 1981

.

-------------------. "The Freeway Paths Are To Be Studied." June 6, 1974.

-------------------. "City Council to Consider North Freeway Resolution Tuesday." October 8, 1981.

--------------------. "Researcher Lee: 'Study Would Reveal Wide Opposition to Freeway Extension'." Vol. 43. No. 20. November 13, 1980.

--------------------. "OHA's Armstrong Working to be the Best." February 25, 1988.

Omaha World Herald. "Circuit Court Decision on Omaha Segregation." June 13, 1975.

---------------------------. "Critics Say North Freeway Became Dead End for Area." November 10, 1980.

---------------------------. "Bloom of Housing Project." April 11, 1937.

---------------------------. "Board Denies Exemption for Church's Housing Plan." June 29, 1982.

---------------------------. "Church Gets OK for Apartments." January 12, 1982.

---------------------------. "Salem Baptist Church Starts $40,000 Annex." August 18, 1955.

---------------------------. "What Do UNO's Black Students Want Today?" May 31- June 1, 1978.

------------------. "City's Choice of Appraiser Irks Negroes." The Omaha World Herald. June 7, 1970.

Ouchi, W.G. (1981). *Theory Z.* Reading, Massachusetts: Addison-Wesley Publishing.

Parker, A. (2006, January). Building a diverse biological community. *BioScience,* 56, (1).

Qadeer, M.A. (1997, Autumn). Pluralistic planning for multicultural cities: The Canadian practice. *Journal of the American Planning Association,* 63.

Rasmusson, E. (2002, October 7-13). Brooklyn bank lends itself to investing in minorities. *Crain's New York Business,* 18, (40).

Roach, R. (2002, December 19). Opening doors to homeownership. *Black Issues in Higher Education,* 19, (22).

Rypkema, D.D. (2003, Winter). The importance of downtown in the 21st century. *APA Journal*, 69, (1).

Satieglitz, O. (1999, Spring). Advocacy planning and the question of the self and the other. *Critical Planning.*

Selby, E. & Marian, S. (1971). *Odyssey: Journey Through Black America.* New York: Putnam Publishing.

Smith, D.A. (1999, July/August). *Emerging markets.* Franchising World, 31, (4).

Smith, R. George. "Dying Neighborhood Seeks New Lease on Life." Omaha World Herald. December 1, 1991.

Stewart, Douglas E. (1964, March 7). "Conditions of Omaha Non-White People: An Overview of the Socio-Economic." *The Omaha Star.*

----------------------. (1964, March 13). "Conditions of Omaha Non-White People: An Overview of the Socio-Economic (Part II). " *The Omaha Star.*

Sullenberger, T. Earl and J. Harvey Kerns. (1931). *The Negro in Omaha: A Social Study of Negro Development.* Omaha, NE.: University of Omaha and Omaha Urban League.

Taylor, M (2000). *Top down meets bottom up: Neighborhood management.* Homestead York: Joseph Rowntree Foundation.

----------------------. "N. Freeway Foes Reject Alterations in Design of Road." *The Omaha World Herald.* November 19, 1980.

----------------------. "Economic, Social Issues Divide North Freeway Opponents, Backers." *The Omaha World Herald.* November 27, 1980.

Tuchmann, R. (2005). Public projects and citizen participation: The challenge of coordinating meaningful public involvement over time. *Boston College Environmental Affairs Law Review,* 32, (2).

Tulloch, D.L. & Shapiro, T. (2003). The intersection of data access and public participation: Impacting GIS users' success? *URISA Journal,* 15

De Viggiani, N., Jones, M. & Naidoo, J. (2004). Growing together? Involving black and minority ethnic groups in community horticulture. *Journal of Community Work and Development,* 5.

Virginia Tech University & the American Institute of Certified Planners (1999). Partnerships and participation in planning. Retrieved on August 22, 2006 from http://www.uap.vt.edu/cdrom/intro/number3.htm

Wagner, C.G. (2004, January/February). Renewing cities and suburbs. *The Futurist,* 38, (1).

Wallis, A.D., Crocker, J.P., & Schecter, B. (1998, Fall). Social capital and community building (part one). *National Civic Review,* 87, (3).

Wooten, J.P. (1982). The urban planner as educator: An analysis of the factors affecting participation of inner city blacks in the urban planning process and the use of a learning module in alleviating such factors as viewed from a housing perspective. Retrieved on September 3, 2006 from http://digitalcommons.libraries, Columbia.edu/dissertations/AAI8222514/

Zaferatos, N.C. (1998). Planning the Native American tribal community: Understanding the basis of power controlling the reservation territory. *Journal of the American Planning Association,* 64, (4).

Zerschling, Lynn. "Relocated Family Seeking Help on Repair Bill." The Omaha World Herald. October 1, 1980.

--------------------. "Opponents Question Need for Apartments in Salem Church Area." Omaha World Herald. December 3, 1981.

The Keys to Empowerment In North Omaha: A Critique and Prospective Paradigms

INTRODUCTION

The area of town known as North Omaha has been the repository for stigma, stereotypes and vitriol from the city – the same entity that "empowerment people" seek to align themselves with - for over a century. A key to understanding the breadth and depth of this citywide belief that North Omaha is not worthy of saving can be summed up by Solomon (1986) where he asserts that, " … stigmas, " ... have a collective quality. That is, in any given social unit, there is likely to be a high degree of consensus about what is considered a stigma" (Solomon, 1986: 65). In this case that social unit is the white majority of Omaha, so much to the point that many black people are even beginning to believe in the negativity.

And Becker and Arnold write,

> Broad views about what constitutes stigma are generally shared by
> members of a society. They will hold common beliefs about both
> the cultural meaning of an attribute and the stigma attached to it ...
> (Arnold and Becker, 1986: 40)

In this case, the beliefs about the central city are shared, and the beliefs about the future of the central city are being projected as being just as negative as the present. Since the same group is in a position to define what is "good and bad" or what is "clean and dirty," then it is clear to me that the future will represent the same stigmatized views of an area that exist in the present.

KEY: AVOID EXTERNAL DEFINITION

> Attributing responsibility to stigmatized persons for their condition
> helps to distance an observer from those persons and from the
> stigma itself ... (Gibbons, 1986: 125)

For over a century, the major newspaper in Omaha has worked to define the identity, purpose and direction for black people living in that city. Where many newspapers have altered those tendencies and have indeed, even opted to hire black reporters and columnists, the *Omaha World Herald* hangs on to its conservative mannerisms and tendencies and as a result, remains one of the most racially biased newspapers in the nation.

And yet, this newspaper, which has never had more than three black reporters (out of a staff of more than 60) in its 118 year history, has the gall to write editorials that have to do with "race."

On December 14, 2004, I wrote a response, which included a re-write of the entire original editorial, to the World Herald editorial called, "Interracial Barometer: A Horrendous Asault Brings Reminder of Decline in One Type of Racial Bigotry." What this means is that four or five white men, who form the editorial board, got together and decided that in all their divine wisdom, they were going to shape a social opinion having to do with race. They were going to select the specific subject area and in essence, sit there was judge, jury and executioner (in this sense, the proper word would be "executor").

My response, titled, "The "Barometer" Needs Fixin,' expresses my contempt, not only for the Omaha World Herald editorial board, but for their jejune analyses of history, race and interracial sex (miscegenation).

Following is an essay that contains both the World Herald editorial and my analysis, paragraph by paragraph:

INTRODUCTION
When a newspaper historically known as racist publishes an editorial on race relations, their motives are automatically racist. But in the case of the recent editorial, "Interracial Barometer: A Horrendous Assault Brings Reminder of Decline in One Type of Racial Bigotry," (December 13th) more was displayed that the newspaper probably intended. Following are my views on this article, an article crammed with lies, historical distortions and the World Herald's misinformed manifestations of social reality.

This short analysis of that article should serve as the basis of serious study and discussion regarding media credibility (or lack thereof), the role that race plays in analyzing social issues and, as I taught Tom Shaw several months back, the impact that bias has on editorial boards, most of which are lily-white as is the World Herald's.

The article will also be used as but one more indicator to tourism entities that Omaha is not yet ready to deal with racial diversity.

THE ARTICLE: RACISM AND RELEVANT RESPONSE

Because the Omaha World Herald lacks racial diversity and indeed, uses white women to cover stories in the black community, its journalistic credibility should already be called into question. The fact that they see nothing wrong with this state of affairs is also an indicator of their collective ignorance of race and more importantly, of how the world is changing around them as they apparently opt to stand in place.

The article begins with the following description:

The windows of Joseph Parks' Massachusetts house were smashed. He then was hit in the head, beaten, dragged to an apartment and stabbed in the chest with a knife. Burning cigarettes were placed on him. Racial slurs were written on his back. He was called a disgrace to his race, thrown out of a vehicle and dragged to the railroad tracks. Why? Park is a white man who once dated a black woman.

What was just described has happened to hundreds of thousands of black men over the years. When it happened in the South, the news media avoided printing these stories for the most part. When it happened in Omaha, the news media, led by the World Herald, did the same thing. In other words, the very institution that was supposed to be committed to providing news to the people was selective in what it chose to print. Why? Because of white racism, that's why.

Now we have a white man who has been degraded because of his association with a black woman. But the World Herald doesn't provide context. Was the man killed? Or was this one of those "warnings" that white folks gave their fellow race members for what they called "mongrelizing"? Without informing us of these facts, the World Herald is again showing how piecemeal and partial its reporting and even its editorializing truly is. It makes a big difference if the white man was killed or just beaten badly; it makes a difference how far back the "dating" went and what kind of relationship the two had. Was she his long-time companion? A concubine? A prostitute? What?

With this fundamental truth and contextual set of questions out of the way, journalistic rubrics that even the most defensive and ignorant individual can understand, we can proceed to the following passage:

An appalling story, from which society can take two things. The first is encouragement. Despite the hateful, disgusting display of racism inflicted upon Parks, it's a story that thankfully has become a rare one told over the years.

First of all, the World Herald is in no position to inform "society" about how many things they can extract from a given story. This is ethnocentrism in its purest form: because these white males say there are two points, that is what every reader is supposed to believe? How about readers who have learned to read critically and can therefore think for themselves? It is not their role to tell the reader how many points a story contains: it is their job to present the story for the reader to glean. They could have wrote, "An appalling story, from which society can gather AT LEAST two points." But that would have been too much like real journalism, wouldn't it?

Secondly, the first thing we can take from the story is encouragement. Though Parks was beaten (and we still don't know how severely), we are supposed to be thankful that this story "has become a rare one told over the years."

This is called conjecture. Conjecture is, "Reasoning that involves the formation of conclusions from incomplete evidence." I have already informed the reader of this paper that white newspapers covered up, completely hid or otherwise circumvented stories regarding interracial relationships. So then, how can these nimrods conclude that the race hatred has declined just because the stories have?

As black people, we know about how the white man covers up stories. One white politician who was found dead a few years back was praised about what all he did. What wasn't mentioned was that he was found in an empty North Omaha house dressed in women's clothes. The World-Herald decided they didn't want the public to know. The World Herald itself went out and bought in a polygraph examiner during Hal Daub's mayoral campaign against Brenda Council and they HID the truth but printed what they wanted the public to know. When a black child was used for a Goodfellows campaign a while back, the World Herald changed the gender and race of the child – because THEY felt it was the right thing to do.

So I am making two points here: first, the World Herald's track record disqualifies it from making any believable points regarding interracial relationships when they cover up the ones taking place right here in their back yard and secondly, that their conclusion that such incidents are diminishing is "jive-time journalism" and nothing more than an attempt to appease white suburbanites by convincing them that race relations are "getting better." Racism is alive and, as such, interracial hatred is never going to be "rare." As Fanon taught, "a racist in a culture of racism is therefore, normal."

The article continues:

Gone are the days when a black man was lynched for dating, or even speaking to, a white woman. Gone are the days when interracial couples had to go to court to challenge the legality of their marriages. Gone are the days when the majority of people in this country considered the union of people from differing races as wrong.

The World-Herald's definition of "lynching" is not appropriate and therefore, their conclusion about the diminishing of lynchings is inaccurate. According to the late, great sociologist Oliver C. Cox, in his magnus opus, *Caste, Class and Race*, a lynching takes place any time a group of white men use their numbers and race to attack a single black man. Is this behavior on the decline?

What about crowds of white boys throwing soda on black men at a basketball game? What about the white judicial system ganging up on young black men and giving them time away from their families? What about white cops who single out black men and ram plungers up their asses (Abner Louima case) or gun them down "by accident" as they did Amadou Diallo? In fact, every cop killing is a lynching because it involves a system (white cop is sanctioned) against a lone black person.

It stands to reason that the World Herald would consider such actions on the decline. The newspaper has historically looked the other way when such "lynchings" occur. They did it when Vivian Strong was killed, did it people like Kellin, Ammons, Bibins were all killed by racist cops. None of them had guns. That was a lynching. So when these white editorial writers talk about "declines" they cannot even make that stick here in Omaha, let alone on the national level!

As for the white woman, perhaps the editors should read my 180-plus page response to a recent article that appeared in Newsweek. The Newsweek article was titled, "The Secret Lives of Wives," but it missed so many points I had to respond. In like manner what the World Herald doesn't understand is that the white man has conceded his woman to men of color. He knows what she's about and she's sick of him for the most part. True enough, television and movies don't reflect this reality – yet. But they soon will.

With that understanding, there is no need to lynch a black man for dating or marrying a white woman. That is the white system's way of getting to "Slaves" for the price of one. In many cases she's isolated and shunned and forced to live with black folks. In most cases they both work so the system wins. It's about the money, not about a black man taking one of their blondes away. The fact is, Malcolm X wrote that the act he was most often asked to perform as a pimp was to have sex with a white woman while her husband watched. And this is still going on, right here in Omaha, today. And the World Herald's editors know it all too well.

The issue of interracial couples having to go to court to challenge the legality of their marriages – this was never a major issue or concern. There were widely publicized cases when it happened (again, the media making sure that these cases were publicized, complete with the addresses of the couple involved), but these people knew who was in charge of the courts: the same white boy who is in charge today. The World Herald is grasping at straws in order to buttress its lies. And they should be ashamed.

But the final lie, the deathblow, is where this team of white men claims that the days are gone when the majority of people in this country "considered the union of people from differing races as wrong."

Say what? On what planet are these fuddy-duddies residing? Later, in their own essay, these same men write that, *"Even today, mixed couples are still subjected to disapproving looks, rude comments and silent, yet noticeable, signals of rejection."*

If this is the case, then aren't those looks a physical manifestation that the person doing the looking considers those relationships "wrong"?

But more profoundly, where is the data that supports this incredible fabrication of reality? How does the World Herald know? On what do they base this contention? Because surely, if those days are gone, then gone too would be the days of white people viewing RACISM as wrong! If white people could stop viewing interracial relationships as wrong, this would mean that they would see nothing wrong with the gradual browning of their race.

This would mean that they accept people of color. And this would mean that white racism is on the decline. Anyone who believes that white people are less racist than they were 400 years ago is either naïve about race relations or a total idiot. These crackers are just more afraid now because black people are not as controlled as we were back then. Their fear fuels their racism as much as their hatred did back then. But the effects are still the same: look at the murders of blacks by white cops, look a the prisons and take a long look at the black unemployment rate. Racism has not subsided or decreased; it has merely changed (but not in its intensity).

When those days are "gone," so too will be white folks (as they define themselves today, at least). But once you have a distorted view of social reality (as evidenced in the World-Herald's stories on "black progress" that have permeated its pages this year), any conclusion you arrive at is going to be warped. For example note the following excerpt:

The lack of stories like Parks' is a sign that society has come a long way in its acceptance of interracial unions. But that doesn't mean there isn't more to be done. An impetus for growth also can be taken from this story."

The World Herald again errs, much akin to their earlier perceptual mistake: it is not "the lack of stories like Parks' that is a sign that society has supposedly "come a long way," it is the lack of reporting and media coverage of these stories that is the flaw. The media wants to "play nice" and not report issues of race against interracial couples because it has to take into consideration the city's image, the impact on tourism, the politics of the discrimination, the status of the couple being harassed and so on. The World-Herald knows this: they didn't report those beatings that Daub used to administer to his Asian wife, Cindy, did they?

But even if the World-Herald was correct and the incidents themselves were on the decline, how is this a sign of society coming a long way? This goes back to that white man's thinking that Gunnar Myrdal helped to create in his study, An American Dilemma. All the time the white man felt that what black people wanted was sex with them when, in reality, interracial sex ranked last among the things blacks wanted.

The white man's fears of interracial sex have always been rooted in the way that his mind works: because he raped black women for centuries, he felt the black man wanted to do the same thing to the white woman. This is how the myth got started and the myth, in turn, fanned the hatred that white men had for black people, in general.

Interracial dating and marriage. This was the first thing that those white boys in South Africa "allowed" when apartheid was crumbling. Not more jobs, not better housing, not more liberal policies toward economic development. No. The first thing they said was, "you may now screw our women." Look it up. This contention in itself is racist and a definite put-down of black woman, an issue I will address more thoroughly in a few minutes.

Because the newspaper knows it is lying, it has to qualify its claims that America has come a long way. So they add in the worn cliché, "But that doesn't mean there isn't more to be done." The first thing that should be done is that the World-Herald – along with the rest of the American media – should stop lying. White boys in England still refer to white women who date or marry black men as "slags."

College campuses are filled with white women dating black athletes who have to hear the names they are called in doing so. The campus newspaper doesn't cover these things. The local newspaper, because they need advertisements from the university, don't address it. But just look at who is used to recruit black athletes: white girls. Black people have known this for years. The white man knew, but he was making money prostituting those coeds, so he kept quiet.

These are but a few facts that should show you, the reader, "there is a great deal to be done." There is as much to be done today as there was to be done back in the 1950s, a time the white man dubs, "the golden years." Why were they golden? No black people to worry about. Their sports teams didn't have to compete against us, and white women knew their "place" so the white man had it all to himself. He could act "cool" because there were no brothers to compete against.

But after the Black Power Movement and the Civil Rights Movement loosened things up, white records in sports fell one by one. The white man's control began to falter, and his manipulated "domination" of popular culture disappeared. The "golden years" of the Cleavers of "Leave It to Beaver" and "Donna Reed" were gone. He's tried to relive those times in his movies and TV shows ("Happy Days"), but he knows his time is past. So he pretends as if interracial relationships are more accepted, but offers on evidence to prove it. This is a racist approach in itself: these writers are saying, in essence, "it is true because we say it is so."

These people claim that, "an impetus for growth also can be taken from this story." And what is that? They explain:

It wasn't along ago – 2000 – that Alabama finally removed a law banning interracial marriage (though it hadn't been enforced in years). That same year, Bob Jones University ended its ban on interracial dating. And while society has traveled far in its ability to be open-minded, there still are some people who react negatively when a black man and a white woman, or a Latina woman and a white man, or any other combination, are dating and marrying each other.

You call this "evidence"? One of the most racist states in the union, one that still flies the Confederate flag, decides that it shouldn't be legislating morality and you call this progress? You call it a sign of growth because Bob Jones University ended its ban on interracial dating? You know why they ended it? Because Clinton threatened to take away their Federal dollars, that's why! So once again, the white man had to be bribed to do the right thing in regard to displaying some "humanity."

Having shot down the two examples that the World-Herald office as evidence of "growth," these nitwits with notebooks nevertheless have the gall to claim that society "has traveled far in its ability to be open minded." This has not been established in a single thing that the newspaper has written down. Look at their own city: what is there to point at that shows equitable race relations? The black community is as segregated today as it was in 1950 – the only difference is that the area is larger.

Look at their own newsroom: no blacks in the 1800s and only three in the newsroom today. How can these liars draw conclusions about change when they, themselves, have resisted change? The World Herald, in a hypocritically moralizing tone, writes that "there are still some people who react negatively when a black man and a white woman, or a Latina woman and a white man, or any other combination, are dating and marrying each other."

Few people get angry when a Latina woman and a white man are together because many Latinas have white skin. Unlike the black woman, who is stigmatized, the Latina has the stereotype of the "hot Latin" working for her. Where OWH editors got their information is beyond me. As for a black man and a white woman, this is the most hated relationship by far. Others pale (no pun intended) in comparison.

The twin myths (both concocted by the white man during slavery) of the black rapist and sacred white womanhood still exist today. In another major paper, I look at movies like "The Pelican Brief," "Drive," "I, Robot," "The Bone Collector," and others where a handsome black man is not allowed to be anything to the white female lead but a "friend." This is an extension of the anti-black taboo alluded to earlier.

Those "some people who react negatively"? Guess who most of them are? White males – like the ones sitting in that editorial room writing this bullshit for the gullible Nebraska public to take in. The article concludes:

Even today, mixed couples are still subjected to disapproving looks, rude comments and silent, yet noticeable, signals of rejection. So take some comfort in knowing that most of those who find love outside their race aren't subjected to the horrors that Parks faced. But remember that even one such case is one too many.

Mixed couples? Does the World Herald care enough to provide an operational definition of what they mean? Are they talking about interracial couples? Are they talking about couples from different ethnic groups or religions. Because a "mixed couple" and an "interracial couple" can be two different things.

Furthermore, the editors order the public to "take some comfort in knowing" that "most of those who find love outside their race aren't subjected" to what Parks was subjected to. How does the lily-white editorial board of the OWH know this? Where is their evidence? Are they speaking locally, statewide or nationally?

This brings us to a final point – the title.

How can one incident be a barometer of race relations on any level? How can a "horrendous assault" show a "decline in one type of bigotry"? Even if racial abuse DID decline in that one type of bigotry, would that be enough to offset the institutional manifestations that plague people of color day by day and year by year? Of course note.

When racists like these write about issues of race, they show how little they care by not providing hard data or documentation. They have a preconception about what they want to write about and what they want their conclusion to be. This biased approach is what I tried to tell reporter Tom Shaw about when he made the asinine statement about reporters being "objective" … The interracial barometer, at least the one that the World-Herald is in possession of, is clearly broken.

And it'll take more than a room full of old white men to fix it.

My advice is therefore to never allow external definition of anything that has to do with you, yours or your community. In a city like Omaha, that means having some kind of checks and balances such as the ones I've created: a River City News Council that keeps an eye on the media and its images of blacks; the North Omaha Critique Committee, created back in 1978, and was so shocking to the white mind that it got an article printed in the major newspaper.

Under the headline, "Media Watch By Minorities is Beginning," the article appeared on October 9, 1978:

> Several Omahans say they have become "watchdogs" of the media in an effort to ensure equality in the coverage of minority events.
>
> The North Omaha Critique Committee, formed in August, checks the local and national media for items which portray minorities in a negative way, said Chairman Matthew C. Stelly. "Much of what we see, read and hear in the media is often racist as well as sexist," he said. "Because of the intentional miseducation of minorities, many don't have the chance or the channels to respond to the vile statements leveled against them."
>
> Stelly, a senior at the University of Nebraska-Omaha, said the minority community here has talented writers and< "We intend to use our abilities to expose, correct and rebuke any detrimental images."
>
> **30 Members**
>
> "What the organization is about is defense of our interests and development of our potential," he said. "These are rights that cannot be given, only exercised." The group's motto is: "To Scan 'The Man' is Our Master Plan."
>
> Stelly said there are about 30 "people of color" in the organization. Each member must subscribe to the World-Herald because "there is no way a person can critique the newspaper by reading it in the library," he said. If members read something they think is derogatory to minorities, they can write a rebuttal which will be submitted to The World-Herald's Public Pulse or Another Point of View.
>
> The person who writes must have a legitimate complaint about something affecting the minority community, he said. Articles must be approved by him or Vice Chairman Jeffrey Patterson before they are submitted.
>
> **Focus on Newspaper**

       "Nobody speaks for the black man better than a black man,"
Stelly said. Right now the group is mainly focusing on The World-
Herald, but radio and TV stations soon will be checked, too, Stelly
said.

       Plans call for the organization to publish a magazine called
"Knocking on the Door." "What we need is a vehicle that will
enable us to freely express our feelings about our conditions," he
said. The magazine will contain short essays, poetry and some
critiques of films and TV shows. Stelly, who came to Omaha from
California last year, said there is a similar organization there which
was set up by the Pan Afrikan Secretariat. He said the Omaha
critique committee "seeks to bridge the gap between the North
Side and other communities.

       "We realize that much of the polarity around the race issue
stems from myths, misconceptions and malicious misinformation.
If we can convince one person per day that they have been
brainwashed, we will have made an accomplishment that will raise
Omaha to a higher level of human existence."

That was 34 years ago, and never really got off the ground because it only
existed in my head. But that put white folks on alert, and that is what these "negro
leaders" are going to have to do. The key, as I say, is to reject in detail, defiance
and self-determination, any image or assertion that is imposed on you by your
oppressor. This action is not only defensive, it is also developmental.

KEY: DEFINE, AT THE OUTSET, WHAT "EMPOWERMENT" IS

For anyone else this would be a no-brainer. If you don't know who you are,
then you can't know who your opposition is. And that is the problem with the
Network. They chose a word they'd heard before (from me and the titles of the
conferences I organized long before they came into fruition) and didn't bother to
learn what it meant. I don't mean go by definitions that you got from what your
funding sources tell you: I mean take the traditional definition and then shape it in
your own image and interests.

Empowerment as it relates to what: making white people more powerful and
therefore more in control of North Omaha, or empowerment in the sense of taking
existing black institutions (what few there are) and using them to build a power
base the way the Triple One Neighborhood Association and Parents' Union
worked to do from 1994-2000 (before I left town).

The name of your organization gives you purpose, identity and direction. Look at the NAACP – National Association for the Advancement of Colored People. Although whites were involved in the founding, black people took control from the outset. The scope is defined ("national"), the orientation is established ("association") the purpose is clearly laid out ("for the advancement of") and so is the major constituency ("colored people," which, in those days, was what Black people were called). The Urban League was founded to help those blacks migrating from the rural south to the city (hence, "urban") and it's orientation was established ("league).

When I created the Triple One Neighborhood Association and Parents Union, I first created a "triple one paradigm" – a model, and then I defined on paper, and then on television in front of thousands of viewers, what I meant. "Triple One" refers to the poorest zip code in the state (outside of the Native American reservations) and that is "68111," in the heart of North Omaha. The neighborhood association meant all black people, however, that is why I defined the boundaries to be all inclusive of North Omaha, also including brothers and sisters from "68110," "68104" and "68131."

Once you have purpose, identity and direction, no one can take that from you. In Omaha the so called leaders involved in recent years appear to have it all ass backwards. They want to call themselves "100 Black Men" (as if they have exactly that number of that this small number is their goal), "100 Black Women" (same problem), and so on. Even back in the day when we were truly courageous, our organizations made it clear what we stood for: Ideal Improvement Club, Mothers for Adequate Welfare, and so on.

When you take a word like "Empowerment" and then add the word "Network," people in the black community think you're talking about helping them by networking with other black people. But that is not what these negroes had or have, in mind. Their network consists of anyone who will give them money, anyone who will claim to be a "partner," and their idea of "empowerment" is to kowtow and cater to the needs of the social order. They want to be all things to all people, "not just the blacks."

For that reason, this paper is important. My views may be in the minority, but they are rock strong and accurate. I'm used to being in the minority when it comes to working with these silly people. As the saying teaches, "You can tell when a genius is on the scene because the dunces immediately form a confederacy against him."

Let's now take a critical look at Omaha's self-proclaimed "African-American Empowerment Network."

<u>The African-American Empowerment Network</u>

The name of the article that I am about to analyze on the following pages is "Power Players, Ben Gray and Other Omaha African-American Leaders Try Improvement Through Self-Empowered Networking." The article is written by a wannabe journalist named Leo Biga, who, like a growing number of white people, appears to be obsessed with black folks. Other than the obvious lies that the headline conveys, there are a number of additional errors that will lead to clarity once corrected. The African-American Empowerment Network has major problems ideologically, internally, and programmatically. I will now explain why this is the case.

To begin with, "power players" is an exaggeration. None of the men mentioned has any power because if they did, they wouldn't be begging for collaborations with and input from other people, but would be engaging in development on their own. To use that term is Biga's idea: these men know they have no power and would never present themselves in such a way. This is one more example of the white liberal attempting to define issues that do not concerne him.

Biga has no idea that using that phrase, "power players" could serve to alienate people from Ben Gray and the others that he has mentioned in his article. He doesn't know how black people think. Black people know that any time a white periodical prints something calling any black man (other than State Senator Ernie Chambers) in Omaha a "power player." All they hear is the word, "player," and based on historical record, black people in North Omaha have been "played" enough, by both white elites and their black lackeys.

The articles begins:

> It may have been 2007 when northeast Omaha's depressed
> African-American community reached its limit. A demographic
> bound by race, history, circumstance and geography seemingly
> exhaled a collective sigh of exasperation to exclaim, "Enough
> already!" Longstanding discontent over inequities in income,
> housing, education, economic development and opportunity
> solidified into resolve by a people to take action.

This paragraph is more racist than the movie "Birth of a Nation," and is filled with nothing more that Biga's uninformed assessments and understanding of race relations and black history. Let me break it down so you will be able to see that not all racists wear sheets or swastikas.

How would Biga know when black people in Omaha reached "their limit"? He says that "it may have been 2007" – where is his evidence. Why did it take so long? Is this must another example of the white man "saying so" and therefore that's the way it must be? As a journalist he offers up not one iota of evidence of how he arrived at this date and how he concluded that the black community had reached its limit. It is all conjecture – racist conjecture.

He adds that blacks are a demographic (he must be talking about black people who, by the way, are not a "demographic" anywhere but on the white man's charts and statistical tables) "bound by race, history, circumstances and geography." But he doesn't say how all this came together. Why is it that black people can be "bound" by all these things and still not produce anything? Why is it that blacks, with all these potentially unifying variables, still remain powerless in a nation where power is valued above all else. Without using the word "racism," Biga and people of his ilk talk of "circumstance," but those circumstances are still dictated by racist decisions made by the people with the power.

Where did this "exhalation" come from? The collective sigh – how collective was it? Was it everybody or just the Christians? Was it a few or the entire community led by the negroes that Biga talks to? Why is he lying and using anecdotes to describe a very serious situation? I'll tell you why: because it's about black people, that's why. And when the subject is black people and North Omaha, people like Biga don't care about diplomacy OR accuracy!

This collective sigh produced the exclamation, "Enough already!" That just happens to be almost the same "slogan" that the negroes put on yard signs and posted all over the black community. The exact slogan was "enough is enough." In the black community we have a saying: "You got to bring ass to get ass." That means you don't say "enough is enough" unless you have something to back it up. And the people that made the signs, like Biga the journalist, are seriously lacking.

"Enough already!," or what? In typical Batman saves Gotham City type comic book hyperbole, Biga claims that the longstanding discontent over various inequities somehow "solidified into resolve by a people to take action." Who were these people? Was it only black people? Was it blacks and their white masters? Where is Biga's information, where are the names, dates and places that could be used to fill in these gargantuan gaps in his historical ignorance?

No matter. It was just a substanceless introduction that led to nowhere. Without mentioning a single name or incident, he then slides from the land of the generic into what the real subject is: the self-proclaimed African-American Empowerment Network. Of that Network, he writes:

> Nearly four years ago, a coalition of local blacks decided to rebuild the community from within. They formed the nonprofit African-American Empowerment Network. The effort was inspired by author and television/radio talk show host Tavis Smiley in his best selling 2006 book, *The Covenant with Black America.*

Where did Biga arrive at the statement that black people decided to rebuild the community "nearly four years ago"? That would mean that black people didn't deal with this issue until the 21st century! The fact is, I had been writing proposals, essays, news articles, reports, black papers and so on, directed at political leaders at all levels, black people, the ministers and so on, and even coined the term "self-empowerment" as far back as 2003. Where were these "negroes" then? When I was sponsoring community development conferences in the early 1990s, where were these people? The ones whose names you are reading in Biga's document were nowhere to be found.

When I outlined the TripleZip Agenda, a comprehensive plan for North Omaha, did any of these people respond? No. When I laid out "North Omaha 2000" in 1995, as a project of the Triple One Neighborhood Association, did Biga, Ben Gray, Willie Hamilton or Willie Barney come forward with any support? Of course not. Biga's attempt to "date" when black people came to their senses (which most still have not yet done) as being only four years ago is another racist slap in the face of North Omaha.

What is this "coalition of local blacks"? Who does it consist of? And why do these blacks continue to form "coalitions" – which are formed to achieve a short-term goal, and then disband – instead of rockstrong organizations the way Triple One did? And why do black people in Omaha continue to get inspiration from outsiders like the fly-by-night and effeminate Tavis Smiley? How did Biga find out who the source of their inspiration was? And why would these fools admit to the media that their inspiration came from some outsider who, for one thing, has been besmirching the name of Barack Obama just because Barack couldn't attend one of his bullshit sessions and sent Michelle instead? Who does Tavis Smiley think he is?

But this is the kind of leadership that black North Omahans are attracted to. People like George Frazier, a motivational speaker that has no solutions to black people's problems. People like Stedman Graham, Oprah's flunky and another person who is only around for photo opportunities. North Omaha suffers from low-self-esteem and believes, like whites in Omaha, that the only good ideas are ideas that come from outside of the area. Tavis Smiley is no more qualified to issue or offer a "covenant with Black America" than a wino is offering up a diagram for a laser gun.

Then jumping forward as if the Empowerment Network's existence is a millennium long and therefore irrefutable, Biga continues his fluff-filled flurry:

> Omaha's Empowerment Network targeted 13 areas for improvement. Efforts by the Network and partners are the latest attempted remedies. In the 1940s and '50s the De Porres Club pressed for civil rights. In the '60s the Citizens Coordinating Committee for Civil Liberties or 4CL, took up the banner. Well into the '70s federally funded programs and agencies spurred by the Great Society and its War on Poverty operated here. At various times the Urban League of Nebraska and the Omaha Chapter of the NAACP have led on social justice and community betterment issues.

What were the thirteen areas targeted and how were they decided upon? Were there any areas that had to do with the racist neglect of the city? Was there the formation of a "liberation lobby" to go regularly to Lincoln to put North Omaha's concerns on the political map? Or was it more of that social work/welfare type shit, where the "13 areas" represent 13 different types of begging from the white man's institutions and where the blacks involved get their palms greased for serving as "liaisons" and "partners"?

Now all of a sudden the Network has "partners." Where did they come from and why can't they just be a part of the Network? I'll tell you why: because they're white and they have power and white people don't want to be involved in any Network where they (the whites) won't hall full power. So they claim to be "partners" and in doing so, they hoard all the resources to themselves and are able to dole out just enough crumbs to the Network to make it appear to be a collective effort.

"Attempted remedies"? Isn't it strange that if you chronicle the history of the entire city of Omaha, the only "attempts" at remedies have something to do with North Omaha? Why are there so many failures? Why so many "oops-we-did-it-again" programs and projects? Because the city, even in its allocations of crumbs, never said that they would spend money on meaningful projects or beneficial programs; they just said that they would "allocate some money." So when that money gets mismanaged, stolen or embezzled by someone, the city doesn't care because they can just sit there and say, "well, ya can't say we didn't try!"

Then the insults continue with Biga reducing the century-plus of black struggle in Omaha to one major incident per decade! He mentions the DePorres Club, which did a lot more than "press for civil rights." It was the DePorres Club, usually chairing meetings at the Omaha Star, that helped highlight housing atrocities and employment discrimination. This is how our history gets trivialized, through white writings such as these.

The fact of the matter is, mid- to late-1940s found increasing numbers of organizations being created that would seek to pressure employers into providing jobs for Black people. One such organization, the DePorres Club, was founded in 1947 by Father John J. Markoe, who had come to Omaha a year earlier. Smith (1980) writes:

> Named after St. Martin DePorres, a Black Latin American clergyman, the DePorres Club, although organized by Catholics, sought to bring together people of all faiths to fight racism. The primary force behind the organization was Father John Markoe, a Jesuit priest who was on the faculty of Creighton University … Father Markoe considered racism a sin, and refused to deal with it gently. His preferred method of confrontation, rather than conciliation, and as a result of his guidance, the DePorres Club brought to Omaha its first round of civil rights demonstrations … (p. 25).

The first meeting of the DePorres Club took place in the home of Mrs. Aleane Carter, mother of Great Plains Black Museum founder Bertha Calloway. According to historian Smith, "in addition to Mrs. Calloway, there was [white civil rights activist and President of the DePorres Club] and Father Markoe. There were also about six or seven Black and White students (Smith, 1980: 76). Jesse Allen, during several major interviews that I had with him, also mentions others, including John Orduna, Herb Rhodes, Sr., John Butler, Richard Turner and Ola McRaney.

According to Eve Hanna, a white woman who was interviewed during an Oral History project, the group, of which she was a member, was organized by people affiliated with Creighton University, and they "conducted many civil rights campaigns. This group broke Coca-Cola and Reid Ice Cream Company because of job discrimination against black people. The DePorres Club was also responsible for winning an important civil rights court decision. The incident involved a 12-year-old Black youth who was refused admission to a swimming pool. The youth was awarded damages of about $200 (Hannah, 1980: 18).

Another one of the early civil rights cases and the court victory that followed, involved a "Mr. Taylor." According to Mrs. Hanna, Mr. Taylor was employed at the Urban League. He was refused food service at the Omaha airport, and the case was taken to court. Mr. Taylor won the decision and was awarded one dollar for damages (Hannah, 1980: 18).

There were some who opposed what the DePorres Club was trying to do in the area of civil rights. But one of the unsung heroes of the DePorres Club was Omaha Star publisher and founder Mildred Brown. When it was rumored that "established negroes" were opposed to the civil rights protest group, the following editorial appeared on the front page of the February 5, 1960 issue of the Star under the headline, "Agitation …" Following is an excerpt:

> Lately some whites and some Negroes (who should know better) have counseled a go slow approach with regard to the many assaults on the rights of Omaha's Negro citizens. Main target of this kind of criticism is the DePorres Club. Some are saying that it has "set progress back" because of its picketing of the Omaha School Administration. These hand wringing do-gooders and some who style themselves outspoken leaders want this paper and the DePorres Club to adopt a head-bowed, hat-in-hand method of commenting on the daily instances of wrong done to Negroes.
>
> This paper is told to speak more softly until "Things can be worked out." We say NO to such suggestions. We stand solidly behind the DePorres Club and its fighting program for arousing the conscience of the people of Omaha to correct the social injustice against the Negro people. Let there be no doubt that we will not shrink from our duty to speak out for those oppressed citizens… (p. 1)

Not to sell the DePorres Club short the way Biga did, recall that also on February 14, 1960, at a conference in Fremont, Nebraska sponsored by the National Conference of Christians and Jews, the DePorres Club ventured forth and presented Governor Brooks with a petition that called for ending racial segregation of teachers and discrimination in the Omaha Public Schools. The organization showed just how organized it was as members distributed handbills during all three days of the conference (p. 1). The group also presented its motto: "Do Something in 1960" to educators who were in attendance.

One local writer claims that in the 1960s the 4CL – which stands for Citizens Coordinating Committee for Civil Liberties -- "took up the banner," again reducing one of North Omaha's most progressive and productive decades to one group. There was more to it than "taking up the banner." The 4CL bought the community together on major issues, and they also worked for black people regardless of denomination. In fact, they played a major role in bringing Malcolm X to Omaha.

The group was founded during the spring of 1963 by four African American clergymen: Reverend Kelsey Jones, Rev. Rudolph McNair, Rev. General Woods, and Rev. R.F. Jenkins. Again, Smith:

> The 4CL was a grass-roots community organization. While whites
> were never excluded, it was always made clear that the group
> existed primarily to mobilize the black community. Large numbers
> of people turned out for its meetings, as well as for the
> demonstrations (1980: 27).

The leader of these men was probably Rudolph McNair. McNair was born in Kansas City, Kansas in 1923, the seventh of eight children of Mr. and Mrs. George McNair. His father was a contractor while his mother was a housewife and quite active in the affairs of the First AME Church.

These men were no rookies, but came to the fore with experience. Following his graduation from Sumner High School, the Rev. McNair served five years in the Army, including a two-year European Theater tour-of-duty during World War II as a sergeant-technician. He retired from the Army reserves in 1964. After active military service, the Rev. McNair worked for the government in the post office, Veterans Administration and the Army Reserves. It was a position as a civilian administrative assistant at Fort Omaha's USAR School which brought him to Omaha in 1958.

Rev. General R. Woods was born on June 23, 1909 in St. Louis, Missouri. Woods was a professional musician several years before entering the ministry, and played trumpet, trombone, tuba and bass violin in jazz orchestras (Omaha Star, 1972: 1).

By the summer of 1963, the civil rights movement in Omaha was gaining momentum and respect. The mayor of the city had appointed a Biracial Committee of which Reverend Jenkins said, "Well, I don't think too much of it because it was just a front that did practically nothing, so I paid no attention to it" (quoted in Smith, 1980: 93). (NOTE: The exact same tactic would be employed some 37 years later by Mayor Hal Daub through the creation of a Race Relations Commission. More on that later in this book).

Unlike the Empowerment Network that talks but doesn't get involved in the streets in leading the community, in October of 1963, the 4CL stood all of Omaha on its head when Reverends R.E. McNair and Kelsey A. Jones joined with a number of demonstrators in the City Council chambers and sang and demonstrated during an October 22nd City Council meeting. All were arrested, with McNair and Jones charged with disturbing an assembly (1964: 1).

At a mass meeting of Zion Baptist Church on Wednesday, January 8, 1964, 4CL Vice President told the audience that the group would "increase the intensity and tempo" of their activity during the new year, and that "If the hallmark of our efforts in 1963 was 'Freedom Now,' it will be 'More in '64'" (Omaha Star, 1964: 1). Furthermore, at this meeting,

Furthermore, Biga can only talk about the War on Poverty when it comes to the 1970s, which in reality was perhaps the second most progressive decade in North Omaha's history. For instance, Senator Ernie Chambers got district elections for the Omaha School Board in 1975, and for the City Council in 1979; soul station KOWH came on line in 1972 based on community demands, not individuals the way Biga would interpret it. And what about the fact that in July of 1971, the Black Studies program at UNO officially got its "Department" status? And in 1975, the Great Plains Black Museum became a reality. But all Biga can write about is Lyndon Johnson's "Great Society" concept and the War of Poverty – which, of course, failed.

Biga's research includes some mention of the Urban League of Nebraska and the Omaha chapter of the NAACP, but fails to specifically cite examples. In failing to do this, he lies by *omission.* In playing up the African-American Empowerment Network and their alleged "accomplishments," he lies by *commission.*

But no matter what white man is writing it, they can never leave out the "blame game" to make young people believe that North Omaha is the way it is because of "black riots." The following paragraph is so typical:

> When the last in a series of major civil disturbances in the late 60s badly damaged the old North 24th St. business-entertainment hub, many businesses left. Few new businesses have opened. Northeast Omaha's chronic gun violence contributed to the perception of an unsafe environment. It is regarded as a mission district dependent on government assistance, social services and philanthropy.

What these white people don't ever mention when they discuss how the "riots" tore up 24th Street, is that the businesses that were burned and damaged the most were the ones that were owned by white people and, specifically, Jews. These were the people that had ripped them off for decades, and the riot gave them a chance to get payback. This was not something random – black people knew what they were doing. It wasn't as if they had seen a lot of development money coming down the pike, anyway. White history writers (not historians) like Biga might do well to remember this important fact.

And further, what was the cause of those civil disturbances? Did black people just want to randomly commit acts of vandalism and destruction as whites would feel most comfortable believing? Of course not. What was unique about Omaha is that there were three riots, all of which involved looting and justifiable violence: July 3, 1966 and then another one in August that lasted three nights; March 1968, payback for a racist speech by George Wallace followed by a shooting of 16-year old Howard Stevenson; and 1969, 3 days of looting and rioting following a police shooting of 14-year-old Vivian Strong, killed on June 25, 1969. The physical damage was "payback" by a community that was united in its hatred of racist abuse by the police and the system.

Businesses were lost and few opened, but the ones that did were black-owned this time around. But Biga seems bent on justifying his belief that North Omaha was worthless until the Empowerment negroes came along. Take note where he writes that "Northeast Omaha's chronic gun violence contributed to the perception of an unsafe environment." What chronic gun violence are you talking about? I just showed where those riots were a response to cops gunning down black kids. Senator Chambers has documented scores of cases of police shooting down black citizens. The Omaha Police Division walks around in paramilitary gear as if Omaha was a major city. And yet white writers like Biga make it appear as if it is the black man's use of the gun that is the problem. *The hunter has an entirely different viewpoint when the ducks have guns.*

The perception of an "unsafe environment" is based on the white perception that black people are the majority in North Omaha and that means that is one place where they can't call us "nigger" and get away with it. When they are defenseless and can't flex their muscle, they use the psychological defense mechanism of transference to make the victims appear to be the culprits. Evidently Biga buys into this distorted piece of sociological history.

Then comes another insult and interpretation by the uninformed Biga. He states that North Omaha "is regarded as a mission district dependent on government assistance, social services and philanthropy." The question that he should ask, instead of wasting ink kissing the collective black asses of the Empowerment negroes is, "if this is true, then what made that area so dependent on the government dole"?

Here's the answer before moving on to Biga's next barrage of drivel: if North Omaha became enriched, Omaha would lose almost all of its Community Development Block Grant funding, which averages about $5 million a year. They would lose most of their Community Service Block Grant money, which goes mostly to ENCAP, a poverty agency. And they wouldn't qualify for the police grants like Weed and Seed and Project Triggerlock. So it's got to remain poor and that's what they do: allow a few to escape through jobs and the rest are there so Omaha can get money from HUD to build "affordable housing" on the fringe of the area to get more to move out. The ones who stay behind will be just enough to constitute that "pocket of poverty" that every city needs in order to qualify for the CDBG money. Does Biga know this, or does he care enough to find out?

Contradictions and game-playing abound and self-proclaimed writer Biga is too blind to see it. Check out the following excerpt:

> President and consultant at Innovations By Design, LLC, Tawanna Black, also vice-chair of the board for the Network, and co-chair for the race relations covenant, summed it up. "In the absence of African-Americans in powerful political or economic positions to drive this, small changes have occurred but nothing major. The Network really flips that theory on its head and says,"Why are we waiting for the power to be given? Let's own the power that's within.' It's an empowerment thing. It means more than just a name on a piece of paper. It's really what it's all about empowering people to take control of themselves. A process committed to that is completely new in this community."

Tawanna Black doesn't know anything about black people. She's married to a white man and owns a boa constrictor, and doesn't even live in Omaha. She was bought in for who knows what reason, but since she's arrived she's had some powerful jobs. They put Ms. Black in charge of a Midtown project where Mutual of Omaha and others lied about being a blighted area so that they could receive Tax Incremental Financing. Now they've got shops and businesses surrounding the district, a hotel and movie theater, all of this with Mutual of Omaha as the hub.

Why would the Network have a "race relations covenant?" Let them tell it, everything is just peachy-keen when it comes to race relations. If the Network is interracial, why would there be such a need since their "target" is North Omaha? This is nothing more than window dressing, akin to the "race commission study" that was conducted in 1997. Who is going to sign a covenant on race relations? This is as shallow as former President Bill Clinton's "apologizing" for slavery. The apology, like the covenant, is only the beginning. My question in both cases is this: where are the financial reparations for the decades/centuries of abuse?

If Ms. Black knows there is an absence of African-Americans in powerful political or economic positions, then shouldn't job one be trying to locate or develop some? Of course not because this would challenge the status quo – white folks in charge, even when it comes to black-oriented projects. So what do they do in terms of "flipping that theory on its head"? They say the very same things that I have been saying since 1977 – turn our power inward. I even provided them with a model: the Triple One Neighborhood Association and Triple One Parents Union. They watched and saw what I was able to do with these two groups, representing the families and youth of the "68111" zip code (hence, "triple one"), the poorest zip code in the state of Nebraska.

Then Ms. Black says, "let's own the power that's within." How sophistic. If there is no power then what are you going to own? What she should be saying is let's develop our power potential from within our own ranks. What did Stokely Carmichael and Charles V. Hamilton write more than 40 years ago? *"Before a group can enter open society it must first close ranks."*

Furthermore, by stating that "we must own the power within," this doesn't challenge the status quo, once again. As long as white people have the real power, these negroes are willing to concede that and then try to "own" something somewhere in the black community, then report back to the white man with their findings. You what this kind of person was called back in the day? An overseer. The only power the overseer had was over the enslaved folk out in the field, and other than that, he was nothing but a flunky and snitch for the white man.

Is this the kind of "power" that people like Tawanna Black want to own?

What she's saying about empowerment is really self-empowerment and I've got three consecutive conferences to back up the fact that I've been talking about this concept since the beginning of the 21st century. So when she says that" a process committed to that (self-empowerment) that is completely new in this community" is an outright and absurd lie.

People who don't study look stupid when they try to make socio-political statements or draw up plans. I've proven that throughout this paper, from the writings of Leo Biga and the World Herald to negro leaders in North Omaha, having been duped into thinking that they have "juice." More evidence lies ahead. For instance, note the following:

> "There's been a lot of psychological damage done to us as a
> people. Historically we just allow things to happen to us and what
> we have to do is starting taking control of our own destiny and that
> means also having skin in the game," said Omaha City
> Councilman and Network violence intervention-prevention chair
> Ben Gray.

How silly. We're not psychologically damaged because we "allowed things to happen to us." Those things happened despite our resistance to them. His statement smacks of those foolish beliefs that black people submitted to slavery. Nothing could have been further from the truth. When there were efforts afoot to take control of our own destiny, I was present when Ben Gray personally used the microphone and his control of it to turn those efforts back. He's turned those efforts back everywhere he's gone. He's one of the reasons why white folks are so deeply involved in the business of the black community.

Then he says that we have to have "skin in the game." What "game" is he talking about? If he's talking about the race situation in Omaha, this ain't no game.

And perhaps the key to his on-going failures are revealed in his statement about having skin the game. Do you know what that means? It mean's just being there; it means just sitting at the table and saying nothing. It means just breathing while other people plan and talk. Skin just means you exist. Karenga (1967) wrote that, "Membership in the black community requires more than just physical presence." Having "skin in the game" is Ben Gray's philosophy (the terminology was recently used during a speech by New Jersey Governor Chris Christie) on community development because when he just sits there he's probably getting paid by the opposition. I say if you go to a meeting and nobody knows you've been there, you wasted your time and everybody else's as well.

Jargon. Clichés. Possibly some old rap lyrics. *Anything to quote rather than some coherent strategies for struggle.* For instance,

> Empower Omaha drafted a rising-tide-lifts-all-ships community covenant. Through monthly community meetings, periodic summits and prayer walks, neighborhood cleanups, block parties and surveys, the Network interfaces with residents through a North Omaha Neighborhood Alliance.

"A rising tide lifts all ships." "Pick up the bottom of the barrel and everything in it is lifted by extension." "A stitch in time saves nine." "A bird in the hand is worth two in the bush." Good Lord, man! Don't these people see how stupid they look? Ten years from now if anybody reads that newspaper and Biga's article, they are going to scratch their heads and ask, was everybody in the Network retarded or on the pipe? Because that's sure what it sounds like.

Not a coherent thought or logical plan among them! They just meet, choose up sides as if they're about to play a game of kickball, give themselves some titles and that's it! Ten years from now will North Omaha be any better off? Probably. Ten years from now will North Omaha black people be any better off? No way! This is not about black people hunkering down and turning their power inward. That was already being done before the white man interloped into the area back in the early 1960s (a point that even the sophistic Biga will acknowledge). And from then it was downhill. We had a few spikes during that time, but those were periods when black people reacted to situations, discrimination and neglect and scared white folks into doing something.

Look at their "strategic plans:" prayer walks, periodic summits (meaning meetings among themselves), neighborhood cleanups, block parties and surveys (why survey the obvious? The need is starting you straight in the face!). This is why white people laugh at us behind our backs. This is why Omaha is an invisible blip on the map of major cities. This is why so many black kids are getting the hell away from that town and heading elsewhere. This is why there is a brain drain among all young people because the maltreatment of North Omaha is so obvious and glaring, even white kids can't take it any more.

And yet these people talk about planning for the future? And then, even in the midst of their buffoonery, they have the gall to make statements such as those which follow:

> "We keep the community engaged, we listen to the community, we write down what they say. I think that's how we get the buy-in from the community," said director of operations Vicki Quaites-Ferris. "Most things implemented actually come as a result of listening to the community."

These lies are being shared with Biga because the people telling them know that this white man couldn't know the truth. It's a fluff piece, an interview being conducted by a race relations novice. So they lie. This woman, who is director of operations, would not make these statements to a black publication of any merit because the community would read it and know that she was lying.

For instance, what "community" do they keep engaged? How do they engage them? What have they done besides the neighborhood watch, block party stuff mentioned earlier? Has the community become so engaged that they (the Network) would not be needed in, say, three years? That is the goal of a good organization that is out to uplift a community: to put itself out of a job. If they did their job, the community that is so "engaged" would eventually become empowered.

They claim they listen to the community. Does the community even know when the meetings are being held? Why would you write down what "the community" says in this day and age of tape recorders and video cameras? Where is the evidence that the community has bought in to what the Network is doing? Was there a survey? Is there a support list? And when she claims that most of the things that have been implemented (like what?) have been a result of listening to the community, then I have a question: of what good is the Network? If the community has the ideas and is so engaged, then the Network is reinventing the wheel and should disband. As Judge Judy says, "If you tell the truth, you don't have to have a good memory."

Next come contradictions and as a result, more confusion:

> Highlander Neighborhood Association president Kristina Carter said the Network's an integral part of neighborhood cleanups. Network strategies encompass neighborhoods, housing, employment, education, family, faith, crime, etc. The strategies come from community leaders, residents and best practices in other

> cities. Not a direct service provider, the Network partners with
> others to support or facilitate programs.

When my neighborhood association – the Triple One Neighborhood Association and Parents' Union – was one of seven neighborhood groups statewide to win the "Project of the Century" award back in 2000 from the Urban Community Improvement Association, Highlander was one of the other six. During that time they were opening up learning centers after school for young people and were doing an adequate job in that area.

I don't recognize the name Kristina Carter, but I do know that Highlander did a lot more than just clean up the neighborhood. And if the Network is an integral part of these cleanups, then they are simply re-inventing the wheel: this is what the Ideal Improvement Club was doing back in the 1940s (along with other community activities). Then all this other stuff is added regarding housing, neighborhoods, employment, education, family, faith and crime.

Here's what I want to know: where is the evidence of Network involvement? What are they doing in terms of affordable housing, helping with rent and so on? What are they doing in the area of education, since black kids in the Omaha Public Schools are having major problems? Where is evidence that they are stabilizing and/or assisting with the defense and development of black families?

Nowhere to be found. That's why in the next sentence Ms. Carter states that the Network is "not a direct service provider" but indeed, "partners with others to support or facilitate programs." So I ask again, of what good are they? This so-called "Empowerment Network" is not about empowerment: it is a social service liaison, a referral agency – a middle man. They have no power to provide direct services but that is what the masses need: direct relationships with those who claim to be their leaders. Instead, they farm the work out to whom? Social Services? Workforce Development? Family Housing Services? This may be necessary, but it is not sufficient – especially when you are playing around with and mouthing platitudes regarding "empowerment." How can you empower others when you, yourself, are lacking power?

As stated, I was having Empowerment Conferences every year, from 2001-2004. None of these people attended a single one of them. I gave out awards, fed the community, and had the event at the Omaha Opportunities Industrialization Center, in the heart of the black community, so the people would know that Triple One didn't just talk and try to lead by proxy: we were directly involved in the bread and butter issues that impacted their lives.

Knowing this, check out the following attempt at an explanation to get "dibs" on empowerment and show a (feigned) concern about the condition of North Omaha:

The Network was in place before a 2007 Omaha World-Herald series revealed black Omaha poverty rates as among the nation's worst. What was already known is that many youths underachieve in school — only half graduate. There is an epidemic of sexually transmitted diseases, a preponderance of single-parent homes and little economic development or opportunity. Newly detailed were high jobless rates and low household income levels. Freeway construction disrupted, some say severed, a tight community. As restrictive housing practices waned, upwardly mobile blacks moved west. Others left the state. Many feel the city needs to make an "It stops here" pledge.

Again, it is imperative to blame North Omaha for its plight, blame the residents for their condition. If not, the only other choice would to be to blame the white people whose decisions and neglect led to the negative demographics that the Empowerment Network is constantly citing.

If the Network was in place before the poverty rates were released, then why didn't they know about the rates beforehand? The key to leadership is information, or don't they know that? You would think that a group that is essentially nothing more than glorified social workers would at least understand social dynamics.

So after citing Omaha's high ranking in black poverty, one would think that the inevitable follow up would be for this group of "leaders" to outline why that was the case. What are the socio-political, financial and educational factors that led to these statistics? No, not the so-called "empowerment" negroes. They immediately allow Biga the reporter to jump into dogging out the kids and talking about under-achieving in school, about low graduation rates. That's Ben Gray's area as the leader of the so-called African-American Achievement team. Doesn't look like much "achieving" is taking place, does it?

Then, another right cross: not only are the kids being blamed for not having any brains but they're also responsible for the spread of STDs! Then there are the single-parent homes which are also our fault, and very little economic development or opportunity. These are two different things: economic development is the result of a plan; opportunity is a human right. The fact is, white folks have been in control of both these areas which explains why the community is deteriorated and why opportunity – except for a few well-placed negroes – is non-existent.

The article claims that a preponderance of joblessness and low housing income levels are "newly detailed." Bullshit! As far back as *The State of Black Omaha Report, 1978*, statistician Manny Martinez documented not only low housing income, but also median housing value and a plethora of other issues that were overlooked in the subsequent reports that would appear over the years, many of them co-opted by the University of Nebraska Omaha's Center for Applied Urban Research (lot of good they've done over the years).

So far the article by Biga, with the blessing of the Network, has managed to blame the black community for the condition it is in. There has not been one mention of any improprieties on the part of the city or the state and the entities that are supposed to be addressing the problems of that area. There is not a single mention of Senator Ernie Chambers who has bought this information to the fore long before the Urban League report of 1978 did it. This is a fluff piece. It is poor journalism. And the Empowerment Network, based on the statements of its self-proclaimed "power players" appear to be nothing short of a group of loquacious quislings.

The Network was in place before 2007, evidently didn't read any of the State of Black Omaha reports, evidently didn't see black men getting shot down by cops and black prostitutes being propositioned by the same; they evidently didn't see or hear what I had been laying out, idea and proposal by idea and proposal, for North Omaha's uplift. When and how did they get on the scene? What are their community credentials?

Biga – with the Empowerment Network's blessing –continues to lie and distort the social history of North Omaha. For instance, he writes that "freeway construction disrupted, some say severed, a tight community." Where were the Network people when Senator Chambers and I were bringing together the UNO campus and the community to oppose that roadway? The ones who are saying that the freeway severed the community were shouted down by the same white people that the Network now caters to and hobnobs with. One of those persons is now Mayor, and his name is James Suttle. More on him in a minute.

Biga, in his incredible ignorance of urban planning and Omaha history, comes to the conclusion that "restrictive housing practices waned" and "upwardly mobile blacks moved west." If these housing practice waned at all, it meant that they existed at one time. And if they existed at one time then what prompted them to "wane"? The economy! The attitudes behind the practices didn't wane, though. Black people moving out to west Omaha did so as renters and those who purchased homes ran into more racism: redlining, steering and over charging by area banking interests. Why didn't Biga mention that?

And what is an "upwardly mobile black"? Does he mean those with good jobs? Because good job or not, if you were black in Omaha in 1970 you still could only live in North Omaha or face ridicule and harassment by those suburban white folks. And as reliable studies show, those who move out west do not cut their ties with North Omaha, because that's where they have to go to get hair cuts, go to the beauty shop, get their nails done and visit family and friends. Biga is, once again, confusing *appearance* with *essence*. This is what happens when you don't do your homework.

He adds that, "others left the state." Why would that be? Why doesn't he write, "others left the state because, while more than qualified, they simply could not find work in a city as racist as Omaha." This statement is far closer to being the truth than what he wrote. He makes it sound like black people were cowardly and "hatted up" because they couldn't take the pressure. What he is describing are the actions of cowardly white people and a concept known as "white flight." Again, he should be consulting urban planning scholars: no other race could stand the abuse and humiliation that black people have had to undergo simply in order to eke out a quiet existence in a segregated ghetto. That's not because of the lack of courage; that's because of the pre-eminence of white racism.

As a result of all of these "observations," what does Biga come up with, and what do the negro leaders endorse? "The city needs to make an "It stops here" pledge." What is "it"? Racism stops here? White women cruising the community looking for young black bucks stops here? Liquor stores all over the community stops here? Abuse of federal funding that should be getting spent on north Omaha but instead is spent on parks downtown stops here? Silly white boys acting like they know something about the black experience and expose their ignorance in writing stops here?

What is needed is more than a "pledge." Do you know what a "pledge" is? It is "a solid promise or agreement to do or refrain from doing something." Would this pledge be legally binding? How would it be enforced? What would prompt the city to pledge to do something that would cost it billions of dollars if they did, indeed, stop "it"? Making a pledge is a gesture or a symbol and most pledges are made to be broken and are shallow – as in the "Pledge of Allegiance" which is filled with lies that you are supposed to believe actually exist. Why would people with no morals make a pledge and expect others to believe it? This is the best that these people can come up with.

I have an idea: why doesn't the so-called "Empowerment Network" make a pledge to stop cavorting with the enemies of the community and selling North Omaha acre by acre? Why doesn't it make a pledge that you can't be a part of the Network unless you live in the community that is being impacted?

Biga hand picks the black people he talks to, which is why he interviews people who are both safe and lacking in knowledge:

> Rev. Jeremiah McGhee doubts the larger community yet
> appreciates a revitalized north Omaha is good for all of Omaha.
> The city has managed a united front against gun violence. The
> Network has endorsements from Mayor Jim Suttle, Omaha Police

Chief Alex Hayes and some 100 public-private partners for the
Omaha 360 anti-violence coalition.

How did Biga find Jeremiah McGee, a so called "reverend"? The word on the street is that this guy marries young couples and links the wedding to some kind of voodoo rituals. I don't know if its true or not, but this much I do know: he's a sellout and will do anything for a buck. But then, this is the kind of black person that Biga is comfortable around. It's almost as if he (Biga) has some kind of "bootlicking sixth sense." He knows not to mess with Ernie and when he asked me about an article, I told him to get lost (and a few other choice words).

The point here is that the preceding excerpt features McGee and then it makes a reference to "Mayor Jim Suttle." This is the man who helped spearhead that freeway that was mentioned earlier, remember? He was the one who lied and did whatever he could to get the money to force that freeway through the heart of North Omaha. Remember? And now here is the Empowerment Network aligning themselves with him. "The friend of my enemy is my enemy."

I don't know the police chief, but he was black, and now he's retired. All I know is that when you align yourselves with cops, what you're doing is ingratiating yourself to them. You helping them to harm our kids in most cases. These people want to befriend cops so that the cops won't arrest them when they come staggering out of one of these bars or commit an act of domestic violence. They turn our kids over to them, and they trust them. These acts, in themselves, should show the true character of the Empowerment Network.

And that so-called "Omaha 360 anti-violence coalition" is a joke.

For one thing, 100 public-private partners are just signing on because how could they not? What do you say when someone calls begging you to be a partner to "stop violence in North Omaha"? Well, you're white and you know the blacks are violent so you say, "sure, I'll help." So now you can become a partner. No response on letterhead, nothing in writing, no contract "pledging" that you'll put in work. Just a claim that, "I'm in!"

And check out the name, "Omaha 360." Do you know what a 360-degree circle is? It means you've come full circle. So they start out without a plan and not knowing what to do and that is where they end up. That is what the name implies, does it not?

Biga continues editorializing, but the contents of what he says (not the manner in which he writes it) also shows complicity by and from, the Network:

Connecting the dots, it became clear that despair is rooted in
certain realities: entrenched gang and drug culture; fractured
families; a lack of positive role models; barriers to educational,

job, home ownership and business opportunities; a sense that no one cares.

Connecting what "dots"? What a foolish concept: when you're dealing with social issues it's not about connecting dots, it's about developing a plan and then approaching the collective problem using an ecological (contextual) approach. Evidently the Empowerment Network doesn't know this. When you connect dots from one problem to the next, all that does is reinforce the stigma that already exists: the problems (dots) are the result of black people's inability to "get with the program." Nothing could be further from the truth.

That connecting the dots concept and the addition of the word "despair" reminds me of the "cycle of despair" that Weinstein and Fantini wrote bout in the middle 1970s in their book, *The Disadvantaged*. It was just another way of dealing with the so-called "cycle of poverty" and admitting that there were no solutions. But of course there are solutions, but they are rooted in undoing the cycle, first and foremost! At the base of the problems that are mentioned is the white abuse of the system and the racism that is a part of dealing with the black community in the same way that you deal with blacks on an individual basis: with disdain-and-how-dare-you.

Then Biga (and the Network, by extension) believe that despair is rooted in what they call, "certain realities." He's listed them, but let me regurgitate them and I'll include what I believe to be the source or basis of each of these "realities."

Entrenched gang culture: How did the gangs get to an "entrenched" status? The gangs are here because the kids who are involved in gangs live in North Omaha. So the kids are entrenched because they're trapped in a situation where they realize they live in a city that continues to abuse, neglect and deprive their parents. The source of gangs: bad police work and low-income status.

Entrenched drug culture: The drug culture is entrenched because everybody is taking some kind of drug. Within North Omaha alone there are about five Walgreen's Drug Stores, and there are also CVS Drugs and other "pharmacies" including those at Baker's and Albertson's (Save-On Drugs). As for street drugs, the need for them is obvious when life-chances are sabotaged. North Omaha has been a "social experiment" for decades, and the drugs came in, just as they did in Los Angeles, as a tool of control. The source? A drug culture that wants to distinguish between "prescribed" drugs and "street" drugs although in many cases, the residual effect is the same.

Fractured families: It's easy to blame single-parent families for problems that are actually community-wide. The other agents of socialization available to young people include the schools, the media and their peers. These families are not "fractured" because the extended kin and pseudo-kin networks more than compensate for the absence of a parent in the home. Source of the problem: The media and social work view that the family is the problem, a tangle of pathology, a cycle of despair and so on. All these, in combination, lead to internal, psychological and behavioral manifestations of "despair."

Lack of positive role models: If the individuals who make up the Empowerment Network consider themselves role models, then THAT seems to be a cause for despair, not any LACK of them! The problem is that what the decision makers consider "positive" may not be all that positive in the eyes of young people. Politicians who take bribes, get caught gambling away more money than a black family of four earns in a year, people on TV hobnobbing with the policymakers who debase the community, these are the people being pawned off as role models. What is the source of the lack of positive role models: a definitive statement on what constitutes "positive." When black kids see the media and black and white politicians insulting Senator Ernie Chambers – the only man they respect – this only makes them want to further reject the people who are claiming to be "positive role models." You have to be a man or a woman first – that's an ascribed status. A role model is an "achieved" status and the people whose names have appeared in this paper have not done that. They are "dubbed" positive role models by the people who aren't affected.

Barriers to educational opportunities: In Omaha, the barriers are the fact that there are no opportunities for the black child to learn about himself. The curriculum is lily-white and the only time blacks are mentioned is as slaves or during civil rights discussions. Add to that the fact that black kids are more likely to be placed in EMH classes than in Gifted and Talented, and it is clear that the decision makers are creating the obstacles. Blacks in OPS fare so badly that few can pass the entrance test given out by nearby University of Nebraska at Omaha and may be getting "steered" to Metropolitan Community College, a 2-year school in the heart of North Omaha.

Barriers to job opportunities: The main barrier to job opportunities in Omaha is the lack of transportation. Want proof? The data from 1990, taken from the 1990 census, gives us an idea of the differences between black and white relationships to the issue of transportation when the context is the city of Omaha:

Table 3. Transportation access by race

Mode of Transportation	Omaha MSA (whites)	Northside residents (Black)
Automobile	86%	70%
Carpooling	12%	19%
Metro Area Transit (bus)	2%	11%

SOURCE: 1990 Census/Chart by Uhuru Sasa Research Institute

Furthermore, Omaha's black community is a place where, in 1978 it was reported that fully 45% of residents lacked automobiles (Urban League of Nebraska, 1978: 20). Five years later nothing had changed. According to an August 7, 1983 article in the Omaha World Herald documented that, "Nearly 45 percent of the households on the Near North Side have no cars. So residents walk or rely on taxis, buses or rides from neighbors and relatives to get to stores along Ames Avenue or shopping centers to the west."

Barriers to home ownership: What is the source? To begin with no job which as I say, is related to and rooted in the lack of transportation (and of course, job discrimination by white decision makers). Black home ownership has decreased, even since the 1920s. Want proof? Take note of the home ownership ethic that was observed in a December 14, 1928 editorial in the *Omaha Monitor* newspaper:

> There are some features about Omaha that perhaps we do not appreciate as we should. Among these should be mentioned the largest percentage of home-owners. It is stated upon the authority of real estate men that 30,000 of the homes in this city are owned by them that live in them. Omaha has 51,000 homes, and 30,000 of these, think of it! More than 60 per cent, or three out of every five of the homes in this city, are owned by the occupants. This is a record unequalled by any other American city. We can point with commendable pride to the fact that Omaha holds the record for home ownership. And it is noteworthy that our own race contributes to this splendid record, the estimate being that 45 per cent of the Negroes are home owners (Omaha Monitor, 1928: 2).

Across the nation black people are facing "obstacles" (mainly the banks, job discrimination, etc.). For example, according to the *2002 State of Black America* report, 2002,

> Compared with whites and the rest of the nation, blacks are still stuck in the pre-civil-rights era when it comes to owning their homes. For whites, homeownership rated is 74 percent. For blacks, it is 48 percent – the national rate in the 1940s (Omaha World Herald, 2002).

More recently, Edney (2004) documented that, "within the African-American community, les than 50 percent of U.S. citizens are homeowners, compared to 70 percent for whites" (p. 11). Home ownership among black people in North Omaha has actually decreased since 1928! The outcome is described, but the "reality" lies at the door of a system whose banks, other lenders and discriminatory real estate representatives work in cohesion to manipulate where and how black people live. This then, is the source of despair, even in the face of the fact that so many black people are so desperately trying to achieve an American Dream that is really, as Malcolm X said, an American "nightmare."

Barriers to business opportunities: Here are the facts that Biga came up with (probably provided to him by someone black and then he omits the source so that people will think that he actually engaged in some research): *"A recent Pew Partnership for Civic Change report found that of 33,000 metro businesses, only 200 are black-owned – most are single owner-operator endeavors."*

And that's the way it was in Milwaukee as well: most businesses have one employee and that one employee is the owner. So what is the Omaha Small Business Network doing? It was charged with assisting with the startup of small businesses. What is the City of Omaha doing with the CDBG funds that were supposed to assist, not only through OSBN, but as a primary venture, to help provide jobs and opportunities for residents of the "pocket of poverty" as they call it? Therefore what is the source of the barrier? Who controls the economics? Who controls the allocations processes? Who performs intake and the application process? It's surely not North Omaha's blacks.

A sense that no one cares: This is nothing but anecdotal foolishness. If despair is rooted in a certain reality, and that reality is that no one cares, then explain this: where are all those Christians who are sitting in Salem Baptist Church, Zion Baptist Church, Mount Moriah Missionary Baptist Church, Pleasant Green, Paradise and all those other institutions every Sunday? If the Empowerment Network just got with the program in 2007, then what would they know about a sense of not caring on the part of residents that they have very little contact with or concern about? Where have they been all this time?

Where is the evidence? For over a century black people have believed that somebody cares about them. Now here comes Biga, listening to numbskulls, who want to believe that the issue is that there is despair because black people don't think anyone cares. The issue is that black people know that the city administration doesn't care, and that is the source of the problem. These people are a small minority of the population but they hoard the power and decision making. The Network, as I've stated earlier, is simply comic relief, window dressing and "affirmative action" evidence that the otherwise lily-white city is doing it's "garsh-darndest to help the negro people."

In absence of a plan and an historical understanding of the situation, the pity party for North Omaha by those who claim to be leaders, continues:

> Douglas County Treasurer and Network chair John Ewing knows
> it from his former career as an Omaha cop and Empowerment
> prayer walks and community meetings. He said residents
> complain of violence, lack of economic opportunities, that they
> feel abandoned, neglected, overlooked, forgotten. It leads to a
> sense of hopelessness. And northeast Omaha's lost some 11,000
> households over time. A diminished tax, voter, consumer base
> diluted the minimal clout it had to hold public and private sectors
> accountable the economic and social ills.

Prayer walks. This man was a cop, and he didn't do anything to stand up for the black community. No one really even knew who he was until he ran for public office. Now that he's not a cop he wants to act as if he's some kind of civil rights leader. It is difficult to know where the words of black people end and where Biga's editorial meddling begins. At any rate, the following statement is shared: "He [Ewing] … said residents complain of violence, lack of economic opportunities, that they feel abandoned, neglected, overlooked, forgotten. It leads to a sense of hopelessness."

This is how it was planned. Do you think that white people would be letting these kids run all over the place shooting guns if the guns weren't aimed at other black people? Of course not. Do you think these white people would be allowing housing stock to deteriorate unless they had a long-range plan? Of course not. All of these feelings – neglect, abandonment, being overlooked, forgotten – these descriptors beg the question, "So what? Where were you?" These feelings are not new? What did you do about it when you were a cop?

Some 11,000 households were lost "over time." How much time? Over a decade? Over 5 years? Since the 60s riots? How long. Households were lost but that doesn't mean that they're not still in the area. They were lost, not to Omaha, but to that particular demographic. These are people that moved to another zip code or area. These are people who are among those that Biga claims moved to west Omaha. When you say that someone or something is "lost," you owe it to the reader to explain why it was lost. Households don't disappear on their own.

More gloom peddling leads the writer and his negro friends to claim that, "A diminished tax, voter, consumer base diluted the minimal clout it had to hold public and private sectors accountable the economic and social ills."

The tax based is diluted because of all those damn churches in North Omaha! Every time a nonprofit sets up, that means that no taxes go into that structure and that means less money for area schools. There are a total of 458 churches in Omaha and 116 of them are in North Omaha. What does that say? So before you start looking to the stars and some chicken-eating preacher to save you, just think about the fact that every nonprofit program, agency, organization or entity in an area further deprives that area of the taxes that a for profit business would be paying in.

Voter base? What does that have to do with accounting for economic and social ills? Since when have politicians and elected officials cared about North Omaha. I am of the mind, looking back, that black people in North Omaha were better off before Senator Ernie Chambers fought for, and got passed, the district elections format. The piss-pot poor leadership that we've had since then, especially on the City Council and the Douglas County Board, is so weak, mealy-mouthed and uninvolved that I don't think that at at-large election producing a white man could have done the community much worse. At least we could lay some white guilt on a few members of these boards and win some concessions. But with black people like these in power, we have to deal with white racism on the outer ring and "buffer negroes" on the inner ring.

The consumer base would not make or break the area because ever since "integration" came, black people have shared their shopping priorities between white store owners in North Omaha and white supermarket owners on the fringe and beyond. The supermarkets that do serve North Omaha charge more for the food and offer lower quality and less options. The consumer base, according to the Greater Omaha Chamber of Commerce, in 2004, Black people in Omaha had a total purchasing power of $593 million dollars. That was eight years ago and the figures are probably either about the same or lower. But that's still a powerful chunk of money not to be spent in the area where you live. Those who have transportation go where the sales are and for the most part, that's Wal-Mart, Baker's, Albertson's and No-Frills.

Now these various "bases" – tax, voter and consumer – didn't dilute the minimal clout that the area had to hold public and private sectors accountable for economic and social ills." Biga has been attempting to read an urban economics text and doesn't understand that these principles essentially do not apply to black communities and their relationship with the white power structure. As I have shown in my brief notes earlier, voting doesn't work because the people we vote for do not see our community as a priority. Taxes are cut because of the proliferation of nonprofits organizations. And the consumer base, when provided with options, is smart enough to go where they can get the biggest bang for their buck. Small stores have to charge more because they cannot afford to purchase in bulk the way large supermarkets can. So if you had a shopping choice, which would you use?

Ben "The Apologist" Gray is always good for "explaining away" issues that defend the powers that be. His ancient and almost decadent views on social reality would be laughable if not for the fact that Omaha is filled with black and white people who are so gullible that they believe what he says. For instance, take note of the following:

> "There's been a lot of benign neglect that's gone on in north Omaha by the majority community and I don't hesitate in saying that because it's a fact," said Gray."But what we've got to do now is rather than point fingers and place blame put together the necessary mechanism to fix it. We've got so much work to do and we've got so many areas that we're operating in."

Benign neglect. This is a term that was popularized by former President Richard Nixon during his term. And it meant paying little attention to black communities just the same way that Ben Gray does today. So one the one hand its prophetic and on the other hand, pathetic. More specifically:

> Benign neglect was a policy proposed in the late 1960s by New York Sen. Daniel Patrick Moynihan, who was at the time on Nixon's White House Staff as an urban affairs adviser. While serving in this capacity, he sent the President a memo suggesting that "the issue of race could benefit from a period of 'benign neglect'. The subject has been too much talked about....We may need a period in which Negro progress continues and racial rhetoric fades." … However, the policy was widely seen as an abandonment of urban (particularly black) neighborhoods … (Wikipedia, 2012)

So if there is any "benign neglect" taking place, it's on the part of the Empowerment Network! They are the ones who minimize the impact of race; they are the ones who avoid "racial rhetoric;" they are the ones who have abandoned urban neighborhoods and essentially turned them over to white developers and the city of Omaha. Ben Gray's words speak volumes – but not in the way that he thinks.

And he acts as if he says something that is profound and confrontative when, in reality, it is flattering to white people. How? The neglect that black people have been victimized by has not been benign – it has been malignant! The definition of "benign" in this case, is "showing or expressive of gentleness or kindness." How is the city's neglect, after intercepting hundreds of millions that our poverty qualified them to receive, even close to being "kind" or "gentle?" The term "benign neglect" was coined to cover the ass of a man who hated black people. Now the apologist, Ben Gray – who will do whatever it takes to support the system -- is doing the same thing.

He sounds just like the white man who is saying, "patience is a virtue" or another one of their pacification favorites, "let's forgive and forget." Now that they've stolen everything and have black people in various forms of servitude it's time to do, just Gray said, "rather than point fingers and place blame put together the necessary mechanism to fix it. We've got so much work to do and we've got so many areas that we're operating in." And that is why the Empowerment Network is a reactionary and anti-black entity: they all believe that the system is the solution and that black people ought to forget the past and move on to a future that is guided and directed by the same white folks that tried to destroy the community in the first place. Their track record speaks for itself.

One step out of slavery, two steps back into it. That is the goal of the next "power player" who is one of the key developers of this "Network." He is a man whom I respect very much and I sat across the table from as he explained what his purpose for the Network was. That purpose has evidently changed. According to the article by Biga,

> Davis Companies CEO Dick Davis spearheads a formed Economic Strategy Taskforce whose goals address economic viability. Those include preparing every African-American for a sustainable living-wage job; moving persons from unemployment or underemployment to full employment and from jobs to careers; encouraging entrepreneurship by increasing access to credit and capital. The Network endorses a from-birth-to-career strategy.

Within a limited context such as Nebraska in general and Omaha, in particular, just how much of a strategy can you develop? When Davis and I met, I gave him a list of national foundations, locations and deadline dates for applications. This was a strategy: to go outside of Nebraska and use Davis's business background to solicit funding from outside. He must have totally disregarded my work and, in fact, his own initial goals (at least, as they were explained to me). Let's look at the preceding excerpt and count the conceptual errors in logic.

To begin with if you're at the point where you've formed an Economic Strategy Taskforce, your goals have got to be more than just addressing economic viability. Viability of what? The community? The financial climate? The people that you want to employ?

Then the goals that are listed are not goals in a climate like Omaha's: it's more of a wish list or a list of "ideals." Goals, for one thing, have to be attainable and realistic. Check out these goals outlined by Dr. Davis and let's see how realistic they are.

One of the goals is, "preparing every African-American for a sustainable living wage job." How do you do that? Don't you mean every "qualified" black person? And if that is the case, then what kinds of living wage jobs are you talking about? Will the jobs match their qualifications or are you just trying to get them into the workforce? How do you define "sustainable?" Nebraska is a right to work state and as such, thousands of black people have been "let go" for a number of reasons because the workforce doesn't even have to have a reason.

Another goal is to "move persons from unemployment or underemployment to full employment and from jobs to careers." How will that get done? Will employers allow this to take place? How will this impact on those who are receiving pensions or some kind of aid – they are only allowed to earn so much money on a job, right? Before a person is moved from unemployment or underemployment, shouldn't there be some kind of transition program to prepare them for returning to the workforce and having to interact with or deal with people who may have "attitudes" about race?

A third "goal" is "encouraging entrepreneurship by increasing access to credit and capital." This means "special arrangements" with banks and other lenders because the "encouragement" is going to have to be backed up with something. Furthermore, increasing access to credit and capital is not enough: its gaining or getting your hands on that credit and capital that is the best "encouragement," is it not. We've always had access to these things, but it was the same kind of access that a homeless person has to walking into the Ritz Carlton; you might walk in, but that don't mean you're gonna make it to the front desk!

As evidence that these well-meaning "goals" are really nothing more than an idealistic wish list, take note of the fact that, "The Network endorses a from-birth-to-career strategy." How can you endorse a "from birth to career" strategy when along the way, you will be confronted by and with institutional arrangements that may not be in your corner, from schools and the media to the cops and the courts? Furthermore, why "birth to career"? Why not make it from birth to the grave?

And furthermore, why a career? Unless that place you work has your image and interests at heart, all a career ends up being is a lifetime of indentured servitude! There's a difference between a job and a career. If you want black people to have a career, make it something that is about helping other black people. As one cultural nationalist taught, "If you are black, your purpose is to build black" (Karenga, 1967). A career is defined as, "an occupation or profession, esp. one requiring special training followed as one's life work." If Davis can get people long-term jobs, that's alright. But a career means you're dedicating your life to what you do. Who wants a career as a janitor or a grave digger? It's jobs that black people want because most black people don't want the responsibility that comes with a career. They love white people so much that just to receive a paycheck from a white company is their ultimate goal. Careers, like these ideals set forth by Dr. Davis, are dreams.

Moving right along:

> Davis has long been active, starting black businesses and providing
> college scholarships to black students. Entities like the African-
> American Academic Achievement Council, 100 Black Men, 100
> Black Women, the Omaha Economic Development Corporation,
> the Urban League of Nebraska, along with black churches, have
> done their part. Pockets of progress have appeared in some new
> home construction, a few business parks, a refurbished section of
> North 24th St. and new quarters for anchors Salem Baptist Church,
> the Urban League and Charles Drew Health Center. Nothing large-
> scale has been attempted.

None of the groups mentioned really do anything for the community as a whole; none of them understand the importance of the ecological approach. They carve out a little niche and even their names are insultingly narrow in their goals and vision. What white group would call itself "100 White Men" or even "100 Men" for that matter? Why limit yourself by a number? I've never heard of "100 Black Women," but it figures that a group like that would pop up in competition with black men. What about "100 Black People"? The separation of the genders is one reason why we remain fractured and fragmented when it comes to the need for collective struggle. White women support their men in upholding the racist system; we want to knit-pick about how we respond to it.

Two of the groups above – the Omaha Economic Development Corporation (OEDC) and the Urban League – have no real track record working with the entire community. The Urban League, having gotten away from housing and employment, is really nothing more than a glorified social service agency, first under the corrupt George Dillard (17 years as director) and now under ex-police chief Tommy Warren. OEDC is the group that the city uses as its "negro pawn" when it comes to tiny development projects, most of them irrelevant except for small pockets here and there.

What does it mean that these groups have "done their part"? Why not elaborate on exactly what these groups are doing, because it's a fact that the majority of black people sure don't know. Some of them target young people and claim to be mentors, while others, as stated are into social services and referrals. But none of them is about the community as a whole. And as we know, *to divide the process is to deform the product.*

And what is a "pocket of progress"? Progress is not a static essence – it is on-going. How can you call it a pocket of progress and then cite "some new home construction, a few business parks, a refurbished section of North 24th Street,, and new quarters for anchors Salem Baptist Church, the Urban League and Charles Drew Health Center? Furthermore, most of this "progress" took place in the middle

1990s, so what Biga is doing is mixing different "happenings" and trying to make it look like a consistent on-going plan when it is not.

They mention Salem Baptist Church. Since when did they do anything for anyone but their own coffers and congregation members? Salem Baptist Church? Salem Baptist Church benefited from the North freeway's intrusion. In fact, Salem was one of the structures that was initially relocated. The church building and the land it was on was sold to the City of Omaha for $150,000.

> The Rev. J.C. Wade, then the church's pastor, said, "It was like losing a loved one to some of us. Some of the people grew up there, but they've adjusted well." Two other area churches were forced to move as well. (Trandahl, 1972).

The money generated from the sale of the church enabled Salem leadership to purchase the land and build on a new location, 3336 Lake Street, in the heart of the black community. Estimates on the value of that structure range from $350,000 to $425,000.

By the early 1990s, Salem was talking about expanding, even though it was already the largest church in North Omaha. The church purchased the huge space on the southwest corner of 30th and Lake Streets, left behind when the Hilltop Projects were torn down in the summer of 1996. The $4 million church, which is now standing, boasts some 50,000-square feet. As one 1996 article reported,

> The Salem Baptist Church, which was established 75 years ago, has been discussing for about three years the need to expand. Its current church is at 3336 Lake St. – about a block from the Hilltop site. There are about 2,500 members, Watson said, 650 of whom can sit in the sanctuary at any one time. In the last eight years, Salem's membership has grown 50 percent, said Watson. "We don't project that kind of growth is going to slow down." Salem Baptist ministers to the "whole person," Watson said, which includes serving social and educational as well as spiritual needs. He said a larger facility will help the church better meet the human needs of north Omaha. "We want this to be an anchor of the community," Watson said (Gonzalez, 1996: 2).

So Salem had moved from a place where people met to oppose a freeway to being the beneficiaries of the sale of property that paved the way for the freeway. Now with its new church atop a hill on 30th and Lake Street, Rev. Maurice Watson claims, "We pledge to make the Hilltop property the most beautiful and productive area in north Omaha," and added, "We will transform what once was a repository of despair, drug abuse, crime, gangs and violence into an oasis of hope" (Gonzalez, 1996: 1).

The project even had the backing of the Omaha World Herald. In typical "manipulate black leadership" fashion, take note of how the major newspaper pumps up a project which, at that time, existed only on paper:

> There ought to be an extra spring in the performances of the Stepping Saints, the drum-and-dance corps from Salem Baptist Church in Omaha. That's because there is good news indeed in the Salem Baptist community. The 75-year-old congregation has announced plans for a new church and school on the site of the former Hilltop Homes low-rent housing project.
>
> "An oasis of hope" – that's what Rev. Maurice Watson, pastor of Salem Baptist, called the proposed $4 million campus. The campus would offer physical education and social programs as well as worship services and education. The 16-acre plot is on the south side of Lake Street, between 30th and 33rd Streets.
>
> **The project would benefit Salem Baptist**. It also **should** help bring stability to the surrounding neighborhood.
>
> Watson said the current church, about a block west of the proposed new site, seats 650 people. With membership growing 50 percent over the last eight years to 2,500, Watson said, Salem has been looking to expand.
>
> The new campus also seems to fit the Omaha Housing Authority's plan. OHA owns the property and has been working on a plan to restore vitality to the section of Omaha immediately east of 30th and Lake. That target area would be well-served by the enhanced presence of Salem Baptist as a community resource center.
>
> How heartening it is to see a venerable Omaha church stake out a bold course for the future. Federal and local officials ought to move quickly to facilitate the sale of the site to Salem Baptist. **Close the deal** and let those saints go stepping as proudly as ever into the next century (Omaha World Herald, 1996: 6—emphasis added).

Even the world Herald saw that Salem was going to be the sole beneficiary. Note where the article says that the project SHOULD help bring stability to the surrounding neighborhood. White people know that churches don't turn communities around – economic development does; retail outlets do; banks and other financial "anchors" do. Not churches. So where does the World-Herald get the idea that this religious institution – which takes money from the congregation but gives nothing financial back – going to stabilize an entire neighborhood when, since its congregation members are there for help and salvation – it can't even stabilize THEM??!!

No sooner did they purchase the property than did Salem decision makers sell a chunk of it to Walgreen's and now, to the east of the church on the hill sits a new Walgreen's Drug Store. And contrary to what was promised, the area surrounding the "church on the hill" has actually deteriorated and those "programs" that were being promised and bandied about have yet to materialize in the year 2012 – fifteen years after the earlier pledge was made.

The reason why I spent so much time sharing information about Salem Baptist Church is because it is the foundation for how the Empowerment Network got started. So this says a lot about how the product would be formed: it is a church that doesn't get involved in the important issues of black people and, in like manner, the Empowerment Network – despite the easily assembled lies of Leo Biga – seems to have the same method of operation. More on the Willie Barney/Empowerment Network/Salem Baptist Church connection in a few minutes.

So Biga takes projects from the mid-1990s and mixes them more recent activities (while naming none) and makes it appear as a "pocket of progress." What Salem did to benefit itself is the same thing that all the rest are doing: running to the white man, hat in hand, and claiming to want to "stop the violence" if they can get paid for it. Progress?

Total confusion, as I charged earlier. According to the article Teresa Hunter – another nearly invisible "leader" that Biga somehow dug up – serves as co-chair of the Network's housing development covenant, said "We work within the framework of what's already going on, trying to make it cooperative … Why are people still falling through the cracks – what else do we need to do?"

Why was this statement even left in the article since all she does is show that she doesn't know which way is up? And yet, she is the director of an agency that is charged with locating housing for people who need it. This is not the exception – it is the rule when it comes to North Omaha negroes.

The article about "empowerment" continues on:

> Where most Network players are native Omahans like Hunter, the driving force is a transplant, Willie Barney, who until recently was a strategic consultant. The Iowa native worked in media marketing for Lee Enterprises and moved here for an Omaha World-Herald post. He worked on Salem Baptist Church's administrative team when he galvanized efforts to create the Network. He served as the Network's unpaid president and facilitator, then as a consultant, and is now its second paid staff member.

"Network players"? Did these negroes give Biga permission to refer to them in such a way? Is this an abbreviation for the "power player" lie that was a part of the headline? Most of the "driving forces" behind anything in the black community are transplants. But if he's from Iowa, he's not a real transplant: a hick is a hick. Not only that, but he worked in media marketing and when you look at his contributions to black life in Omaha, that's about all you'll find: free publicity, free marketing, free public relations – whether deserved or not.

Then Barney jumps from the pan into the fire by moving to Omaha to work for the Omaha World Herald. I did the same thing when I arrived in Omaha: I typed the want-ads for the World Herald and learned everything I could about racism in Omaha and at the newspaper from Rudy Smith, the only black in the photography department and Sibyl Myers, the only reporter on staff. Of course Barney would join up with Salem Baptist church because the negroes in Omaha are quick to point out that Salem is the biggest and many (not all) say that it is the oldest black church. In addition, that is where all the bourgeois negroes who think they're special attend church.

Now Barney is a paid staff member. What is the source of their revenue? How much is he being paid? Is this some of that Suzie Buffett money? Is the source somehow linked to the city of Omaha? What are their fundraising and long-time economic development plans to sustain the organization? Remember what I've been saying: the hand that feeds controls. How can you be about "empowerment" when your very financial base is one of dependency and reliance on the same system that has worked to destroy the community that you purport to want to protect?

> "In evolving over time we've stayed true to our mission," said Barney. "We said we want to be positive and pro-active and to build partnerships … with the entire city. It has to be bottom-up and top-down for it to be anywhere close to being successful — individuals, families, leaders at all levels working together collaboratively."

What does this have to do with North Omaha? You heard it from his own mouth. He said that they want to be positive: sometimes in order to obtain a positive result you have to be willing to tackle the negative, like for instance letting these white people know that what they're doing is not charity, but a form of "reparations" for more than 100 years of neglect and discrimination. But the Empowerment negroes don't have the guts to do that because it would be threatening their funding source.

Barney says they want to be pro-active, but if you want to be proactive you have to have a direction and a philosophy. To be proactive is "serving to prepare for, intervene in, or control an expected occurrence or situation, esp. a negative or difficult one." So the problem is the abuse of North Omaha and the people responsible for it are not North Omahans. So in being proactive, Barney and those of his ilk would have to be prepared to address a situation that is negative – meaning discrimination, segregation and racism. But they cannot do that because they are in bed with the discriminators, the segregationists and the racists!

Barney says that he wants to build partnerships with the entire city. Biga may have misconstrued his words, but I don't think so – Barney probably got verbose and said so much that the editors had to cut some stuff out, hence the ellipses. But he said enough: he wants to build partnerships with the entire city. Here's the question that this transplant from Iowa should ask: where, in the annals of history, have whites in Omaha sought to build any partnerships with North Omaha black people? I'm not talking about the tokens that they handpick, I'm talking about black people whose lives are in disarray? They haven't, so why do we always have to be the ones who want to build bridges and bridge gaps and all that? Because those doing it don't know what to do and they want to get paid. So they "go along to get along," as the saying goes.

Barney said that, "in evolving over time we've stayed true to our mission." That is an admission that everything that I have charged the Empowerment Network with is true. They have not stopped selling out North Omaha for a single minute; they have stayed true despite the fact that their anti-violence "programs" have failed, despite the fact that they haven't provided any housing, haven't created any meaningful, sustainable jobs, and certainly haven't change the physical plant of North Omaha. So they will remain the same; the "evolution" will only take place as the conditions change. But they won't change because they'll be too busy staying "true" to their mission. And that mission is to make sure that the relative positions of blacks and whites – the powerless and the powerful – does not change to any marked degree.

Then Barney foolishly tries to delve into management principles when he opines, "It has to be bottom-up and top-down for it to be anywhere close to being successful — individuals, families, leaders at all levels working together collaboratively."

There's that word, "collaboratively." And what he has just described has never taken place in the history of Omaha. The only time it comes close is when white people are threatened with major protests, race riots or some other form of confrontation. The Martin Luther King Jr. "kiss the other cheek" crap does not work on these people. The ministers are afraid and they claim to be tight with God. So where does that leave Barney and those negroes who are seeking to work from the bottom up and the top down? How asinine!

And with their philosophy (conciliation, accommodation, acquiescence) and origins (Salem Baptist Church) laid out, the foolhardiness just keeps on coming. Observe:

> The effort started focusing on seven core areas: jobs, business-economic development, education-youth development, voting, violence prevention, housing-neighborhoods-transportation and engagement. Evidence of the Network's wide reach was seen during its annual Harmony Week (May 21-29), when dozens of organizations and thousands of people across the Metro participated in expressions of unity and community engagement. In 2009 the organization opened an office in the historic Jewell Building in the heart of North O, across from the Omaha Star.

What effort? Earlier Biga wrote that Omaha's Empowerment Network targeted 13 areas for improvement," remember. Now it's seven areas that they are "focusing on." Focus is nothing unless it is followed up with a coherent plan on how to address what you're focusing on. And since they have no solutions they engage in foolishness and frolic as evidenced by its "annual Harmony Week." This is something that has always been used as a public relations campaign; have an event, give away free food, take photos and make sure the media is there. And because there are a lot of people in attendance, silly journalists like Biga can conclude that it is "evidence of the Network's wide reach."

But the preceding excerpt contains another key: the one that shows the interlocking directorates that exist in most "movements" that take place in Omaha. That is where the same people are working for different groups but make sure that the same goals and inactivity remain par for the course. It's similar to "six degrees of separation:" The Empowerment Network is housed across the street from the no-longer-relevant Omaha Star newspaper. It is in a building that is historical, but is also owned by the Omaha Economic Development Corporation, a shill for the city powers that be. And if OEDC is involved, that means that the city is not very far behind because that is who OEDC director Michael Maroney reports to and receives his piecemeal projects from.

So in addition to financial control by Suzie Buffett, we can now see that this so-called "coalition," this "network" is really nothing more than an adjunct to the city, just like NOCD was back in 1972 when it was formed. If you know your history, you won't fall prey to manipulated manifestations of it as in this case: the same old scams with different appearances and "players."

These people seem to think that marketing and public relations (remember Willie Barney's former job in Iowa) is the same thing as tangible production or community success. Read the following:

> The Network boosted its presence via an expanded website, Facebook page and Revive! Omaha Magazine, which Barney's SMB Enterprises LLC publishes. A TV spot features Network leaders reciting, like a creed, the Empowerment credo: "We can change Omaha. It's time to rebuild the village. Family by family, block by block, school by school, church by church, business by business. Each person doing their part. Working together, let's transform Omaha. Do your part. Live the covenant."

Websites and credos – all public relations. Talking about what they "can" do, but not doing it. Citing idealistic platitudes as if they were accomplishments. All this has been done, on a lesser technological level, of course, throughout the history of community development efforts in Omaha. Barney publishes a magazine and probably pays himself; he sells ads from which the revenue also probably goes into his pocket. Add to that the fact that he is on the payroll, and it is in his best interests to keep his mouth shut and, in exchange, the white man will let him wallow in his substanceless inactivity.

But there's more

> The Network's first full-time staffer was Quaites-Ferris, a former deputy assistant to former Mayor Mike Fahey said. Three-and-a-half years in, the Network has a track record. Barney said whatever course the Network adopts, it relies on others to carry it out. "At the end of the day it's ENCAP, the Urban League, Omaha Economic Development Corporation that are doing the work. But I think because we're here we've helped facilitate potentially more partnerships than would have happened before."

If it is indeed true that "three and a half years in, the Network as a track record," then produce it. List the accomplishments, not the intentions or plans. List how many families you've helped and jobs you've created. Three and a half years and you have a website and a credo.

Another connection is Quaites-Ferris, who worked for the Mayor of Omaha. All these connections and the people can't see that there is no way that the Empowerment Network could be independent? Barney can't cite examples of this "track record" they've got because anything that they do is going to have to have the blessing (read: permission) of the powers that be, the Omaha elites. And if he is bragging about "the work" that the Urban League, ENCAP (formerly Greater Omaha Community Action) and OEDC are doing, then he's citing three groups that have done even less than the Empowerment Network.

These are groups that have been around for decades, and have nothing to show for it but social work. They do nothing for the masses of people and can't get involved in any problems against the city because they, like the Network, are beholden to the city. OEDC gets CDBG money from the City of Omaha Planning Department, ENCAP survives off of Community Service Block Grants, and the Urban League is a site for the Nebraska Department of Social Services. None of them would dare bite the hand that feeds.

It's a lost cause. The Empowerment Network is the latest in a long string of "minority fronts" that the City of Omaha comes up with whenever they feel their federal status (grant money) may be threatened. And in the final analysis, its all about the money.

Barney boasts that the Network has, "helped facilitate potentially more partnerships than would have happened before." And that is their claim to fame: becoming partners with groups that have been here longer than they have and, as a result, should have been doing more.

Even the quasi-critics of the Network display an abysmal ignorance of the gravity of the situation, akin to those Native Americans that sold out their own people to the U.S. cavalry. For instance:

> Malcolm X Memorial Foundation president Sharif Liwaru said
> he feels the Network's facilitator rather than direct service
> provider role "is still hard for people to grasp."Barney concurred.
> While Liwaru and community activist Leo Louis feel the
> Network effectively engages established organizations and
> leaders, they advocate more outreach be done to new, more
> loosely organized groups as well as to youths. "We're doing
> more to really make sure it is an inclusive process," said
> Barney."If they don't come, we'll go to them, and we're not
> perfect, we make mistakes, but we keep pushing forward."

There is nothing "hard to grasp" about a group of people who pontificate, put signs on lawns claiming that "enough is enough" and then whenever you hear about them, they're having meetings, talking with the police, and socializing with some of the people who are a part of the on-going problem. Maybe Liwaru doesn't want to admit what he knows – but he's not stupid.

Biga calls someone named Leo Louis a "community activist." I always wanted to know how such a title is bestowed. I figured it out: white people use it has a warning label for people who are working for a group or cause they they (whites) don't agree with. I never met Louis and I wouldn' t know him from Adam's house cat. He has no record to speak of, but just because this white reporter referred to him as a "community activist," he's already got my approval. Why? Because I'm sure that Louis didn't introduce himself as, "Hi – I'm a community activist." This is a label that white people reserve for those who have not bought into their program.

Barney claims that Network is doing all it can to make it "an inclusive process." Earlier he talked about bottoms-up and top-down strategy. But here is the clincher: that strategy was applied only to people who they (the Network) consider to be "worthy." If the process was inclusive, then the product would be inclusive and diverse. It is not; the Network consists of people who think they are leaders but the people they are supposed to be serving are left to social service agencies and the usual do-nothing groups like the Urban League, the NAACP and on an economic level, OEDC.

> In mid-2008 the Network noted workforce development gaps for at-risk youth and launched a life skills and jobs program. No one wanted a summer like 2007, when there were 31 reported shootings in 31 days during one stretch. Program participants included kids failing in school and drop-outs , ex and active gang members.

The first thing the Network should have noticed was the "workforce development gap," as they call it. When I met and talked with Dick Davis, he had it – unemployment – as a priority on his list. But now this group is doling out chump change short term jobs and trying to call it a victory. Every summer the government would provide funding for youth jobs. Then it started drying up but cities picked up some of the slack. What the Network is doing is nothing new and its nothing profound. It's a fearful response to the gun violence and this proves what I said earlier: if you want to get the white man's attention, you have to use violence or the threat of it. That' all he knows.

As for the kids failing in school, Ben Gray is a part of the Network. He's supposed to be the director of the African-American Achievement Team – although he dropped out of college himself. There was no progress and, in fact, on his watch, the test scores for black kids have gotten worse. Aren't any of these guys accountable to truly act in a way that leads to "empowerment" and not pacification or placation?

Here was their strategy:

> Barney and Gray contacted employers to secure 150 paid internships. The program was repeated last summer, with enrollees split between returning and new participants. Barney said many "transitioned back into school, some went on to get GEDs and others got offers for fulltime work." 2009 saw hundreds more jobs created by federal stimulus funds and private donors. The Urban League facilitated.

Internships? Assuming that Biga is using the terminology that he got directly from Gray and Barney, this approach to jobs is, at best piecemeal and at most, elitist. An internship, by definition, is *"any official or formal programs to provide practical experience for beginners in an occupation or profession," or a position as a participant in such programs."* This is what college students do to gain experience; these young kids need full-time, permanent jobs, not a chance to get a whiff of what it's like to get a check and then, in a few weeks the experience is over! Where is the community on this "internship" approach to jobs for young people? Internships, but the very name, have a time limit!

Then Barney says that they "transitioned back into school." This goes to the heart of what I said: internships are for students and those who plan to go to school. This is an elitist program when you consider the fact that most of those youth don't want to go to school, have been pushed out or have dropped out. Where is the city's contribution? Where is the spending of the CDBG and CSBG monies? Why should these people be waiting for stimulus funds? And these private donors are rich – why doesn't Buffett contribute some of his billions to a long-term job effort? Why do black kids always have to be guinea pigs so that megalomaniacs and pseudo-leaders can make the white man think that they're "on the job"?

Then Biga and the Network, undoubtedly working in tandem, flip the script:

> Minus any federal funds in 2010, the number of summer jobs provided at-risk youth this year will be closer to 500, rather than last year's 800. "In a lot of instances we basically have to start from scratch — we have to teach people how to fill out an application, how to successfully interview, how to do some things we take for granted," said Gray. "This is a big job because you've got to change attitudes as well as change behavior. Neither is easy, but you've got to get it done because the only other choice is to build more jails and at the end of the day that's costing us three to four times as much money as to provide jobs and job training and proper schooling."

There was supposed to be a plan. The largest church in the city was where Barney laid it out. Gray is on the city council and has access to funds. He carries water for a Mayor who has access to a contingency fund. What is all this about going back to the basics or starting from scratch? This is re-inventing the wheel: programs, assuming black people are stupid, take them back to how to fill out an application, how to successfully interview. According to Gray, these are things that "we take for granted."

How could he take it for granted? He had one job for over twenty years carrying a camera. Before that he enlisted in the military. Where is his experience filling out an application? The problem is always the black community, a community that worked harder than anyone else when there was work. No one works harder than black women, for starters. Gray doesn't have confidence in his own people, which is why he paints a picture of (1) acceptance of the piecemeal programs offered or (2) risk being locked up.

His appeal is to the system because that is who builds the jails. He's looking at black employment as a "savings" approach to community development – the market approach. At no time does Gray use the history of neglect and abuse by the system to get it to do the right thing.

Clearly, these men are not economists or job creators and, in fact, they are poor planners. More evidence follows:

> Barney said the group launched a multifaceted violence prevention collaboration. "It's not just telling folks, 'Don't do this,' now we're providing options." Impact One Community Connection, formerly New World Youth Development, was formed to do gang intervention-prevention. The Network also collaborates with ENCAP, the Eastern Nebraska Community Action Partnership (formerly GOACA).

Earlier I offered insights about the importance of nominality – that is, naming something. From your child to an organization, a name is the first thing that anyone comes into contact with, plain and simple.

So they've changed their name from New World Youth Development – grandiose and untrue, to Impact One Community Connection, a definite downsizing in scope and of course, so generic that it means all things to all people. Impact One? What the hell does that mean?

The Network "collaborates" (there's that word again) with ENCAP, which is formerly GOCA (not "GOACA" as Biga writes). So what? ENCAP is a social service agency that provides mental health counseling, free groceries and rental assistance. Over the years what else has it done. It's always had leadership that was more likely to take a few days off and meet some woman in the park than planning for North Omaha. From Charles Lane to Dr. Ben Ebong to Karen Shepherd to whomever is running it now. GOCA is a social service approach to community development, not a social engineer.

People with a limited track record in their commitment to the major issues impacting North Omaha (police brutality, utilities assistance, racist evictions and other housing discrimination issues, mis-education of kids in the Omaha Public Schools, etc.) continue to attract Biga in his painting of a portrait of profundity:

> Teresa Hunter said she, Barney and others were impressed "a
> group of youths wanted to continue meeting and talking about
> the issues and the remedies. They wanted to keep coming back
> and to make a change." In turn, said Barney, participants "were
> amazed somebody cared enough to spend all that time one-on-
> one with them and to help them get a job. They will flat out tell
> you no one has ever given them these opportunities before. Even
> some of the kids on the street that everybody totally discounts
> and that people said there's no way you're going to reach, well,
> we reached them."

Who cares if these people are "impressed" with kids wanting to talk about issues? Had they approached them earlier they would have known it long ago. Had they not assumed that young people "didn't care," they would have learned it long ago. Had they been involved in the community's concerns, they would have known that. These people are afraid of black kids, and that's the problem. Whatever the white man says about these kids, these negroes believe it. And the only time that they're "impressed" is when the kids come out to one of THEIR programs where they have those kids sign in and then they can run to the white man and say, "See boss – we had good attendance." Either that or turn the sheet over to the police for review. I wouldn't put anything past people like these, who admittedly work so closely with those who have only done harm to North Omaha.

Barney claims that kids told him that no one has ever given them these opportunities before. That is a lie. To begin with, opportunities have never been in short supply: black people get "opportunities" all the time. But the issue is what is the source of this "opportunity" and where is it going to lead you? Going to a meeting and learning how to conduct yourself in a job interview is an "opportunity," but without a guaranteed job, it's nothing more than an exercise in futility.

The Empowerment Network has the opportunity to do right by North Omaha, but the proof is in the pudding: as long as they don't make decisions on their own, as long as they cater and kowtow to whites with power (while they have none), the opportunity is going to have the same conclusion as many opportunities that are provided to you by an outsider: *non-productive*.

If you close your eyes and talk to Barney, Hunter, Gray and the other self-appointed leaders, you wouldn't be able to distinguish between what they say or what some white suburbanite has to say. There is nothing culturally inclusive about their plan or their attitudes. Using the deficit model, they assume the worst about North Omaha and view themselves as "missionaries" who are hell-bent on "helping out those savages." The same tactics that white folks, using the social work approach, have historically approached North Omaha.

Continuing:

> Recruiting them, he said, was largely the work of the late Roy Davenport and of Gray. Both brought longtime gang intervention experience. The Network's aligned itself with the Omaha Police Department, particularly the Northeast Precinct, and North Omaha Weed & Seed to do Safe Night Outs and other efforts for improving police-community relations. Gray, who leads an emergency response team, said street work is where it's at in reaching past or present gangbangers.

The late Roy Davenport and his "Ambassadors program" was actually something I advised him with. He didn't even have a name for it and I came up with "ambassadors." Then I never saw him again because somehow, he got hooked up with Ben Gray. What Biga doesn't mention while he drops names and pretends like he knows the history, Davenport got into some trouble of a sexual orientation nature and was afraid that the other person was going to go public; so Davenport killed himself.

Next, they admit that they work with the police. When Triple One worked with police the cops were African-American were black and they cared about and lived in the community: Danny Hayes, Tariq Al-Amin, Marvin McClarty and so on. These guys are working with white cops and the Northeast Precinct is not the most progressive place in the world. If Weed and Seed is involved, then there's grant money somewhere down the road. "Safe Night Outs" is a national program and the Network needs to stop taking credit for it.

Now Biga's own words and beliefs mix with Ben Gray's as he writes, "Gray, who leads an emergency response team, said street work is where it's at in reaching past or present gangbangers." This is supposed to be a news article or a feature – who used the term "gangbangers"? This is what pisses these kids off: they are labeled and black people accept those labels. If Gray said it, he should be ashamed of himself as an elected official; if Biga came up with it based on what Gray said, then they should both be ashamed. But weak minds think alike, and this is but one example.

Look at how Gray re-invents the wheel and describes and takes credit for the actions of what many others have done long before he was on the scene:

> "You got to meet them where they are. If you are not willing to get out in those blocks, in those neighborhoods, in those houses where they live, you are not going to reach those young people. You gotta be at the hospitals, you gotta be at the funerals, you

> gotta be constantly talking about not retaliating … about going in
> a different direction. That's very time consuming, painstaking,
> difficult work and there are no set hours. We have ex-gang
> members employed through Impact One. They monitor the
> streets on a regular basis."

When did Ben Gray ever "get out there" in the neighborhood other than to campaign for office (and it's doubtful that he even did it then)? Ben Gray knows there are people out there who don't like him because he's known as someone who will do anything for a buck and that he's linked to Suzie Buffett, a white woman who calls the shots for the black community's main politicos (Brenda Council, Chris Rodgers, Ben Gray). If he went door to door he wouldn't be able to control the response because he'd be on someone else's property. If Ben Gray is nothing else, he is a control freak, but he only seeks it when he's got the upper hand (a microphone in his hand, the city council seat, etc.) He's outlining a strategy that any community organizer would undertake – that doesn't mean that he did it.

Take note of where he thinks the young people are: hospitals and funerals. That's after the fact contact, in my book. If you go to their houses, then what are you saying to them? Gray never personalized the process or the strategy. He says "YOU" gotta do this – that doesn't mean he did it or has the guts to do it. Maybe those "ex-gang members" (in reality, there is no such thing – "blood in, blood out") are the ones he uses to go door-to-door because he claims they "monitor the streets on a regular basis." Are they paid or are they acting as volunteers?

Since he thinks he's a leader, he feels that his kudos and approval means something. Check it out:

> Gray lauds the Network for "putting its neck on the line" to even
> do this outreach, saying it's a microcosm for how a wounded
> community can heal. "We have people that have been
> disappointed so much they're not willing to necessarily buy-in
> until they have seen some stability in you going down the road
> getting a few things accomplished, and then you'll hopefully get
> that groundswell of people that will come on board with you."

Which members of the Network are putting their necks on the line? Is he implying that all of them do? Is he? If you are doing outreach, why would you be putting your neck on the line if you have credibility? Is he saying that young kids are "dangerous"?

Then comes the closest thing to a confession of inadequacy that you'll ever hear from Ben Gray. It's where he says, *"We have people that have been disappointed so much they're not willing to necessarily buy-in until they have seen some stability in you going down the road getting a few things accomplished, and then you'll hopefully get that groundswell of people that will come on board with you."*

It's because of people like him, getting caught time and time again in things that are later swept under the rug. Impregnating an intern at KETV not once, but twice. She's still in Omaha but doesn't want to bring attention to the fact that she sued KETV and finally won – he helped her do it. Why isn't this public? What about the consecutive lies that he told about taking over as publisher of the Omaha Crusader, lies that served as stall tactics more than anything else? And where is that big time attorney that he was supposed to bring in to defend black police officer Tariq Al-Amin when the police department was trying to fire him for statements they say he made (actually, it was me) on a cable television program?

Where was the response to Senator Chambers' Omaha Star essay about how he (Gray) lied about having met with and interacted with Malcolm X? What about his flip-flop on a vote that bought CVS Pharmacy to an area of the city that was outside of his district? Why the 24 change of mind? Bribe, perhaps?

People talk, and this is the talk on the streets. It reached me all the way in Dallas so if that is the case, then the streets of North Omaha must be permeated with these kinds of allegations. Some of them I know of personally, so there can be no doubt that when Gray talks about people being "disappointed," he is a part of the reason for that. The Jews give him an award and he literally disappears from involvement in community coverage while serving as host of "Kaleidoscope."

I don't know Barney, *but you judge a man by his words and his works*. If his words are any indicator, then he is yet another in a long line of "sunshine soldiers" who march out to "save North Omaha" and then end up working for and with the city administration. Take note of the following general truisms and vanilla philosophy with no mention of race, discrimination or any of the things that are at the base of the problems he claims to be combatting:

> Barney said the Network "has the opportunity to really make a tremendous difference. Some of it will be over time, some of it will be dramatic," such as the 36 percent reduction in gun violence in July-August 2008. Barney said he's sure some people feel the Network effort is not open enough, or that they don't have a voice. He wants them to contact him. "We'll sit down and we'll meet and we'll listen and try the best we can to make adjustments." "We are building a long-term foundation. We're getting more and more people engaged, more people are stepping forward. That doesn't mean the violence is going to stop today or next week. I keep saying to folks, 'It did not happen overnight and it will not be solved overnight. 'We've seen some things slowly move in the right direction."

The Network has "the opportunity," he says, "to really make a tremendous difference" and "some of it will be over time, some of it will be dramatic." Every single person in Omaha has the opportunity to make a tremendous difference, but very few *seize upon* or *take* those opportunities. That's essentially the difference between leaders and followers.

Additionally, with "over time" and "dramatic" are not opposites – something can be done over time or in the short term and still be dramatic. This is what happens when people who can't think on their feet get interviewed and when the person doing the interview is editing their words. The Network has had more than ample opportunity, but an organization without a sense of direction is like a rat on a treadmill: movin' but not going anyplace!

You cannot take a two month reduction in anything and consider it a trend or a success. There are a plethora of variables that would go into a reduction of gun violence, including the fact that those acts of violence were instigated by the police and as such, the perpetrators are locked up; the fact that the police upgraded their patrols; the fact that in response to these shootings, the people in the area became more aware and more careful about where they were going. This alleged "decline" in gun violence cannot be laid at the door of the Empowerment Network and anyone who thinks that is an idiot.

If he's sure about something, why not act on it. If you are being accused of not being open enough, then change it. Why should people have to contact you to do something that you claim to already know? When my constituents said that I was too forceful at meetings and intimidated them, I stopped going to meetings and handed the agenda, the plans and the gavel over to Robert Bauldwin. That is what leaders do: they make decisions and they realize that the organization and the effort are more important than their presence. If they are real leaders, their presence will linger on even when they are not physically there.

Even if people do contact him, he offers them nothing in the way of a guarantee – he doesn't assure them that the problem will be fixed. Instead, what does he say? *"We'll sit down and we'll meet and we'll listen and try the best we can to make adjustments."* Try as best we can? Perhaps, in the final analysis, this is all that the Network will ever end up doing – especially once the money dries up and they are left only with the depth of their commitments and convictions.

As if the flimsy explanations and jejune excuses were not enough, now comes more "explanations" from Barney:

> Barney said he's sure some people feel the Network effort is not open enough, or that they don't have a voice. He wants them to contact him. "We are building a long-term foundation. We're getting more

and more people engaged, more people are stepping forward. That
doesn't mean the violence is going to stop today or next week. I keep
saying to folks, 'It did not happen overnight and it will not be solved
overnight. 'We've seen some things slowly move in the right
direction."

It should be clear after reading my analysis that the Empowerment Network
leadership doesn't have a clue. The man who was the brains behind it, Dick Davis,
drew up diagrams, charts and had models that I personally saw. I don't know if he
turned it over to the wrong people or what, but this is not what I saw when I was in
his office working to develop long term strategies. And for the record, I was the
one who bought the concept of "empowerment" to North Omaha; it was only after
I left for Dallas and my assistant, a senior brother named Henry Mason died, that
the conferences stopped being held and the empowerment concept was put on hold.

The article (mercifully) concludes:

> Geraldine Wesley with Long School Neighborhood Association
> embraces the Network "getting people's hopes up to empower"
> North O, adding, "If they carry out all the things they intend to do, it
> would be good." "Well, right now its just ideas, there's nothing
> concrete as far as I know," she said. I am waiting for the results. It's
> going to be a long process, I know that. I hope I'll live to see it."

Hope. Dreams. Wishing. Have faith. Keep on believing. I sicken of these
types of platitudes as our community suffers, not on only a daily basis, but on what
seems to be an hourly basis. There are people who are ill and can't get around,
there are people who are hungry and who are wondering how they are going to
feed their children, there are people whose utilities have been shut off, there are
people whose cars sit in the driveway because they can't even afford a gallon of
gas. And then you have people prancing around the community talking about
"empowerment" and they can't even help pay one light bill?

That was one of the knocks against the Black Panther Party back in the day.
They would talk all this stuff about revolution, but the question would come back
from some other group or individual, "how can you talk about revolution and you
can't even take out one police station?" The Panthers, to their credit, did create and
pioneer the feeding of kids in day care and they did other good work as well. But
this Empowerment Network is not feeding anybody, and no one's life is being
improved because of the Network's presence. They take on no issues, they don't
advocate and they won't lobby.

These have been my views of the Empowerment Network. I'll put my 25-
plus years of experience and community development up against anyone in that
Network any day of the week. It should be clear who would be victorious.

<u>Understand the Politics of Race and Reality: The
1997 Race Commission Study</u>

As you can see in the previous section, much of the black leadership doesn't have a clue; like birdies in a nest waiting for the mama bird to drop a worm in their collective mouths, these black "men" are nothing more than comic relief for the powers that be. No one who knows anything about community or neighborhood development could possibly be taking them seriously. Read their words again: if they had even a scintilla of dignity, they would retract those words and leave intelligent statements to people who know what they're talking about. But they are not alone.

I selected the following report and analysis (only the "Introduction" section has been analyzed in this paper) to demonstrate that naivete (ignorance) about race relations even impacts on those who are supposed to be major decision makers. The conclusions of the race commission's report have long been forgotten but that was because they were "forgettable" the minute the ink dried: no concrete ideas, grandiose and irrelevant quotes and a plethora of conceptual mistakes that I was more than happy to point out in the analysis that follows.

You have to understand your own direction and vision and as importantly, understand the role that "race" has played in the development of Omaha. If you can do these two things, you will be miles ahead of the men and women who were interviewed in the previous section.

Following is my analysis of the introduction section of the 1997 "race commission" study that was conducted by the Omaha city administration and a team of more than 100 people, hand picked by then mayor Hal Daub.

**The 1997 Race Commission Study and Its
Introductory Comments:
Retrospective Critique and Commentary**

In January of 2000 when the city issues a study which claimed that race relations were never better, I was angered by such a false conclusion. At that point I issued a "counter-document," in rebuttal to a "report" that was subsequently issued.

The method was not a new one. In fact, it represented what now, in retrospect, appears to be an historical tendency, documented in a work written in 1971 called, *Odyssey: Journal Through Black America.* In one segment, long-time Omaha dentist Earle Person had this observation:

"When the whites put together their new downtown area, their slogan was: "Can do." We [blacks in Omaha] saw that the slogan for the Near North Side was: "Won't do." The prime movers just say, "Well, we'll try a few little things, form a committee, call in an outside research organization, make a study." And they do survey after survey after survey, and al of them get stuck away in some file..." (Selby & Selby, 1971: 290)

How prescient Person was!

North Omahans – the most oft-studied group in the history of the city and, as a result, we remain the poorest. Why? Because if we empower ourselves, there will be no one else left for them to study; no one else for them to exploit; no one else for them to document as being poor, and then taking that information and sending it to Washington, D.C. in exchange for Federal grant monies!

The city's philosophy, based upon the research of their spending patterns, appears to be clear: if they are going to do anything to help North Omaha residents, it will *only be if there are Federal grant dollars available*. Even in this "race report," as you will see, the employment section tells the reader that the key is the "economic development section" of the report. And when you turn to that section, all you see being discussed are Enterprise Zones – a federal program! The message: if blacks want jobs, then they had better pray that Enterprise Zones works! Meanwhile, local employers will continue to discriminate, refuse to hire, arbitrarily fire and otherwise neglect any blacks who apply for jobs in the conventional manner.

Generally speaking, the "Report" by the so-called Commission would receive a grade of "D-minus" if it were handed into me in a college-level course. Take note of what these white people and their "colored quislings" have done. They begin with a report on race and divide it into sections. But alas, each subcommittee digs in only to find none of them knows anything about race relations and indeed, that they are themselves at least partially responsible for its existence. So what do they do? Each section degenerates into a "how to guide"! And that is what you can expect if you read a copy of it: a dialogue on how each of the areas – health care, housing, education, employment, economic development and media – can improve its training, its outlook, its promotional materials, its examinations, its recruiting and so on. Very little in terms of concrete ideas about how each of these areas has harmed North Omaha.

The fact of the matter is, there can be no serious social change if the players who prevent such change are in charge. This is a common sense reality that the "leadership" of Omaha appear to be too ignorant to understand. As I've written elsewhere,

> Black Omahans , with few exceptions, have very low self-esteem
> and apparently do not care what takes place in their community.
> Whites have traditionally known this, and they knew it as far back
> as 1977. The Urban League quotes "one city official who has
> boasted that 'Omaha today is host to one of the neater, more law-
> abiding black ghettos in the country." (Urban League of Nebraska,
> 1978: 7) And in a 1977 survey by WOWT, it was found that race
> relations, as a perceived problem, ranked tenth behind such areas
> of preoccupation as recreation, transportation and city sewers.
> (Stelly, 1998: p. 12)

The Commission was an inept, cowardly group of people who didn't attend most of the meetings. Dr. Everett Reynolds of the Omaha NAACP documented the poor attendance at many of the meetings, and the black community knows that this is just another, in a long line, of attempts to make it appear as if Omaha is changing for the better and that race relations are improving when, in reality, nothing could be further from the truth.

On the cover of the document is a quote by of all people, Robert F. Kennedy Jr. A savior to many, Kennedy's track record with blacks is questionable when you remember the role he played in the arrest of Dr. Martin Luther King Jr., and his incessant attempts to try to get civil rights advocates to "slow down."

No Kennedy had any love for black people. And, like far too many white people, he was a racist. But these white people view him as a liberal and a progressive. So the question is, why would Hal Daub, a conservative Republican who is also a racist, have a quote from Robert F. Kennedy on the cover of this report? Why would Hal Daub have a picture of the hands of black and brown and white kids joined together when, in reality, he has hurt the families of brown, black and red people ever since he took office?

With such hypocrisy evident on the cover of the report, you can imagine the depth of contradictions that lie within the covers. Following is documentation and discussion of the foolishness, shallowness and perfidious contents of the *Omaha Commission on Community and Race Relations Reports and Recommendations, December, 1999.*

The Name of The Organization

While claiming that there was no governmental influence or input into the document, the very fact that they call themselves a commission puts the lie to such claims. A "Commission" is defined as "a group of people given official authorization to perform certain functions or duties." Furthermore, in her section of the report, Director of Job Training Diane Thomas puts her report in memo form, addressed to guess who? Mayor Hal Daub.

None of the people on the Commission understand the gravity of the race problem in Omaha. But they do, however, have one thing in common: they all benefit from it. From Eddie Staton, who will do anything to remain on the government dole and Danye Etchinaw, a woman who belongs to the money-grubbing organization which calls itself La Belle Afrique, to Carrie Murphy who works at the racist KMTV-Channel 3 and Rita Melgares, queen of the conservative Latinos, they are all Daub supporters on some level, or they are the minions of people who ARE Daub supporters.

And this explains why the report amounts to nothing even resembling a relevant report. That is why they call the group who wrote it the Commission on Community and Race Relations. Had they left out the community, the lack of experience and knowledge on race issues would have been even MORE obvious; by adding the "community" dimension, those who miss the boat – meaning most of them – can claim that they were speaking "generically" or "didn't see race as a concern."

Kellie Paris-Asaka, the director of the Human Relations Department, appeared on Channel 7's "Kaleidoscope" on January 9, 2000. She was concerned about the criticisms of the report and made some statements which showed that, indeed, there is an ulterior motive to the recommendations put forth in the Commission's report.

For instance, she expressed disappointment that the City Council did not allocate her the $40,000 she needed for a "race survey." But she claims that she still wants the money and, if the Commission no longer wants a survey, she hopes "we can use the money to effectuate the recommendations of the Commission." Well, before her appearance, nowhere in the document does the city, the county or anyone else devote or commit money to any of the "recommendations" in the Report. On the contrary, one of my major criticisms is that what few good recommendations there are appear to be part of things already taking place. No money then, was committed.

One thing about her appearance was that she admitted that this was the best that she and her cohorts could do. In her words, "I put a lot of work into getting this report published … it was a powerful recommendation … this was a sincere effort to start a dialogue on race relations in Omaha."

Back in 1995 when I went on the air on Channel 22, I vowed to the community that it was my goal to take the issue of racism out of the bar and the interracial bedroom and to raise it to the level of social debate. Ernie's show came along and did the same thing. Programs like "Black Male Roundtable,"""The Khalil Ben Ashanti Hour of Power,""""Protecting the Village," and "Show of Truth" did the same thing. The Triple One Neighborhood Association and the Parent's Union, both created by me, did the same thing in the areas of community development and education, respectively.

How then, can Ms. Paris believe or open her distended mouth to say that this poorly written document and its pretentious authors have "started a dialogue on race relations" or anything else, for that matter? When I was addressing the race issue on my show, it was people like Paris and her cronies who were cowering at home gasping for air and acting shocked and amazed. Like her boss, Mayor Hal Daub, she is a hypocrite.

She told "Kaleidoscope" host Ben Gray that it was the findings of the Commission that "race played a significant role in" the particular problems that the Commission addressed and finally, that "race is an issue." Where has this silly woman been for the past decade? She handled the Crossroads Mall case back in 1995, after I brought the parties together and exposed the racism in the case. *And she was so inept, she had a fling with one of the plaintiffs and ended up losing the case, anyway!* This is the kind of track record that the woman who now heads the Human Relations Department brings with her. And if she couldn't handle an easy, slam dunk case like *Kemp, Kemp and Colthirst vs. Crossroads Mall and Simon Management*, then who is she to make it appear as if she knows anything about race, racism or race relations? Like her boss, she's a jack of *few* trades and a master of one: tommin'!

She claimed that the survey was "a tool to measure progress." Here's how you measure progress in race relations: look at the segregation of Omaha today and compare it with segregation of 10 years ago. Is there any change? No. Are more blacks being hired? No. Has the relative income between whites and blacks narrowed? No. If there was no racism, would there be any need for her department? No. And finally, if there was no racism, why did her own boss, Hal Daub, attempt to do away with the Department as recently as three years ago?

So it's clear what's on his mind: if he can't destroy it because of black community support, he'll put someone in charge of it who will run it into the ground. Enter: Kellie Paris Asaka! Her ignorance of racism shows when Ben Gray asked her why they didn't use the discrimination data from the files of the Human Relations Department or the Nebraska Equal Opportunity Commission. She said that while they had information in the areas of employment and housing, there wasn't enough data in the areas of health care, media, education and so on. After all, she explained, "we determined that racism could go beyond the traditional areas."

Oh, really? Paris is an attorney. The "traditional areas" of discrimination are the ones which paved the way for the others! She knows that housing and employment discrimination were both sanctioned by the system as recently as

1950! She has to know something about the racist mindset because that is what discrimination is: it is the action based on a racist attitude. Now since that is the case, if you find it in an area like employment, that paves the way for the exercise of racism in other spheres: where you can afford to live, how your children fare in school, the quality of health care you receive, where you can go socially and so on. If this woman doesn't know this, then she is an insult to the Nebraska Bar, the North Omaha community and anyone who is sincerely committed to learning about now to improve race relations in Omaha.

To paraphrase an age old adage, you judge a Commission by the reports it bears. And in this case, it is clear that the Commission created by Hal Daub and monitored by Hal Daub reflects the same naiveté, racism and backwardness which Hal Daub exhibits every time he opens his mouth. This kind of ineptitude is evident in his cronies, from Mike Saklar and Brinker Harding, to Jim Cleary and now, Kellie Paris-Anaka.

As stated, this document is an exercise in futility, and starts off with what I view as "grandiose quotes" by the League of Cities.

The first such quote, from the 1991 League of Cities document, titled, "Diversity and Governance," reads as follows: "The first requirement of city leaders is that they embrace diversity and affirm equal rights for all. From that there can be no retreat." This is not true. City leaders need to ACT on that which has already been confirmed by law and by God. Their affirmation is unnecessary if they would but just act.

On the same page is another quote, this one from "Building a Nation of Communities," also by the League of Cities: "Deep-seated problems such as racism, economic exclusion, and a sense of political powerlessness often stand in the way of residents feeling they have a equal stake in their communities' success."

"Often stand in the way"? Are there times when racism, economic exclusion and a sense of political powerlessness WORK for people of color, or anyone else, for that matter? This statement, by being quoted, is a case of the blind leading the blind. This proves that what white people (and their Negro lackies) find relevant, black people feel the opposite about.

To ensure balance, no doubt, there are two more quotes from the League of cities, the 1999 Futures Report. The question at the top of the page asks, "How Can We Undo Racism?" The first answer is "By Changing Ourselves," and the explanation reads,

> On the one hand, working against racism means changing what we, as individuals and elected leaders, are doing to keep racism alive – for example, by separating ourselves, intentionally or not, from

individuals of different races, or by not speaking up when those
around us make racist comments.

The question is, why haven't white folks done it? The answer is, because they cannot. As Dr. Frances Welsing teaches, racism is a matter of genetic survival for those people. If they fraternize and have sex, the product is a child of color. For their own survival on this planet, they must shield themselves from the brown gene, which is both sociogenically and genetically more powerful than the "white" gene.

The second answer is, "By Changing our Policies and Institutions," and the quote says:

> Dismantling racism also means changing the policies and the social
> and institutional systems that allow racism to remain an oppressive
> force – for example, by enabling police to stop motorists because of
> the color of their skin or by permitting banks to treat loan applicants
> of different races differently.

The policies and institutions are aimed at maintaining the white supremacy structure which protects them genetically. Segregation is one way that they maintain social separation. One need only read "The Cress Theory of Color Confrontation and Racism" or *The Isis Papers: The Keys to the Colors* to better understand why white people act so foolishly when they must confront their neighbors of color.

The selection of these quotes shows that Commission members are out of tune with the racial reality of the times. Even the "Negroes" who were members of the Commission, had they cared anything about their white colleagues, would not have allowed these dunderhead quotes to be used. But it appears that neither side really cares about the other and the key was to hurriedly construct a document that the Mayor could use as evidence that he "cares about the negro people."

Well he failed and they failed. Following is evidence of these collective failures and reasons why the Report by the Commission on Community and Race Relations should be read carefully.

And then burned.

Next is the "Executive Summary."

The writers of the report were so limited in their research skills that they attempted to masquerade their shortcomings with irrelevant quotations, outmoded data and generic conclusions. An example lies in the following passage:

> Since the spring of 1998, volunteers from across this city have been
> actively engaged in research, analysis and assessment of race relations

> in Omaha, Nebraska … Racism in all its manifestations is an emotional topic for many, and is extremely difficult to talk about. Members of the committees experienced this as they strived to create actionable recommendations organizations, government and even individuals can embrace and implement. (p. 3)

More than half a year of research by all of these people, and their findings are as relevant as a term paper written by a third grader. The topic is only "emotional" to those who have practiced and benefited from it; blacks, Latinos and American Indians have been dealing with racism for so long, there is nothing to get emotional about. So the statement about emotion shows you which group constituted the majority – white folks. And that is why they "strived to create actionable recommendations" and didn't really create any. They tried to do all they could, but failed. They attempted to find solutions but didn't know how to define the problem, where to look for solutions, or how to analyze what they came across.

Furthermore, what are the academic credentials of these "volunteers"? What makes them think that they can conduct research? Not only that, but the report claims that these people were "actively engaged in research, analysis and assessment of the state of race relations in Omaha, Nebraska." If these people were so smart, they would have already found a "solution." The fact that they are, as a collective, intellectually inadequate can be seen in the difficulty that this town has in luring and keeping major businesses; when all is said and done, the State of Nebraska and Omaha lose out to such hinterland capitals as Alabama and Utah!

But this raises an important point: these people, both subconsciously and consciously, have such a low regard for race relations and improving race relations, that they feel that any layman, any clown off the corner can conduct "research." If we were studying the way to make relations better between white men and women, do you think the League of Women Voters or the Omaha chapter of the National Organization of Women would allow just "anybody" to conduct research in their behalf? No.

Only when it comes to the blacks and the Latinos do these arrogant white people think that they – the source of the problems we face – can also provide the solutions. They want to conduct research and do analysis on data when the problem stares them in the mirror every day; when they are sleeping with the problem; when they are employed by and do the bidding of the problem. This dishonesty is the basis of the report which explains why honest people must reject its contents, root and branch.

The poorly written and shabbily presented "reports" were explained, as follows:

> The reports in this package appear just as members of the
> subcommittees have submitted them. This is the information that
> these volunteers have compiled in each individual committee, on their
> own time over the last twenty months, without influence or input from
> any political factions in the City. (p. 3)

Almost two years of preparation, we now learn. And they want us to believe that during this period, the people who didn't know what they were doing didn't seek any assistance from anyone who works with the city, the university or anyone with expertise that they lacked? This is an absurd lie. The people involved had been benefiting from racism all their lives and most of them live in segregated neighborhoods. When confronted with having to challenge that which has become a way of life, it is no wonder they were left dumbfounded and why, after twenty months, the best they could come up with was 62 pages of dunce-like drivel.

To further the like, a "nonpolitical disclaimer" of sorts was provided by these intellectual midgets in the following passage:

> Subcommittees recruited members who were interested in making
> positive impact in the race relations arena. Political affiliation was a
> non-issue as subcommittees met each week or month to hammer out
> the essentials for improving race relations in our city. They sought
> out individuals who freely gave of their time and resources to look at
> Omaha race relations issues from a 360 degree viewpoint with the
> intent of finding facts, causes and solutions – not placing blame … (p.
> 3)

First of all, these people found no solutions. They simply regurgitated some general truisms that most people already knew. This, again, is attributable to their backwardness and dishonesty. Furthermore, they talk of not "placing blame;" it is not a matter of "blaming" anyone. It is a matter of "attributing responsibility," and we know on whose shoulders segregation, redlining, steering, consumer fraud, pilfering of Federal grant money, mis-education, and police harassment should be placed. It is not a matter of "blame," but a matter of those who practice these things to own up to them and realize that since they are so intertwined with the problem, they cannot possibly be a part of any solution.

If the subcommittee recruited members "who were interested in making positive impact in the race relations arena," why did they not share with the readers of the Report how they went about making those selections? How was the recruitment mechanism set up? Was it by word of mouth? Or was it by picking people who shared the same views and values? And since it most likely was the latter, how can one expect change when what we have on this subcommittee is really nothing more than the blind leading the blind?

How do you look at something with a "360 degree viewpoint?" What is a 360 degree viewpoint? How would you know if someone had the capacity to look at something with this kind of viewpoint? How did those doing the recruiting know who had or who did not have this viewpoint? If the subcommittee knows who has this view point and who does not, then does that mean that the committee can tell who is racist and who is not? The thoughts are flawed because the words used to describe the process are flawed. That is why nothing that comes from such divided approaches and mixed up ideas will work. As Karenga writes, "to divide the process is to deform the product."

The lies continue to mount, as the need to cover up the shabby work increases. Take note of the following attempt at an explanation:

> Cross sections of people from across the metropolitan area participated in the Omaha Commission on Race and Community Relations. Individuals from all walks of life were actively involved in all subcommittees. This means that leaders from community organizations, private and public sectors as well as front line concerned individuals were actively engage in the work of the commission. (p. 3)

This is a lie. Ultimately however, what they really mean is that everyone involved was selected, picked or recruited by someone else. And this means that what you ultimately had was a "clique of the unconscious," a coterie of kooks, a circle of pseudo-intellectuals. By banding together, they make it appear as if the issue of race is so complex and that they do not know what the problem is. The more people they recruited, the bigger the problem became because when it comes to race relations in Omaha, white people are the major problem, and their handpicked flunkies of color make solving the problem even more difficult.

In addition to the pervasive stupidity and racism that permeated the subcommittee, paternalism was also present. That is the only way to explain the cultural arrogance that lies behind the following statement:

> People of Color were able to openly discuss how they were affected in the seven focus areas … The impact of those leaders' participation is evident in the community partnerships that have been formed, and small, yet important change that have happened as a result of those forums. (p. 4)

How would white people know if people of color were "able to openly discuss how they were affected"? If these people of color felt some comfortable, then why even bother discussing racism, why not leave everything the way it is now? After all, they are sitting in the midst of racists and they are comfortable enough to say how they feel. This means that "equality" existed in that situation? Where then, is the equality and the "open ear" of the white man in the society at large? Nowhere to be found. And the reason it can't be found is the same reason why it didn't exist at these "playtime sessions" sponsored by the subcommittee: because both sides are being fake, with white people feigning liberalism and black people fooling those whites by "tomming." No sane solution can come out of a situation when the two parties involved are behaving in such a duplicitous and perfidious manner.

The preceding statement claims that the impact of "those leaders" participation can be seen in the community partnerships that have been formed. As a grant writer, I know that the buzzword of the 1990s was "partnership," just as the buzzword of the new century is "collaboration." At any rate, the only partnerships that are formed revolve around going after grant money and then splitting it; the white groups need the minority input for ideas and to meet Federal guidelines, and the blacks need the white resources and clout. This is not a "partnership" – it's an alienated arrangement.

Knowing that they were woefully inadequate, a day late and a dollar short, the charlatans who made up this subcommittee began applying qualifiers to their already shortsighted efforts. At one point they write,

> … **The original purpose of the commission was to assess the status of race relations in Omaha – not "fix" the problem** … The gathering of this diverse group of people to discuss the nature of race relations in Omaha, Nebraska is **a strong first step.** Many recommendations for improvement of race relations in the seven target areas have been made from the best efforts of this Commission … (p. 4—emphasis original)

The first sentence is an outright confession, confirming all that the community has been saying all along: that the subcommittee was a joke and that they were studying what had already been studied to death. By "assessing the status of race relations in Omaha," these lazy cowards relied on information and insights already studied – secondary information. If you want to know the status of race relations in Omaha, you have to interview the people who are the victims of racism, because they know where it comes from, how intense it is and what form it comes in. You don't bring together a cadre of people from the oppressor class and then claim that you want to "assess the status of race relations in Omaha." You know how those relations are because, as a racist, you enjoy the benefits and the segregation that the "status" has brought to you and your family.

Notice that the quote says that the recommendations for improvement of race relations were made "from the best efforts of this Commission." Not from concrete results; not from quantitative analysis; not from objective longitudinal assessment and comparison. No. From "the best efforts" of the Commission. So if the Commission is filled with people who are ignorant of race relations, then their "best efforts" are going to culminate in a collectively foolish conclusion. And that is exactly what happened.

After this confession, the overall weakness and inadequacy of the committee is addressed, in a backhanded way, but addressed nonetheless. Note the following "well-at-least-we-tried" foolishness:

> ... Challenges that Omaha and the nation have faced concerning race relations did not happen overnight. Subsequently, the on-going recommendations and solutions will not "fix" the problem of racism – intentional or not – overnight ... The Omaha Community must be constantly vigilant of inequities or opportunity, and be change-hardy and solution-driven about processes or behaviors that perpetuate those inequities ... (p. 4)

These people are local and they are part of a subcommittee that is supposed to be looking into racism here in the River City. Why then, do they write begin by writing about, "challenges that Omaha and the nation have faced concerning race relations?" The answer is because they know that they failed but they want the reader to know that the entire nation has failed to deal with racism, so Omaha is not by itself. In a word, misery loves company. After indicting the entire nation in an attempt to ameliorate their own racism and segregation-oriented tendencies, the subcommittee then stoops to clichés: it didn't start overnight so it won't be fixed overnight.

These people realize that Omaha is a wealthy city and that racism played a major role in building that wealth. The master of the subcommittee, Hal Daub, knows that it is racism and his hatred of North Omaha that is going to generate Federal dollars for the city—money that he can steer away from North Omaha and use to improve his downtown skyline, build more places where white people can engage in freakishness and frolic, and use to entice more companies into the city, companies that won't hire people of color.

That is why all this subcommittee could come up with, after all those months, is sweet-sounding, liberal rhetoric like that which follows:

> What IS needed if Omaha, Nebraska is to continue to strike to be an inclusive community that values differences of all types, is for MORE

> people to continue to come together in a spirit of unity … (p. 4—
> emphasis original)

And finally, after realizing that their efforts were abysmally inadequate, they conclude, nonetheless, by trying to make themselves look like civil rights pioneers:

> The Omaha Commission on Community and Race Relations has laid the groundwork for open dialog … several of the subcommittees have decided to continue their work by sharing and partnering with community organizations. Let the good work begun by these dedicated volunteers continue. … (p. 4)

This is the product, not of white trash or some high school dropouts. This is the work of the best that Omaha's white community can produce. This is their ultimate effort. And you see what it looks like and what it entails. And as you read it, things don't get better. They get measurably worse.

The next section of this "race commission" study carries the heading, "Overview From the General Chairs." Following is that interview and my analysis of it

***   ***   ***

Racism makes you do stupid things. In order to feign a concern for race relations, Mayor Hal Daub knew that he had to pick a chairman that would make him (Daub) appear "wise." He couldn't pick a white one because that would look like paternalistic racism; he couldn't pick a black one because he (Daub) distrusts and despises African-Americans. He couldn't pick a Latino because it might make the Blacks and other racial minorities feel left out. So what do they do? Three people are picked to serve as "general chairs." The three are Eddie Staton, a system-oriented "Negro" whose words and actions prove he is beholden to the mayor; Rita Melgares, a conservative Latina lawyer; and Roy Smith, owner of a white car franchise and a very rich man. This "menagerie," then, served as the leadership for a "Commission" that was supposed to address race relations with some semblance of seriousness.

The paper is supposed to be apolitical, but what do they write in the document? Take note:

> We want to also express appreciation to Mayor Hal Daub for his support and vision in the creation of this commission. We hope that this will be the first in many efforts to publicly denounce racism and discrimination of all types in Omaha … (p. 5)

If he supported it, then that means he was around when they were writing it. And if the commission was the creation of Daub's vision, then that explains why it was filled with racists and incredibly unqualified people of color. It also explains why the committee's statements, like the actions of the mayor who created it, are also contradictory.

For instance, the commission writes that, "we hope that this will be the first in many efforts to publicly denounce racism and discrimination of all types in Omaha." That statement translates to mean that racism and discrimination are always going to be around, hence the need for "many efforts" in the future. This is the kind of foolishness that exposes racists for the imbeciles that they are. This Commission is surely no exception.

And because they know that they are visibly making themselves look like fools, they immediately launch a reaction formation and attempt to place the blame on those who can see through the cheap scam that they are trying to pull of. They write that,

> … Let the critics say what they will – if they did not actively participate in this process they personify the adage: "If you're not part of the solution, you're part of the problem. …"

The only way to "actively participate" was to be "recruited" by one of the members of the Commission. Therefore, if you weren't recruited, what they are saying is that you are part of the problem – as if they and only they are part of the solution. Anything created by Hal Daub is going to be racist because that is what he is. And those Commission members know what they are doing – they just don't give a damn. And it is this very lack of values and morals which prompts them to attempt to transfer the blame onto others.

The whimpering idiots know their shortcoming, and that is why they cover them up by claiming that they have just started:

> Racism in America has existed for over 300 years. While the efforts and recommendations of this Commission are not a quick fix, it is a beginning …

A beginning to do what? Moving on, they write,

> If change is to happen, it must begin at the top! We challenge all arms of City and County government, as well as leaders of Corporate, community Educational and Religious organizations to take an adamant moral stand of denouncing racism, bigotry and hate. We urge

these leaders to weave a culture of understanding, respect and valuing
of differences among people .. TODAY! (P. 5 –all emphasis original)

This suggestion about change beginning at the top is how racism is maintained. The change has to start at the bottom, collectively amass influence and power, and then influence those at the top with the numbers of people who want to influence and determine new policy. Why would a racist who has things going the way he wants – practicing racism in full view and still not have any opposition from most whites – stop in the middle of the stream and reverse his position? It doesn't make sense, but the suggestion once again shows how silly the people on this Commission are.

How can they "challenge" anyone in the corporate, community, educational or religious community? They are beholden to these interests! That is why the meetings were so poorly attended; that is why of the three General Chairs, only the "Negro" member came forward and tried to justify the contents of the report. This was because that "Negro" was the only one with the tombstone courage to condemn the head of the local NAACP. Had Smith done it, he would be exposed for his racism; had Melgares done it, she would have been attacked by the Latino and Black leadership. But when a "Negro" does it, the attack is legitimized by those white people who believe that he is really a leader. But the black community knows better.

With that said and done, the following section of the "study" is titled, "Recommendations of the General Chairs." The recommendations (pages 6 and 7) are shallow, generic and written as if the chairpersons were in a hurry. Following are excerpts from some of those recommendations:

> … Organizations should create a statement of personal commitment
> of zero tolerance for racism and discrimination and make that
> statement public no later than January 31, 2000 …

A statement of personal commitment? This implies that these organizations should go to each of their employees and get a statement that they will no longer hate black people. No, what we need is an "organizational" and an "institutional" commitment and, from there, an ideological and philosophical commitment that these people will no longer practice the stupid doctrine of racism. We need financial, legislative, judicial commitments – not personal ones. If a white person never says "hello" to me in life, that is fine by me. But that doesn't preclude him or her from supporting and turning their head while their institutional representatives destroy North Omaha and then lie and claim that "the negroes did it to themselves."

Furthermore, *how can a city, steeped in a history of racism and segregation, have the temerity to issue a zero tolerance edict?* That would be self-incriminating! They would have to issue a statement against all of their white leadership, from Daub, McKiel and the County Board, to all of the banking and business interests who are behind the evil that is done to North Omaha on a daily basis. They would have to expose Creighton University and how it controls the board of the Charles Drew Center and how it is gradually encroaching northward. They would have to expose the sexually perverted and racist hijinks taking place at Boys Town, the elitist racism at UNO, and the discrimination at its malls, restaurants and movie theaters.

After the preceding ridiculous recommendation, the General Chairs continued the pattern by suggesting that,

> … People of Color must be vigilant in reporting acts of discrimination and bigotry promptly to appropriate authorities (i.e., -- human resources departments, City Human Relations, Nebraska Equal Opportunity Commission, Urban League, NAACP, ADL , NCCJ, Chicano Awareness, etc.) …

This statement was put in the report to imply that people of color were not reporting incidents of racism and discrimination. This is a dupe. People of color have "reported,""blown whistles" and "exposed" so much, and have paid such a high price for doing so, most of them are just burned out. When they do report such acts, who do they go – the nitwit who now heads the Human Relations Department and claims that a "race survey" would do some good? The same Mayor who, upon learning that a Native American child had gotten shot in the back by a white clerk, basically said "if you shoplift, that's what you can expect?" A police department that is responsible for saturating North Omaha with drugs and arbitrarily arresting black males? An Equal Opportunities Commission that is, at best, a joke?

Then, when you do report these incidents what are you really doing? You are, as Malcolm X would say, "running from the wolf to the fox." The employers who own the big companies are the same ones who backed the racist Mayor we now have. The Mayor controls the Human Relations Department and all of its verdicts. How then, can black people find justice with such an existing state of affairs? Not to mention a judicial system which includes judges who draw swastikas on reports, say "fuck you" to female attorneys, and who allow even worse "pranks" to take place and say nothing.

Black people must fend for themselves and if the Report was honest, that is what it would have said.

But if the preceding suggestion showed an abysmal ignorance of what black people are up against, the following one most certainly over-estimates the moral fortitude of this community's white population when it suggests that,

> … It is the responsibility of People (sic) who are NOT of color to also be vigilant in taking action when they see occurrences of racism, whether it be confronting the perpetrator of the racist behavior or refusing to patronize an establishment who (sic) is guilty of such behavior …

Now the board is asking the racists to spot and respond to other acts of racism! If white people had the collective capacity to do this, there would be no residential segregation in Omaha; there would be no District 66, for surely their racism and the subsequent "white flight" led to the creation of far west Omaha! Those members of the Commission who allowed this report to go public did themselves a grave disservice. Not only did they expose their collective ignorance, but they also insulted the intelligence of those of us who are out here fighting racism on a daily basis. According to them, we are misguided: all we have to do is sit back and wait for white people to put an end to it themselves!

> Have the Human Relations Department; (sic) with community groups (i.e., Nebraska Equal Opportunity Commission, Urban League, NAACP, ADL, NCCJ, Chicano Awareness, etc.) create a community database of verifiable incident reports by December 31, 2000 …

First of all, the Human Relations Department is supposed to be already doing this. But who are these Commission members to talk of "having" the other organizations create a database of future incidents. These groups need to get on about the business of making sure that no more incidents occur! And as for those Jewish groups – the Anti-Defamation League and the National Council of Christians and Jews – they are of no use to the black community whatsoever. They sit on our boards and dominate our lives through so-called "philanthropy," but they are just as responsible for the condition of North Omaha as their gentile buddies are. To even include them in this list is a slap in the face of both the black and Latino communities.

Since Daub is behind this madness, and since the director of the Human Relations Department is his water carrier, what they are trying to do is "control" complaints of racism so that these complaints can be more easily discarded. That is why many of the recommendations have the "solutions" funneled through a department run by a woman who knows nothing about race relations and who was hand picked and appointed by the Mayor.

Still as yet they suggest that some unnamed entity,

> … Create a process where Douglas County employees can register
> discrimination complaints with City Human Relations Department by
> February 28, 2000 …

What has the Human Relations done for the black community in recent years? One of the General Chairmen is a former director and even he, as mealy-mouthed as he has been lately, knows that the work of the Department has been watered down since the times when he held the reins. The Department is intentionally being made worthless so that it can be eliminated altogether – that is why Daub appointed an incompetent to run it. Who else, but an incompetent, for example, would make the following suggestion.

> … Create a citywide public relations campaign to promote valuing of
> differences and reporting of incidents by December 31, 2000 …

Money can now be spent. But on what? A stupid public relations campaign! Daub and Paris-Anaka want that money so badly that now they're grasping at straws. A citywide public relations campaign against racism? Where are you going to put the billboards – in west Omaha? Because you're preaching to the choir if you put them in the north or southside.

The foolishness continues and concludes with perhaps the most absurd suggestion of all:

> … Have City Human Relations host awards event for groups,
> corporations and individuals who contribute to bringing the city of
> Omaha together in valuing differences by December 31, 2000. …

The key to the preceding statement is that the suggestion calls for the Human Relations Department HOSTING an awards banquet. How timely. This is one way to give the department credibility that it lacks. To give this department the power to bestow awards for people who promote racial harmony. This relieves the Department of the responsibility of having to do it! Daub would be present and would give a speech; the Omaha World Herald would be there with cameras flashing. And before you know it, you've got a press release, a campaign brochure and billboards showing how Daub "unified" the city. And every entity that gets an award would represent a real or potential vote.

Secondly, why "award" these groups? If they are so "anti-racist" or progressive, then why should they be awarded for it? This suggestion shows the true commitment of the Commission: surface level only. *Pretend* that you are not racist. *Pretend* that you will work to combat racism. *Pretend* that your Department is committed to people of color when, in reality, you're in the mayor's pocket. *Pretend* that the Report you just produced has real merit. *Pretend* that the Commission you are on is actually working. And then, when you are rewarded for your deceitful behavior, *pretend* that you deserved it.

That was a glimpse at "race and reality" in Omaha. I could have written more but the hour, as the Muslim brothers say, "has been well spent." We have to know what empowerment is in order to internalize it, teach it, and institutionalize it through approaches, paradigms and programs. A key component of empowerment, in order to ensure sustainability of what we hope to implement and inculcate, is mentoring.

Mentoring: Passing the Baton

An old saying from the black power movement days teaches, "You can't teach what you don't know, and you can't lead where you won't go." Young leaders: stick with what you know. There are too many people out there who think that just because they have expertise in one given area, that this gives them the right to rule in other areas. There are those of us who have expertise in a great many areas: but we are few and far between, and the time has come for leadership to take on a laser-focus on key and core issues. That is where youthful leadership comes in and that is why this week's tidbit deals with the importance of mentoring, and while I'm at it, I'll offer up a new definition, one that is more relevant to our future leaders and their roles in the defense and development of the community.

What is a mentor as it relates to communities like North Omaha? In the organizational development game, there is a saying: "A mentor is someone who's hindsight can become your foresight." Oh, if only North Omaha's community-based organizations could practice such an approach! The key to any good organization is continuity, and although groups continue to exist, there are glitches and stoppages in some of the business that needs to get done. This would not be the case if mentoring programs were in place.

In North Omaha, many of the organizations that at one time had value and validity no longer pass muster. And much of the reason for this has to do with the fact that when it comes to organizational leadership, those who had the reins had a difficulty letting them go. A few examples prove this to be the case.

When the Urban League passed down its torch to new leadership, there were systems in place that enabled the newcomers to enter and begin to do their own thing. There was rarely a time when there was on-going continuity: new people came in with new ideas and because the board changed so much, those incoming leaders literally had to start over again with much of what had to be done.

The smoothest transition, to date, took place between the time that George Dean left and George Dillard came in. What few people remember is that during the interim period there was a man named Tal Owens. Tal worked with Dean closely and always had his back; as a result, he learned on the job and when George decided to head off to Sacramento (he is now in Phoenix), Tal stepped in and things were smooth enough to hand over to the eventual new full-time director, George Dillard.

The local NAACP has undergone several transitions but with no mentoring program in place, it has taken a path similar to that of the League. When its most outspoken and many say best, director – Buddy Hogan – served, the NAACP was probably at its highest point. Buddy served for a long time, had media outlets on radio and a weekly column in the Omaha Star, "Buddy's Byline." He was an outgoing leader and as a result when he left, new leadership couldn't fill his shoes. Although Rev. Everett Reynolds came in and lead the organization through tough times, those who preceded him had a difficult time "handing over the reins."

Today's present leadership at both the Urban League and NAACP have their own agendas and are doing the best they can based on what they have to work with. But it would have been much easier had Thomas Warren had a program or paradigm out outline the vision of the local Urban League, and if Tommie Wilson had a guideline that would have helped her move alone lines similar to those taken by her predecessor, Dr. Reynolds.

Look at OOIC. Although it continues to survive in these most tumultuous of times, is there any doubt that its longtime director of 30 years, Dr. Bernice Dodd, should have had leadership mentoring program in place? Is there any doubt that each of these organizations would benefit from an on-going "Leadership Intern" program, where young people could learn about organizational development, community leadership, grant writing and networking?

Omaha Economic Development Corporation had a long history under Al Goodwin and was highly visible. When Al decided to step down and bought in Michael Maroney, the transition was quick and smooth. Why? Because the two had worked together, knew what needed to be done, and Al stayed around as a consultant and, to this day, still knows more about OEDC than anyone. But this is what happens when information is shared and shaped by those with a similar vision and vigor.

The same thing is true of individuals. As great as Senator Ernie Chambers has always been, there was no one in place to continue on his work. Were it not for the 400-page training manual I wrote, one that documents much of what Ernie did, where would the record be that would motivate and inspire young people to earn the art and science of politics using the Chambers style? What will happen to the

Omaha Star if its leadership changes? What about Cox Cable Channel 22 under the leadership of Dr. Everett Reynolds, Trip Reynolds and Everett Jr.?

We need these entities, and we know that those who come behind us will need them. Since this is the case, it is only logical to have programs in place where young people can stop re-inventing the wheel and thinking that they're coming up with new concepts when, in reality, they are only regurgitating what has already been attempted?

John Crosby once wrote that, "Successful people turn everyone who can help them into sometime mentors." In this case, those who lead organizations in areas where there are important sociopolitical concerns can do no less. This is true of organizations ranging from the Chicano Awareness Center, the Preston Love Jazz and Arts Museum and Girls, Incorporated to UNO's African American Students Organization, the Nebraska Black Sports Hall of Fame, Nuestro Mundo newspaper and the Aframerican Bookstore.

If we want continuity, then we have to be willing to pass the baton on to those who can take the organization into the next phase.

<u>Key Issues for Empowerment Network</u>

As you can see in this book, the Empowerment Network is tackling very few bread and butter issues, and when they do talk about an issue like "jobs," it is in a very sterile and generic way. That is why the organization has very little credibility: its orientation and relevance seems to revolve around those who area already well off. That is why in this brief section, I hope to jump start the Network and get the organization on the road to relevance. Following are a few of the issues that they can address, tackle, spearhead and, where possible, actually *solve or resolve.*

Issue 1: insurance for the poor. As of April 28, 2005, there were 195,000 uninsured people in the State of Nebraska, representing 11.3% of the population. A whopping ten (10%) percent of the Metro Omaha population, according to the U.S. Census, is uninsured. "Most are low-wage workers, work in small businesses and either don't earn enough to afford health insurance, or can't afford it and/or aren't eligible for public assistance" (Fredericks, 2005). Those numbers have probably increased markedly.

What the Network should do is get Mutual of Omaha, Prudential and Aetna involved in addressing affordable insurance for the low-income, mainly those who live in North Omaha. One of the founders of the Network, or at least the braintrust behind its embryonic beginnings, is Dick Davis, who is the founding director of Davis Insurance Companies. Behind his leadership, positive steps could be taken to provide insurance of all types to North Omaha residents. This is something that is doable and that the Network should be spearheading.

Issue 2: Taxi accessibility and the jitney stands. This may sound trivial for those who take having an accessible auto for granted. But in a study as cited elsewhere, Omaha's black community is a place where, in 1978 it was reported that fully 45% of residents lacked automobiles (Urban League of Nebraska, 1978: 20). Six years later nothing had changed. According to an August 7, 1983 article in the Omaha World Herald documented that, "Nearly 45 percent of the households on the Near North Side have no cars. So residents walk or rely on taxis, buses or rides from neighbors and relatives to get to stores along Ames Avenue or shopping centers to the west."

There is little reason to believe that these figures have improved over the past 29 years with the economy being what it has been.

The taxicab system in Omaha has always been racist and, as such, there have always been dual systems. Back in the day black folks had access to Unity Cab Company and later came the Ritz Cab Company, the latter located at 2414 Patrick Avenue. When society was legally desegregated, this did not prevent Cab companies like Yellow Cab, Safeway Cab and Happy Cab from nonetheless refusing to take calls from black customers who resided in the "urban core." For that reason, jitneys were formed in order to meet the needs of the neglected black North Omaha consumer.

So racist is the city that even whites in decision making positions allowed the jitney stands to exist, realizing that white cab companies feared coming into the black community, especially at night. Vernacular cab" is a term used to describe a taxi system that is informal. The vernacular cab system in Omaha has been researched by my mentor, Dr. Peter T. Suzuki, a professor in the Department of Public Administration at the University of Nebraska at Omaha.

Dr. Suzuki's research is based on his participation as a patron of the jitneys. He literally went "under cover" for a period of time as a taxi driver for a jitney stand (where the taxis operate from) in North Omaha. According to his findings, vernacular taxi systems typically exist in many larger cities across the United States in minority communities and have "developed out of a common history of racial prejudice and discrimination by the standard White taxi cab companies" (Suzuki, 1991: 123).

The Empowerment Network could stand ready to defend the existence of the jitneys and, in fact, work on ways to empower them and expand their jitney stands. This would mean employment for residents, especially those who are chronically unemployed or retired.

Issue 3: Address transportation issues with Metro Area Transit.

In April of 1987, a group calling itself Citizens Concerned About Transportation, attended a public forum and accused the Metro Area Transit of ignoring the transportation needs of North Omaha. The forum was held by the MAT Transit Advisory Committee, which claims that it "passes along citizens' concerns to the MAT Board of Directors" (Omaha World Herald, 1987)

Another layer of bureaucracy. The so-called Transit Advisory Committee is nothing short of a buffer zone between the community and the MAT Board of directors, much like local "management companies" enable rich whites to control rental housing and never have to have any contact with their black tenants – the management company does all the collecting of rent. During that meeting Ed Neil, then a member of the Committee, claimed that the committee was "the eyes and ears of the community … as far as we are concerned, we are the same as the Mayor's Hot Line" (Omaha World Herald, 1987).

In 1997 or thereabouts, Linda Stone told me that 57% of MAT's bus services were concentrated in North Omaha.

Present at the meeting was Buddy Hogan, president of the NAACP, who reminded the Committee that public transportation is essential to a democracy and should be subsidized enough to serve all those in need.

On Monday, May 23, 2004, Channel 6 aired a segment titled, "Who's Riding the Bus?" The report was horrible. Omaha's public transportation is horribly mis-managed, and the routes are designed to pacify North Omaha, but to also lend itself to the relocation strategy that takes place. By offering transportation to urban fringe jobs, the bus service aids in the "seduction" that lends itself to leaving North Omaha and moving elsewhere, closer to one's job. Slowly but surely, the Metro Area Transit is cutting back its routes. What will befall the black community then?

From the Empowerment Network could spring another version of 1987's Citizens Concerned About Transportation. This would give the Network much needed relevance, visibility and credibility.

Issue 4: Tavern and Lounge Owners Network (TALON): We have a disproportionate number of taverns, bars and lounges in our community. Why not create an organization made up of the owners of these places of leisure and create the basis for the funding of scholarships? Not just academic scholarships, but monies to defray the cost of recreational programs for our young people, monies to send them on junkets to Kansas City, Des Moines, Chicago or St. Louis? If each owner put $25 a month into a kitty, by year's end there would be thousands of dollars that we could use for the benefit of our young people.

Issue 5: Metro Area Tourism Escort Service: I proposed this to Jay Baum, then the director of the Omaha Convention and Visitors Bureau, back in the 90s when a tourist was killed in Miami. The plan would be for Network members to simply screen and hire young black males and give them jobs as escorts for incoming tourists during the summer. With the successful construction and popularity of the Qwest Center and the rebuilding of downtown, such "guides" would be an important addition to guaranteeing the safety of the disabled, the elderly and others who are "new" to the area. This idea could create upwards of fifty part-time jobs.

These represent five more relevant ideas they the Empowerment Network has displayed in its existence. Developing the committee means more than just talking about doing it over lunch with the very people who stood by and watched that same community deteriorate over the decades. What I propose will lend credibility, accountability and relevance to an organization that, based on the word on the streets, exists only in the minds of the membership. As the Christian Bible says, "words, without works, is dead."

KEY: AVOID PLACATION AND PACIFICATION APPROACHES

Throughout Omaha's history there have been ongoing 'programs,' 'projects,' 'models' and 'developments' that have been accompanied by the local media praising the "new days" that were about to arrive in North Omaha. Having analyzed these programs during my writing of the history of North Omaha, it is clear that all of them had something in common: they were designed to pacify and placate, not promote; they were designed to bamboozle, not build; they were all about hoodwinking black humans, not helping the 'hood.

In this section I will deal with three such ploys (there will be references to others). These are: North Omaha Community Development, the North Omaha Rebuilding Committee, and the newest one, a part of the Empowerment Network's "strategy," North Star.

North Omaha Community Development

Back in 1972 there came an organization called North Omaha Community Development – there goes that word "development" again. NOCD was created from a grant that the city received to deal with "development" in the North Omaha area. And after one failure after another, ten years after being "created," NOCD was found to be, as State Senator Ernie Chambers proved, an "adjunct" to the city – a kind of outpost that did the bidding of then-mayor Mike Boyle in exchange for a building, salaries and some "assignments."? There was no intention about empowering the residents of North Omaha.

On August 28, 1981, a pledge was made to the members of the black community by then Commercial Federal Bank to loan ten million dollars in North Omaha for "development." In addition that pledge included a public relations campaign that would promote Commercial's "willingness to loan to North Omaha." None of this came about, as you can plainly see.

Ten years after being created, NOCD came under fire in a January 20, 1982 rebuttal that appeared on the opinion page of the Omaha World Herald. The text of Chambers' essay well documents the role that the city and NOCD played in bilking the government, misinforming the black community, and generally playing games with community projects such as a "black fence" that encircled the old Safeway Building. The fence was removed once Chambers pointed out how foolish and racist the move was.

Now, the essay:

In "Another Point of View" (Dec. 21) Carl Tyler, president of North Omaha Community Development (NOCD) purported to respond to my remarks about NOCD's involvement in the "fence and park hoax" at 24th and Lake. My reply to him is delayed because information I requested Dec. 22 from Omaha Housing and Community Development Director Marty Shukert reached my office Jan. 7. Summarized at the end of this article, it gives food for thought as to why NOCD often assumes the role of apologist for the city.

Mr. Tyler expressed a "wish to set the record straight" because "Senator Chambers made a number of untrue statements." Rather than lay a single untrue statement at my door, he accused The World-Herald of misrepresenting NOCD and executive director George Garnett through "misquotes," "misinterpretations" and "false illustrations."

It is puzzling why NOCD made no whisper of challenge nor sought to "set the record straight" on any of The World Herald's alleged iniquities at the time of **commission;** and when NOCD did decide to object, it was under the guise of accusing me of untrue statements!

*   *   *

The allegedly false illustration accompanied an article extolling redevelopment of 24th and Lake, and NOCD's involvement. NOCD sought no correction, though it's likely that it clipped the article.

While declaring that a park the size depicted in The World-Herald drawing would "eliminate a major (?) manufacturing plant and the jobs that go with it," Mr. Tyler did not "set the record straight" on whether the jobs held are held by community residents **nor** that Canar may soon vacate, despite the enhancement of his property with public funds. Though disclaiming involvement in a "court settlement" that allowed a new face to be erected, Mr. Tyler did not "set the record straight" with an explanation of why NOCD concealed information it possessed about the new fence, and accepted misguided media and public praise for "bringing down" the old one.

Nor was the record "set straight" by disclosing that the Garden Apartments' remodeled units have been priced out of the range of those people whose depressed economic condition provided the **qualifying basis** for the federal UDAG grant which fueled the scheme.

*   *   *

Regarding the North Freeway, Mr. Tyler did not "set the record straight" by disclosing that I provided NOCD and the public with more crucial information than any other source and forced many concessions. His suggestion that I "help plan" any project that is destructive of the black community is traitorous and irrational. I was invited "to become a part of the problem-solving process." The invitation revealed two things:

(1) Abysmal ignorance of the profound political **and** problem-solving significance of my legislative success in obtaining district election of the school board and the City Council; and,

(2) An inexplicable forgetfulness of my intervention in **their** behalf to help solve problems NOCD was having with the City Council and Gov. Thone's office (from which they had been effectively barred).

From Marty Shukert came information establishing a heavy financial tie justifying the characterization of NOCD as an **adjunct** to the city. Since 1977, the city has funneled loans and grants to NCOD totaling $2,046,936. Of that amount, $32,127 was a **grant** to rehabilitate the NOCD building owned by NOCD president Carl Tyler. Another $114,000 in grants went primarily for NOCD salaries. As a **moneyless** "co-developer" of the Garden Apartments, and a shill for Greater Omaha Corporation, NOD received a **grant** of $850,000 and a loan of $300,000 at 3 percent, and a share of the **title.**

As the **moneyless** sole developer of the Blue Lion Project at 24th and Lake, the NOCD will receive a grant of $400,000 and a **loan** of $300,000 and the **title.**

The total amount is public funds. With income derived from the projects, NOCD is empowered by the city to select which persons and projects will receive funds for 'redevelopment" purposes.

Under such a sweet relationship, it is impossible to ignore the truisms that "the hand that feeds, controls" and "the servant does not bite the hand that feeds."

Now the record has been set straight. (all emphasis original)

The editorial appeared in January of 1982, and the concept of "empowerment" seems to be more about empowering the city and its "outposts" in North Omaha than it is about empowering the residents who live in and hail from that milieu. In March, NOCD shows that its allegiance was more to "policing" North Omaha than politicking for it.

In March of 1982, seven years after the City of Omaha had begun receiving millions in CDBG monies, a 12-member committee was formed to study revitalization "and crime" in the area claiming at the time that the 24th and Lake intersection was *"undergoing a facelift, including landscaping and renovation of two vacant buildings into specialty shops, entertainment facilities and office space."* Where is all this?

Later would come claims of $50 million being "earmarked" for North Omaha, various "committees" being set up and promises being made by bank after bank. These tricks and traps continue on to this very day. And the list goes on and on.

And yet the city, with the assistance of North Omaha Community Development, continued purchasing huge chunks of North Omaha – especially North 24th Street – and continued to act in ways not particularly in the best interests of the black community.

For instance, the July 15, 1982 edition of the *Omaha Star* carried an "Open Letter to the Community," written by Woodrow Benford, Sr., regarding bringing in more police to the area! Most of what Benford writes in the letter that follows is incorrect, but it becomes clear that grant monies were available to "police" the black community and North Omaha Community Development – under the guise of "Security Task Force," wanted some of the money. Following is Benford's poorly written letter:

Dear North Omaha Resident:

Due to certain illegal activities occurring in our community, many problems have arisen recently which affect the safety of our loved ones, and enhance the growth of criminal activities in our area, which on previous record was declining dramatically.

The 24th and Lake Street Marketing and Security Task Force has identified a number of visible street crimes which must be curtailed to a minimum at best, so our community will not be viewed or perceived as a hot bed or crime.

Over the years, the residents of North Omaha have consistently complained and requested a positive law enforcement policy against crimes and activities that breeds havoc on our streets and within our various neighborhoods.

These crimes hamper the success of community development activities in the areas of housing rehabilitation and in-fill, commercial revitalization, transportation services, and industrial development. These development activities must go on in a positive manner, so that North Omaha can stabilize and begin to expand and grow towards a resourceful future. Crime has a negative impact on this process. So please support positive law enforcement to assure community growth to prosperity.

However, street crime such as gambling, drugs, illegal solicitation and sales, traffic blocking, drinking, and disrespectful use of person and language are still very visible in our community. Illegal activities of these types deter the social and economic interaction from our youth and elderly, which demises the respect and appreciation of our living environment and cultural life style. Illegal acts project skepticism, unnecessary hardships, high insurance rates, property investment and lost revenue, disrespect of citizenship, blight and deterioration, health and safety hazards, and last, but not least, an overall bad image on our community perspective.

To minimize major crimes of burglary, larceny, assault, and murder, the visible street crime must be eliminated from the living environment. A positive police enforcement policy will be initiated this summer, which will provide for a safer and healthier environment for all to conduct their lives.

Many hours and discussions have been conducted to address the issues of crime in our area. Surveys have been low key, but positive and persistent results have generated strong desires and support for good police protection and enforcement of laws and ordinances which we all must adhere to and abide by. Positive law enforcement can be and is supported by everyone, who wish to live in a safer community.
Respectfully,
Woodrow Benford, Jr.
24th and Lake Street
Security Task Force

The "many hours and discussions that have been conducted" that Benford writes of above can better be understood if we go back four months prior to Benford's essay. Simply put: NOCD had been meeting with the police all along! Then we find a story on page 4 of the "major" newspaper's March 30, 1982 issue titled, "Group Begins Northeast Study." The key areas will be in bold-face type:

A 12-member committee, including four Omaha police officers, formed to study **revitalization and crime in northeast Omaha** will hold its first meeting at 4 p.m. today at the mayor's office.

Police Chief Robert Wadman said the committee, which also includes **eight members active in North Omaha Community Development Inc.,** will discuss ways in which

police can help in the rebuilding of deteriorated North Omaha areas.

The police committee members are Capt. John Mitchell, Sgt. James Skinner and Officers Gerald Paul and David Schlotman. **The NOCD members all serve** on that organization's business development committee.

The committee will focus on the 24th and Lake Street area – **a center of attention during the civil disturbances of the 1960s** – though its interest **will spread farther**, Wadman said.

With the aid of about **$800,000 in Community Development Block Grant money,** that intersection currently is undergoing a **facelift,** including landscaping and renovation of two vacant buildings into specialty shops, entertainment facilities and office space.

A city-funded consultant's study on the 24th and Lake area concluded that **declining population, an undesirable reputation** and a subsequent lack of interest by potential businesses were limiting development.

Wadman said **crime enforcement is a companion to revitalization**; 24th and Lake Streets has a bad reputation for crime, so people would be reluctant to locate a business there.

Wadman said statistics **may** show that the area is not the hotbed of crime most people think. He said **fear of crime may be more substantial than actual incidents of crime.**

He said the idea for the committee came from a meeting between himself, Mayor Boyle, the city's Housing and Community Development staff, Public Safety Director Joe Friend and **NOCD Executive Director George Garnett.**

Any recommendations the committee makes will be forwarded to **Wadman and Garnett**, the chief said.(all emphasis added)

Please remember that a "facelift" is only a "minor change" in something. That means that all that money -- $800,000 – is going for minor renovations. And if you look at the area now – some 19 years after the preceding claims were made – the primary people in the Blue Lion Center are the city's own Job Training program. The "landscaping" did not exist, and the addition of a few benches to sit on is nil because the police cruising 24th Street hassle anyone who sits on the benches!

The seeds had been planted.

The year 1982 came to an end with major projects underway that would do more for non-North Omahans than for the residents themselves. But the veneer was being maintained by NOCD and others. For instance, an event called "Community

Development Day" was held on September 11, 1982, and took place between Charles and Seward Streets along 24th Street. At that time NOCD was claiming to be "an umbrella organization of 14 neighborhood groups" (Omaha World Herald, 1982: 8). The activity included a parade, local politicians like Mayor Mike Boyle and City Councilman Fred Conley, and food, drill teams and booths.

Neighborhood control had begun. That number of groups under that "umbrella" have not quadrupled, but the people in charge are to be found in the City Planning Department. The construction of the Blue Lion Center would become a city-owned property and would not fulfill the claim of "revitalizing business" ("empowerment"?) in the area, or the 1982 "visions" of a consultant sent to Omaha by the Nebraska Department of Economic Development.

North Omaha Rebuilding Committee

Move up a year to 1994, and the coming of a group calling itself the North Omaha Rebuilding Committee. It was largely made up of individuals either directly or indirectly tied to banking interests. Just because they are African-American does not mean that they have the best interests of the community at heart, but they said they did.

Individuals who try to serve two masters oftentimes reveal their true intentions by the "code words" that they use. Such "code words" were present during an "information meeting" held on a Saturday morning, January 15, 1994, at the Omaha Opportunities Industrialization Center. The code words were, "let's forget what happened in the past." In other words, these individuals knew that lenders had discriminated, knew that lenders had redlined, knew that lenders had steered black people away from key areas, knew that lenders had engaged in blockbusting in the past. *Yet these people came to the community and expected the community to believe that these same individuals, who had profited so much for so long had, all of a sudden, decided it was time to reverse that trend and begin doing the black community some 'justice.'*

At this same meeting, called an "information seminar," the banking interests were there with their black-appointed representatives at a meeting that was "stacked" from the outset. It was stated then and reiterated in an Omaha World Herald article that First National Bank would lend $50 million in north Omaha over the next five years, and that American National Bank would "try to lend $10 million over the next five years." (Foy, 1994: 13) There's that figure of ten million dollars once again: first Commercial Federal Savings and now First National Bank. Moving on.

This meeting was dubbed by Lindsey DeBerry (leader of the so-called North Omaha Rebuilding Committee) as "the result of efforts that looked into the

Community Reinvestment Act, saw the need to rebuild relationships between banks and North Omaha." What he really means is that the banks were in violation of the Community Reinvestment Act which called for more banking involvement in lending, in the minority communities. Since these banks were in violation and needed to comply in order to meet FEDERAL requirements, they enlisted the help of two willing individuals, Lindsey DeBerry and John Orduna.

DeBerry and Orduna claimed at the time that their roles were strictly voluntary. In any case, these two individuals are being used by American National Bank to solicit loan applications from the black community, applications which will be made to appear as if American really cares about the community and is doing all that it can. But their own words put the lie to to their alleged intentions. On several occasions, DeBerry made the comment that the actions by the loan program set up by American National was going to *"jumpstart North Omaha."* He said that the proposed loan program would *"have a tremendous impact on North Omaha"* and that it would have a "trickle down" effect. He did not say where the money would "trickle down" from, but we can assume that he meant American National Bank. This is empowerment-type talk, and that was in 1994 – 18 years ago.

An *Omaha World Herald* article called, "Anchor Store Being Sought at 30th, Ames," the following excerpt, along the same lines as Fred Conley's earlier proposal, demonstrates that DeBerry is trying to walk the fence on the issue and, in reality, agrees more with me than with those who support the Renaissance 2000 project:

> "Lindsey DeBerry, who heads two north Omaha revitalization
> committees, said residents must be "empowered" through
> small- scale home- and business-loan programs before north
> Omaha can support major ventures such as Renaissance 2000."
> (Foy, 1994: 13)

There's the word, "empowered." To talk of "empowerment" on a "small-scale" is one of the biggest contradictions and, in fact, demonstrates ignorance of urban planning and community development. The only thing the small-scale can produce is a small scale production--and such productions are not the kinds of facts or foundations on which to build "empowerment"; in fact, such penny-ante, chump change approaches only foster more dependency.

NorthStar

In almost every black community there is a white organization that "hunkers down" or "posts up" in an attempt to appear to be all things to all people. These are groups that are usually steered by white-dominated boards of directors but who may (or may not) march out a few key "negroes" to make the organization appear as if it is black managed – when, in reality, it is not.

Dallas has groups like The Bridge, which serves Dallas' homeless, and there are other more token groups like Dallas Can! and _____. In Milwaukee, funding goes through the typical means: Boys and Girls Clubs, the YWCA and the YMCA and others who organize to dominate and direct the lives of black kids. In Omaha, there is NorthStar, an organization that makes claims of what it is doing but in reality, it is like a quasi-mission, where white college students and adults pad their resumes by making it appear as if they are "volunteering to save the negroes."

This is an organization that is dominated by the money of the Buffett family, Susie Buffett in particular. She already has a child care center in the black community and dominates and finances the lives of three black politicians: Chris Rodgers of the Douglas County Board, Brenda Council of the Nebraska Legislature and Ben Gray, City Councilman. All of then are beholden to Buffett and would never contradict or conflict with anything she says or does. It is white matriarchal control at its finest.

The website asks and answers the question, "What is NorthStar," and here is what is explained:

> The NorthStar Foundation originated in August 2007 to focus on the critical, unmet needs of North Omaha's young males - beginning in fourth grade - with the goal of successfully building them into healthy, educated, employed contributors to their community. Since its inception, NorthStar has examined models nationwide to clearly construct a "vision" for a truly unique, world class program and facility that will provide measureable and transformational growth for these young men. With a relentless focus on helping boys attain high school graduation and be prepared to pursue higher education or gainful employment, NorthStar seeks to change lives, one boy at a time.

The people involved in NorthStar are not educational innovators. They talk of having a unique program but they admit that they 'borrowed' from others in order to get what they currently have. Secondly, at least one of the people involved in NorthStar as a board member – Council Ben Gray – has been an abysmal failure at most education-related endeavors that he has undertaken: he didn't finish college, the African-American Achievement Team that he is the head of is a joke and has perennially failed black youth, and as an individual, he has had no impact on or made any major contributions to, the education of black males in Omaha. These are facts (I deal more with Gray and his wife, the latter who sits on the Omaha School Board, in another section of this book).

So with funding from Warren Buffet's daughter (who wants to dominate the lives of black people in Omaha through her monetary control of what little black leadership there is), NorthStar is yet another white program that uses black kids as a reason to empower white folks and further white privilege in the River City. They strike at the guts of the biggest needs of black people (those needs that generate the most grant money), and then hunker down, get a large facility, recruit minority kids, stock up on white volunteers, and then someone gets to publish an article or essay about how "wonderful" things in Omaha are.

The truth-claims continue in regard to NorthStar:

> At the heart of NorthStar are five program areas of emphasis: Academic Achievement, Athletics & Healthy Lifestyles, Adventure & Experiential Learning, Arts Immersion, and Actualization & Employment Readiness. Through participation in an exciting before and after school model that places youth in a safe, secure environment with mentors, staff and peers who share common goals, success in all five program areas is attainable. Building a team of partners and the needed infrastructure to move from concept through capital campaign to operational reality is a dynamic and exciting process. With a site secured in the heart of North Omaha and corresponding building and program needs defined, NorthStar is moving forward, quietly engaging broad community support. The NorthStar Foundation is a non-profit organization under IRS Code Section 501 (c)(3).

The life chances of black males in North Omaha have not improved on bit since Northstar was built. It is a grant magnet aimed at carrying the dubious title of being "one of a kind." In the same way that Omaha constructed recreation centers following each of the race riots in the 1960s, Northstar serves a more up-to-date purpose: as a repository. But don't get it twisted – in both cases the key purpose is "containment" on some level.

KEY: DEFINE DEVELOPMENT IN YOUR OWN IMAGE AND INTERESTS

Poverty pimping, as it has come to be called (at least by me), is big business in major and mid-sized cities. If you can carve out an area that is considered to be low-income, a ghetto or a barrio, then you can get the Federal money year after year without providing ANY evidence of having done anything positive for that area. Of course, if you did, your area would then become so stable that you would no longer qualify for the poverty money. So the key is, as I've written, to keep somebody poor, unemployed and living in substandard housing.

That would be YOU.

Fraser & Kick begin by stating,

> Most recently community building has been framed as anti-poverty
> work with a heavy component of civil responsibility …
> Communities and residents are viewed as ultimately responsible
> for improving their quality of life in the context of a market
> economy with increasingly limited state support for social welfare
> interventions. This contrasts markedly with models of benefits
> provision for the poor characteristic of earlier decades, and with
> models of community building that historically have advocated for
> the organized resistance of the urban poor against market forces
> and dominant political-economic and cultural practices that were
> disadvantaging (Fraser, & Kick, p. 24).

The concept of anti-poverty is not new, but because of some of the social changes that have been implemented since the 1960s when black people decide to light torches and threaten property in order to ratchet up any morals that the system might have, certain wording has been replaced with more palatable terms. Poverty started out meaning low income ethnic white folks (Italians, Poles, Germans, etc.), and then it began to mean "black" for a while.

But now because of the way that the economy has started to gradually slide, the concept of "anti-poverty" has come to mean just that – *anti- low income*. So now white folks are back in that group again, but the disproportionate numbers and percentages of the low-income are still African-American and Latino. Of course there are poor whites: *but they ain't poor because they're white*. Therefore the area left behind is ripe for picking, and that is what the city elites are doing: targeting these areas for "development" so that their developer friends can get paid and the structures built can add more revenue by being rented, leased out, or sold.

The key is to make all of this business appear to be moral and based on a sincere concern for the poor. But the facts are what they are.

Anti-poverty became a matter of civil responsibility because grant writers started putting together proposals for nonprofit corporations who, in turn, decided to enter the anti-poverty game, using the Community Action Agency models of the 1960s. The funding came fast and furiously as, from what I could see, any organization that wanted to "address poverty" had the right to do it – qualified or not. That included churches, community centers, and even human services agencies like the Urban League. The Federal money, during the '60s and '70s, was pouring in. Names like "Concerted Services" and "Inner City Development

Corporation" began springing up. As they did so, you knew a grant of some kind was in the making. They were claiming to be community development programs but were really "economic development outposts." And only a few individuals and families were "getting developed," if you know what I mean.

That is how, gradually, what the authors wrote, came into fruition as they asserted that, "Communities and residents are viewed as ultimately responsible for improving their quality of life in the context of a market economy with increasingly limited state support for social welfare interventions."

The reason for the marked shift in models and philosophy was that government listened and heard the words "self-help." It is easier to control people if you make them think that they are taking care of their own issues and problems. This meant that the benefits being provided to the poor had to have strings attached and in fact, those strings would be "pulled" by members of their own groups. In that way, if anyone was to blame, it would be the people who were closest to those who needed the help – not the Federal bureaucracy. There can't be "organized resistance" of the people doing the oppressor look the way you do; at least, that was the way it was in the '60s and '70s. "The man" and "the system" were identified by race and class, not by what was being done to harm you.

Fraser & Kick continue kicking knowledge:

> Data from the U.S. Census Bureau (2002) show that official poverty has increased in recent years with 34.6 million people now living in poverty. Of this group, nearly 26 million reside in metropolitan neighborhoods, with the number of central city poverty tracts increasing from 2595 in 1980 to 3221 in the year 2000. Residents of urban high poverty tracts were over three times more likely than those in other city neighborhoods to receive public assistance, and one and one-half times more likely to be unemployed. Over 40% of adults in high poverty urban neighborhoods do not even hold a high school degree (Fraser & Kick, p. 25).

Of course the previously described information is more than likely even worse now with the economy being worse than it was in 2002. So there is a need for these cities to "hustle grants" to the best of their ability and in order to qualify, they have to make sure that there is a low-income area that they can "target" (even the grant applications themselves refer to these areas as "target markets").

One key to keeping the money coming in is to link education with poverty. That is why when you see negative demographics, you will also see information provided, as is the case in the preceding excerpt, that the people in the area lack high school education, lack a diploma or such and such a percentage has a GED and no college. This is only partially true because when race is interjected into the equation, the concept of education and success is markedly altered. The facts show that white high school dropouts earn more than black high school graduates, white high school graduates earn more than black college graduates, and that when it comes down to experience, white people get hired in many cases, after being trained by a black person who they are then promoted over. This is known as "corporate leapfrogging" and once again it shows how "race," not "space," is the final frontier.

Furthermore, by linking education with poverty you can make money on both ends: the area colleges can increase their enrollments and this is especially true for those proprietary schools that make promises about making students employable and work on a strictly cash economy. These schools do to prospective students what the city does to minority communities: exploit ignorance and create a façade that an education can and will automatically change your life. Rooted in this belief is the oft-held contention that jobs and a higher quality of life are what life is all about and as such, the path to these jobs and higher quality of life is via the educational route. As Giachino (2010) cogently contends,

> Education is the path to success and financial stability, but diploma mills have cheapened that truism, and have been expensive for students and taxpayers. With Black unemployment at 16.5 percent and continuing to creep upward, bulking up educational credentials seems like a good idea. Especially given that people with lower levels of education have been pounded even harder in the recession (Giachino, 2010).

In her seminal study, Chung (2008) investigated whether students self-select into the US for-profit colleges or whether the choice of for-profit sector is accidental or due to the reasons external to the students (geographic exposure to for-profit providers, tuition pricing, or random circumstances). She found that find that students self-select into for-profit sector and found that three groups of "significant factors" stand out: (1) choice of for-profit sector is characterized by lower parental involvement in student's schooling; (2) for-profit-bound students are more likely to display high levels of school absenteeism and to give birth as early as 10th grade; and (3) the average predicted probabilities of choosing for-profit sector increase as in-state public community college tuition rises and county-specific concentration of for-profit providers grows larger (Chung, 2008).

Everybody can make money off the poverty game. You can hunker down and start up a nonprofit to tutor at-risk kids after school even without having any credentials of your own; you can hang out a shingle and offer "affordable legal advise" to the community; you can obtain nonprofit status and then beg for clothes and food which you can then turn around and give out – but only after alerting the media and letting them know the time and place so you can stand there and show everyone how much you love the "negroes." And then, from that public relations coup, you can let the public know that "all donations are tax-deductible."

So all that benevolence that you hear about – the United Way, Catholic Charities, the Salvation Army – they don't do it for free. As nonprofits they continue to get money to hire staff, pay office expenses and also create jobs. They might do good work for the poor, but all this is being done in lieu of providing those same poor with jobs. If they did that, then there would be no need for the poverty pimps, would there?

Ask yourselves: what do we need that is developmental? We know that we need jobs, but in the way that the concept of employment is being defined, it is almost synonymous with finding a white man to adopt you. When we think of "looking for job," our view is always outside of where we live and beyond the realm of our community. How can we be organizers if we are dependent upon the source of our problems to employ us? What happens if we do get hired? How far will we be "allowed" to go? Ever wonder why your leadership is so cautious with their words when they're on television? It's because they know "the boss might we watching" and they don't want to lose their jobs.

When you define development in your own image and interests, you sit down and create a wish list. You know the community and what it needs, and you know that before all these grant programs, social service buildings and other "projects" came into our community, the community not only fared better but it looked better. We got by and the "underground economy" went a long way toward establishing security in our community. We settled our own problems and we didn't have the high rate of homicide that we do today. We can and must do better and it begins by looking internally and then building outward.

KNOW YOUR ENEMY

From time to time you'll see an ad or promo addressing, "The future leaders of tomorrow." In reality, that is redundant. But unbeknownst to the illiterates who make money pawning off such distortions as 'cutting edge appeals,' even a mistake in action can produce, somewhere along the line, something positive.

"Future leaders of tomorrow," in the context of this series places the emphasis on the term, "future leaders." What I mean is that they lead the future; they pave the way, define the social realities that, in turn, will lead to a better life for those who need help the most. This week's information deals with some leadership concepts that you will run into from time to time.

<u>Internal Opposition: Provocateurs and Race-Traitors</u>

Over the years, those of us with superior intellect have used that knowledge to create a kind of "hierarchy of consciousness." I'll take the heat although others have also done it: we have wrongly insulted Uncle Tom in our attempts to define those of us who we, as leaders, believe have "sold out" or in some other way, "betrayed" the race.

To begin with, those of you who read the Harriet Beecher Stowe's book, *Uncle Tom's Cabin* (oops! Sorry. I mean those of you who, out of fear of books, saw the movie that starred Avery Brooks). The term was coined after that to mean someone who sold black folks down the river – but why? Uncle Tom, in the end, chose death rather than snitch on the enslaved black folks that had escaped.

But the name refers to his actions: smiling for the master, scratching his head, kowtowing to curry favor, laughing when nothing was funny. This was the behavior that the other enslaved folks looked at with disdain and behavior that would later be emulated by the likes of Mantan Moreland, Stepin Fetchin and to a lesse extent, "Rochester" Anderson. But in the latter case, it was for laughs and the appeasement of Anglos.

"Tomming" was a survival tactic. But here is what no one wants to write or talk about as it relates to the education of our future leaders: I have found that there is a direct correlation between the amount tomming you have to do and the amount of ability and intelligence that you have. Put simply, if you're a moron, then you have to tom a lot in order to get in, get ahead or, as we used to say, "get over." But if you have ability, and you have some semblance of consciousness, you can put yourself in a position where you can not only survive, but also do so with some semblance of dignity while at the same time caring for your families.

Case in point: black women. Now although the term for them is "Aunt Jemima" (who never sold out anyone but was a creation of some pancake people), it is clear that over the years they have played a major role in the survival of black people. During that time they have had to endure untold horrors of working for Anglos in their homes, serving as nannies and the like. They had to smile, laugh and listen to others poke fun at sometimes even watch as Anglos harmed or killed black people. From slavery to the present, this has been the case.

Does that make them "toms"? No. But what they did was in the way of survival. What we have to look at is just how important is what we do to the end result of caring for those we care about? Young leaders have to get other people of color to ask, "is this tommin' necessary"?

Those of us who have our own businesses or intellectual ability have to worry about this less. But in my case (others can pretend they never did it) I have used that term far too often to describe black folks who were simply trying to eke out an existence. Did they betray the race? Did they humiliate black folks? No. And here's why: these kinds of folks are not the exception – they are the RULE!

That's right, I said it: black people, in general, are "toms." I used to get phone calls from people telling me that Senator Chambers was wrong for calling black people Uncle Toms. But I agree with Ernie: look at what we've produced as a race. That is how you judge a group: what do they, as a collective, produce that, in turn, can help them with their own growth and development? When you ask that question you come to a very simple answer: *nada.*

Don't get me wrong, we built this country and we've made others great. But those strong and smart enough to bake the pie should be astute enough to see that once the pie is finished, they deserve at least a slice of it! Our people have "tommed" and, at one time, it may have been a survival tactic. But today, in 21st century America we do it for one reason and one reason alone: because its comfortable and it feels good.

We have gotten away with doing nothing for so long that when somebody does something, we take offense to it. Like our former slavemasters, we look at that person with disdain-and-how-dare-you and work to isolate ourselves from him or her. You've seen it before. The same people that smile in your face and say "good job" when outsiders aren't looking are the same ones that are running back and currying favor, joining their bosses in "dealing with those militants" and those "rabble-rousers."

Tomming is not unique to us. White folks (the original toms) have it down to a science, especially in corporate America. They call it, "brown nosing." I've seen it, and it is hilarious. What is funny is that those who do it share the same fate as the blacks who do: those in power, because of the 1960s and the consciousness that we ushered into existence, know when someone is tomming! It used to fool them; now, for the most part, it no longer does.

So what's the purpose?

If we don't need it in order to survive, then why do it? Furthermore, if we do need to do it in order to survive, maybe we're in the wrong business. Maybe if you have to tom to get a good grade or a degree, or if you have to tom to keep your job or get that promotion, maybe you don't deserve any of it. Maybe all those black people laid their lives down or put those lives on the line so that future generations wouldn't HAVE to tom any more. The early toms knew how degrading the act was, but in the name of future generations, did it so that we wouldn't have to. Feel me?

Understanding now that denunciation rarely leads to definition, I share my information with young folks. Of course I still "dog" people that I think aren't doing what they should be. But just write it off as a personality quirk of mine, but a political necessity for future leaders.

One last thing: you can create more etymologically correct terms whenever and wherever you choose. Rather than using either "Uncle Tom" or "Aunt Jemima," I created the term "Gungamima." Gunga Din was a man in India who sold out his people to the British and when he died, they paid him the ultimate compliment by saying that he had, "a white heart." His betrayal led to the slaughters of tens of thousands of his people. So we take his first name ("Gunga") and add to it that ending of "Jemima," and we come up with a gender-neutral term to be used to those, male or female, who act in a way that embarrasses, humiliates or in some other way harms black folks. "Gungamima."

So remember: if you've got skills, tomming is less of a necessity. In 21st century America, we need to look inward because we have communities that dominate most cities and with numbers usually comes power. The fact that we are still lagging in the power category clearly shows that in the final analysis, tommin' don't work.

Leaders of the future, this is important information. Our numbers are too small to be throwing anybody away. Those that will leave will do so on their own. In the meantime, it is up to us to close ranks, educate ourselves and remember the words of George Jackson: "Every sickness ain't death, every good-bye ain't gone, and every big man ain't strong."

To be continued …

THREE APPROACHES TO NEIGHBORHOOD DEVELOPMENT

I have always informally credited black people with being the originators of the neighborhood movement. I say this because no matter what major city I visit or live in, there are neighborhood associations in black communities, some active and some not. But the key is that these are neighborhoods that were not always black; when our people entered, white folks left ("White flight") and this gave birth to the black ethnic enclaves that you see today.

It is my belief that the formalization of the neighborhood movement came about when outsiders saw the pride that we took in our homes and that indeed, certain sections of the black community were named and referred to by area, usually the street name or the name of some monument or building. Since we were compartmentalized anyway, those in power perhaps got the idea to start a movement (in much the same way they take the credit for inventing rock n' roll and jazz) that would create neighborhoods, with names. The final word is that in doing so, the area would be much easier to define and ultimately, control.

In this section there are three approaches being defined: the social work approach, the neighborhood maintenance approach, and the political activist approach. We will begin with the neighborhood maintenance approach because long before there were these "gated communities" and "neighborhood watch" programs, black people were watching out for each other, having events and cleaning up the neighborhood.

The Neighborhood Maintenance Approach

The early editions of the *Omaha Star* newspaper carried a recurring college on the editorial page called "The Roving Reporter." This was no fluff piece; the questions that were asked were hard core questions and are surely even need of answering even today, more than 70 years later.

In the August 20, 1938 issue, the question posed was, "Do you think North Twenty-fourth street is properly lighted as compared to other neighborhood business sections of the city? To this day, no newspaper poses questions to its readership because, for the most part, they don't care what their readers think – or want. At that time (unlike now) those in charge of the Omaha Star were engaged in community involvement and as a result, they were – in the tradition of the black press – advocates and defenders of black people.

This question posed goes directly to the issue of "place framing," which is what Deborah Martin (2003) outlines in an article titled, "Place-Making: Constituting a Neighborhood for Organizing and Activism." A point where I agree with Martin is where she outlines how space – that is, the setting, geographic location, and socio-spatial context of a neighborhood – influences the formation of collective identities and activist agendas (p. 731). And that is what North Omaha has done for the past decade: provided a "culture" for black people to insulate themselves from the racism that permeates the rest of Omaha. No matter how well off you are of who you think you are – or who you marry – if you're black, you'll come back to North Omaha because, thanks to racial and residential segregation, that is where the "flavor" and the "soul" are at.

This is how the North Omaha community – the ghetto – gave form and function to a number of organizations and efforts that met the needs of the people of various time periods. In this case, the answers to the questions posed by the "Roving Reporter" provide an idea as to what was going on in the minds of ghetto residents and shows that we did not childishly sit around waiting for the white man to come around and give us ideas.

For instance James "Jimmy" Jewell, then the owner of Tuxedo Billiard Parlor, answered, "I think we are slighted as far as lighting facilities are concerned, North 24th Street from Cuming to Lake is not only poorly lighted (sic), but is the last area to be lighted (sic) and the first to have the lights turned off."

Now why would this be the case? Because when services are deteriorating, black people find out first because they deteriorate in our area first. When services are lacking, they begin lacking first in the black community. When Cox Cable came to town, the last area (hub) to get the optimum channels was North Omaha. When Northwestern Bell came, it was North Omaha that was last to get call waiting, call forwarding and the other amenities that those living out west got from the get-go.

Mr. R. Taylor of the Lux Barber Shop said, "I feel we need quite a bit of improvement. It would add a great deal to our business as well as to the appearance of North Twenty-Fourth Street." Mr. J.H. Anderson of Climax Cleaners replied, "That is the first thing I noticed when I came to Omaha – the poor lighting system on North Twenty-fourth street, and I think something ought to be done to improve this condition." Those from outside of Omaha can get a quick understanding of the disdain that the rest of the city has for the part of the area where black people live. It becomes clear right away. But white people don't see it because, in their view, black people get what they deserve. The problem with that statement is that far too many white people in Omaha – perhaps the majority – get far more than they deserve.

People don't have to be literate or eloquent to be able to describe their surroundings and the feelings or "vibes" that they get from those surroundings.

Today, as white folks in neighborhood associations apply for and receive grant money for neighborhood watches, garbage cleanup and other minor details, inner city neighborhood groups like the Ideal Improvement Club in the 1920s and today's own Highlander, Wirt-Binney-Spencer, and Triple One neighborhood groups deal with inner city issues, which include violence and crime. And again, our ideas as far back as 1928 generated questions and answers that are now being put into effect by those who live OUTSIDE of the area.

Want proof? The August 27, 1928 edition of the *Omaha Star's* "Roving Reporter" question was, "What is the best means of eliminating the congregation of boys around our business establishments?" Here are some of the answers.

Mr. A.B. Wright of 2872 Maple said, "What we need to eliminate this congregating is adequate amusements for our young people, like the whites – in the form of swimming pools, playgrounds, tennis courts, and a first class YMCA and YWCA. We are taxed the same sin most instances more than the white people and should have the same consideration for our young people in return for our taxes." Miss Annie Franklin of 3026 "R" Street said, "In order to keep the boys from hanging around business establishments I would suggest more activities at the Recreational centers and nearby parks should be erected."
Mr. C.B. Mayo of 2422 Lake Street replied, "I don't think resorting to law enforcement would e right, because these boys have to have some place to meet, but there should be some adequate form of clean amusements, like playgrounds, and a YMCA to occupy their time."

These ideas are the seeds of what you see today. While neglected by white planners, black people knew had to be done, knew what their rights were and knew that "an idle mind is the devil's workshop." And at least one respondent knew the importance of listening to the young people: "The best way is to have a large social to get them together and reason with them. Let them express their opinion and offer suggestions to find some other means of amusements. And if that would to help, then we should resort to the force of the law." Mr. Charles Walls, a butcher, said, "First you should explain to the boys what harm they are doing to the business by hanging around; and if they fail to heed to your advice, use other devices."

Take notice that the tendency is to look inward first, then rely on outside forces if need be – it appears to be the other way around here in the 21st Century, where black people appear all too eager to bring in racist cops to deal with nuisance issues.

What was just described was the grass roots version of the "neighborhood maintenance approach." Neighborhood specialists Fraser & Kick (2005) define it somewhat differently:

> **The neighborhood maintenance approach** has focused on protecting neighborhoods from perceived and actual threats … Some strategies community groups have employed include peer pressure, political lobbying and legal-juridicial (sic) action. The organizing of community for neighborhood-level improvement and maintenance has been a strategy to assist middle and upper classes as well as in lower-income areas (emphasis original)

When it comes to the low-income neighborhood associations, much of what is described above does not really apply. The "perceived threats" are real when it comes to black people: we don't hallucinate nor are we paranoid schizophrenics. We have endured over 350 years of white abuse, much of it taking place in segregated and/or separated racial enclaves similar to those now being euphemistically described as "neighborhoods." We don't cry "wolf" because, in most cases, the person answering the call – a cop, for instance – is also a part of the reason we are shouting for help in the first place.

Secondly, the idea of "political lobbying" is not an approach that we use in the formal sense of the term. Our version of lobbying, which has bought great success in terms of accomplishing our goals, I might say, revolves around "boycotts," "pickets," "protests" and the like. This is the ultimate lobbying that goes beyond the backroom deals that white suburbanites, because of their contacts and because politicos tend to live in those kinds of communities, practice and promote.

Also in regard to neighborhood maintenance, the authors opine,

> Regardless of the type of neighborhood, organizing community
> toward enhancing, maintaining and protecting neighborhood space
> has been tied closely to land-use decision making and enforcement
> … An estimated one-third of new housing units built in the U.S.
> since 1970 have included some form of privatized community
> association. In lower income neighborhoods community based
> organizations have organized against unwanted land use as well
> (Fraser & Kick, p. 26)

I'm not sure if the preceding statement is quite accurate. The authors claim that, "Regardless of the type of neighborhood, organizing community toward enhancing, maintaining and protecting neighborhood space has been tied closely to land-use decision making and enforcement." The type of neighborhood determines how much attention it will get from the city. That, in turn, is based on how much priority the city attributes to that neighborhood. Need may not have anything to do with it: most black communities are in need, but they get ignored anyway as outside developers buy up land and then sit on it. And, of course, cities ignore certain areas so that they will remain unkempt, undesirable and crime-ridden, which, in turn, generates even more Community Development Block Grants and Community Service Block Grants.

Moreover, the previous statements says that organizing community toward enhancing, maintaining and protecting neighborhood space has been "tied closely" to land-use decision making and enforcement. Again, I beg to differ. What these scholars want us to believe is that what they write are uniform facts and are therefore universally applicable; such is not the case. Those communities with wherewithal and a chance for immediate growth receive the most attention. This is called "the triage approach," akin to a triage unit in the military that helps those patients that have the best chance of surviving. The rest are placed on the back burner, that is, if they are ever helped at all.

Taking over the neighborhood movement is where the real funding is going. One way is by "consolidating" them all, or, as the previous excerpt bore out, simply creating "some form of privatized community association." This is an overseer that will dictate what you can and cannot do to your property and so on. This is not the type of "neighborhood maintenance" program that black people need. This is more of a "fortress" type situation, managed communities high on security and usually gated. One article I read long ago referred to them as "community of interest," where people of similar demographics (elderly, women, single parents, etc.) live in a secured and enclosed area where supermarkets, movie theatres and schools are all provided.

That is what "neighborhood maintenance" has come to: low on the "neighborhood" concept (after all, segregation is segregation) and high on the "maintenance," which means control, surveillance and monitoring. Big Brother has arrived.

<u>The Social Work Approach</u>

In the field of social work there is an approach known as the "strengths/empowerment approach. I would like to briefly share this because it appears to be more in line with what the black community should do and has the potential to do than these "wait for us to build another park" approach that is now being employed in and around North Omaha.

> At the heart of the strengths perspective is a belief in the basic goodness of humankind, a faith that individuals, however downtrodden or debilitated, can discover strengths in themselves that they never knew existed … No matter how little or how much may be expressed at one time … people often have a potential that is not commonly realized. A belief in human potential is tied to the notion that people have untapped, undetermined reservoirs of mental, physical, emotional, social and spiritual abilities which can be mobilized in times of need .. tapping into not what <u>is</u> but what <u>can be.</u> (Van Wormer & Boes, 1998—emphasis original).

This is what I was talking about when I held three "self-empowerment" conferences at the turn of the century. I believe that black people are the strongest people on this earth, and I believe that of that group, African-Americans are even stronger because of that 400 year slavery episode. We may have survived it physically, but we remain scarred because we were never "de-briefed" afterwards. That is a story for another time.

At this juncture we continue to doubt our own power where it matters most. Far too many of us continue to believe that, "The white man's ice is colder than our ice." As the excerpt states, "people often have a potential that is not commonly realized." In our case, that potential has been suppressed by a society that only wants to funnel and focus our powers on bullshit activity: sports, singing, dancing and other forms of entertainment. I believe that we have latent and untapped talent that can enable us to re-create North Omaha in our own image and interests. If others want to help with technical assistance, financing and perhaps some consultation, that is fine: but they have to also be willing to practice non-intervention and watch while we solve our own problems.

To date, they have not been willing to do so. Instead, we are force-fed "hope" and "wishes" and "prayers:"

> Every community, every narrative needs a note of hope. In our own fields and our own ways, we must convey hope … Believing that it can be done, that we can move forward, that people will care, and that we will turn things around is contagious. (Hardcastle, et. al., 2004: p. 217).

There is a time and a place for prayer, hope and wishing. When that time is ill-conceived, and when we opt to engage in these actions instead of watching our backs while other people talk about "empowering" us, we are making a grave mistake, one that we have, unfortunately, made for hundreds of years when it comes to Caucasian people. We trust them and they know that; and that is why the social work approach works so well on us: they have a god complex and a missionary syndrome; to many of us suffer from what psychologist Roderick W. Pugh called, "The-we-ain't-ready-syndrome," along with low self-esteem and serious cases of learned helplessness. Combine these two different areas of thought from these two different groups and what do you have? Slavery, 2012. How then, can we believe that these "empowerment movements" are for our (black) benefit?

We are treated like children who need to be helped, like problems that have yet to be solved. As Gary and Littlefield posit,

> Although Billingsley (1968, 1988) and Hill (172) have documented the strengths of African-American families, the prevailing paradigm for assessment and intervention with *this group is problem focused and deficit oriented. African-American families are generally treated as flawed and dysfunctional units;* little regard is paid to their strengths. Moreover, traditional treatment models are limited in that intervention is *problem specific* (Gary & Littlefield, 1998: 81- emphasis added).

The same applies in the areas of neighborhood development. We are viewed as people to be "taught," "helped," "shown the way." Even the token developers that the city fronts money to and uses to make it appear as if they know what they're doing get no real respect: jive-time, small-time, color-filled projects that are usually nothing more than fodder for the white man's barroom jokes and after-dinner meetings with his cronies.

The social work approach has its positives, but not when the race relations of the players are so skewed and one-sided. Here is how the social work approach is defined by Fraser & Kick:

> The social work approach has focused on service delivery through
> neighborhood-based organizations … Significant resources were
> provide to low-income families, including day-to-day maintenance
> services, human capital development opportunities (e.g.,
> education) and opportunities for activity in political and
> intellectual movements centered on issues of race, class and gender
> … Led by the Progressives such as Robert Wood and Jane
> Addams, the social work approach identified the neighborhood as
> an appropriate level at which to organize and test social reforms,
> but in many ways it left the politics of reconciliation between labor
> and capital to others (Fraser & Kick, pp. 25-26)

Again, their overview is not totally accurate or attributable to the neighborhood context when the variable of "race" is added.

From the top down, those doing the "servicing" and the "delivering" are not African-Americans. They may be ordering around a few people who are black – the way the Nebraska Department of Social Services did when it was closing down black day care centers a few years back – but other than that, the key is to associate all that is about "social" and "welfare" with that which is white. In that way, black youth can grow up seeing white people, not their parents, as their guardians and saviors. Again, Caucasians think in long-range terms (e.g., marathons); black folks, because of our precarious position and condition, have to be concerned about the short-term (sprints) and as such, continue to be open for tricks and scams perpetrated by "service deliverers."

The social work approach is paternalistic and insultingly dominating. Things may have calmed down in the last few years, but ask the sisters who were on welfare what those white social workers put them through. The system itself is rife with rules that are nearly impossible to follow, and even now, with public housing, there is "zero tolerance." What happens when those individuals, like most human beings, make a simple mistake? They're out on the street, that's what.

The social work approach appears to be the approach being used by Nebraska's economic developers in general and the city of Omaha's planning department, in particular – especially as it relates to community and neighborhood development planning. And here's the part where a lack of cultural competency is most clear on the part of the writers. They claim that, *the social work approach identified the neighborhood as an appropriate level at which to organize and test social reforms, but in many ways it left the politics of reconciliation between labor and capital to others.*

What was the process used by social workers to "identify" the neighborhood as the "test entity"? What logic would that make, since the neighborhood is a microcosm of the immediate community in which it is located? For instance, one might take the Triple One neighborhood and work within its boundaries, but there is still an entire North Omaha community that suffers just as much as those in the "68111" zip code! What about 68110? What about 68104 and 68131?

The neighborhood was nothing more than an easy to control area that could be used as a "laboratory" for social workers and their minions to conduct various "social experiments" on what far too many people in the social science field believe to be nothing more than "human black lab rats." This nation's history provides ample evidence that such a perception has always existed and in the scientific community persists to this day.

And where are these "politics of reconciliation"? Are we to believe that because two groups "collaborate" that there has been some type of reconciliation between the two. Maybe the black side of the equation, in Omaha, has led the whites with the power (on the other side) to believe as much. But the fact is, reconciliation is defined as, "restoring of harmony, adjustment of differences." In Omaha, you cannot restore that which never existed in the first place. The history of whites and blacks, North Omahans and the rest of the city, has been, at best, antagonistic. As for an "adjustment of differences," why would whites with power decide to "change" when their attitudes and actions toward black people, including segregation, discrimination and racist application of the law, have generated billions of dollars and one of the highest standards of living in the United States?

So there is no reconciliation between labor and capital when it comes to "others." The "others" – the ones who remain under-capitalized and unemployed – are fodder on which labor and capital feed!

What is more accurate, in my view, is the social work paradigm that continues to view the black community, black families, black men, women and children, as some type of "problem." They have coined such terms as "tangle of pathology," and "culture of poverty." Put another way,

> Deficit, disease, and dysfunction metaphors permeate treatment at every stage of the process, from intake to termination (Cowger, 1994). In the criminal justice system, clients often find their very selfhood defined by their crimes. For such persons, whose views of therapy and of all authority figures are apt to be decidedly negative, a positive approach is essential to establish the one crucial ingredient of effective treatment -- trust. Sometimes one encounter or one supportive relationship -- whether with a teacher, social worker, or priest -- can offer a turning point in a life of crime (Van Wormer & Boes, 1998).

For over a century, with the on-going racist laser-focus of the major newspaper, Omaha's black community has been stigmatized as a crime-ridden war zone with no prospects. The city administration has only acted with sincere benevolence when there was a riot or a threat of one. To this day, it is clear that North Omaha remains stigmatized, which is why these people who are accepting "collaborative efforts" from so-called black leaders do so only when they can pick and choose the "negroes' they want to have interactions with. In Omaha, most white people fear North Omaha, and that is why the deficit model described above in regard to criminals and inmates, can be applied to all of North Omaha because, in the views of the majority population, that's what we are.

This view of North Omaha as a crime zone and blacks as criminals aids and abets in the "angelic" and "missionary" vision of the social worker and the social work approach. These are people who believe that blacks have to be "saved" and "salvaged."

The social work approach is one that is more about paternalism and control than it is about helping the neighborhoods and communities that need help the most.

The Political Activist Approach

I consider myself an activist but I wouldn't use it as a descriptor because, like words like "militant" and "nationalist," you do more to scare your own people than you do white folks. Black people, so brainwashed for so long, have equated having a black viewpoint with being anti-white. Why, I ask, must whites always be a part of your intellectual or perceptual equation? Can't you just love your own people so much that you just don't have time or room for them? That is the kind of "politics" that I'm talking about: helping those that need help the most and, as you know, that means us.

According to the definition by Fraser & Kick, however, the political activist approach,

> … has focused on changing the institutional structures that are viewed as causing poverty and the declining conditions of neighborhoods … Not infrequently they have challenged the existing power structure by developing a community based upon socioeconomic "class consciousness" or based on other identities that have not been expressed spatially in terms of a geographical neighborhood (Fraser & Kick, pp. 26-27).

As usual, these men avoid the issues of race. You cannot talk about "class" without talking about race in America. Many of the poor are black and most of the black are poor – it doesn't get any simpler than that. Furthermore, and as I've always said and believed, there are poor white people – but they ain't poor because they're white!

Changing the institutional structures has not been a priority for several reasons. For one, institutions are designed to perpetuate, not condemn, themselves. So if you want to change an institutional arrangement, the best thing to do is to create what I call "counter-institutions" and deal from a position of power. Individuals, no matter how strong, cannot overcome institutions. You can cite the case of the civil rights movement, but that movement did not change institutions: it simply said, "scoot over – I want to share it with you." That is not even close to the revolutionary bent of groups like the Revolutionary Action Movement, the Weathermen, the Brown Beret or, to a lesser extent, the grandiose Black Panther Party for Self-Defense.

I also differ when they write that political activists have challenged the existing power structure "by developing a community based upon socioeconomic "class consciousness" or based on other identities that have not been expressed spatially in terms of a geographical neighborhood." These identities have been expressed spatially and for that matter, temporally (based on time) as well. Race and class are definers and have an impact on the geographic area. That is what segregation is all about: those in power take race and class and use it to determine what geographic area you are going to occupy: near the bottoms (where the floods take place), close to railroad tracks and noise, near toxic waste dumps and so on. These are but a few examples of "identities that are expressed spatially even though the defining of that space is in the hands of the powers that be (e.g., planners, developers, real estate experts, etc.)

Deborah Martin (2003) outlined a concept called "place-framing." She believes that the neighborhood functions as a site of political activism and further that, "Neighborhood-level activism in the U.S. urban areas increasingly operates in a political context dominated by an elite agenda of urban growth through civic boosterism and redevelopment projects (p. 731).

This is one way to put it; a more accurate way would to say that neighborhood-level activist in the United States inner cities (black and Latino communities) increasingly operates in a political context *dominated by neglect by the elite decision makers whose agenda it is to keep the areas poor* until such time as they can attract enough poverty grant money to relocate those populations and prepare those neighborhoods for the return of their elite counterparts (e.g., white folks).

That "civil boosterism" and those "redevelopment projects" that were referred to are just part of the smokescreen that those in power use to rationalize their incursions into low-income areas. That "boosterism" is nothing but a public relations campaign by the local media to provide support for the "new programs that are on the way," and the "redevelopment projects" are just that: projects aimed at "developing all over again," meaning a re-definition of the area in the image and interests of those who are in power. The indigenous populations, by way of other prongs of the "redevelopment plan," are therefore relocated to other parts of the city through eminent domain, scattered-site housing, apartments that offer affordable housing and other "redevelopment plans" aimed at inducing the poor to move to places that are more "in line with their incomes" and therefore leave the central city to those who want to develop it because of access to a riverfront, a lakefront, downtown jobs, downtown night leisure and other reasons.

A book titled, **Asset Building and Community Development** offers us an explanation as to why people get involved in neighborhood groups:

> Research shows that length of residence and interests in protecting
> the value of the home are strong predictors of membership in
> neighborhood associations. Having children younger than age 5
> also strongly affects membership in these organizations;
> presumably, interests in safety and education are the motivating
> factors in this case (Green & Haines, 2002: 72).

The preceding definition falls short. While having children who are young and concerns about the community are important, what about the political issues? *People who join neighborhood associations are people who want to get involved in addressing problems – and prospects – taking place in the community.* Those problems are, at their foundation, usually political in nature.

Then there is the statement by Martin that "place informs social action." While I agree that this might be the case in most instances, it is social action of some kinds that define place. For instance, there would be no "black community" in Omaha were it not for white flight. Therefore the actions of those who wanted to leave the area gave birth to a community that is now known across the state as the "near Northside" of Omaha. So action precedes place, and once place is established, more action is needed and used to either maintain a place or relocate it.

This is where political activism begins and ends: addressing the time, place and circumstance under which behaviors take place, behaviors that may shape policies and laws that are imposed on neighborhoods. Any political activist has the right to analyze, then address, what those policies and laws are.

Finally, in regard to the political activist approach, Fraser & Kick opine,

> The political activist approach to organizing neighborhood
> community has arguable declined in prevalence since the 1970s, as
> global recession motivated U.S. corporations to move offshore,
> and the state began to dismantle social welfare programs (i.e.,

> emergent neoliberalism). In accord with the neo-liberalist response to urban problems in the late 1970s and 1980s, the state has significantly decreases funding for programmatic efforts aimed at inner city neighborhoods specifically, and urban areas more generally … Together, these factors have shaped current configurations of neighborhood-based organizing, spurring community building as the dominant strand of supported neighborhood organizing (pp. 28-29)

The political activist approach to organizing neighborhood and community has not declined or increased except in response to the conditions of that particular neighborhood or community.

For instance, in the previous excerpt, the author claims that political activism has declined. What is this premise based on? Did they conduct a survey or study? Who did these men talk to? If they are so certain, then why would they then add the qualifier, "arguably" in regard to the alleged decline? And why would political activism decline since the 1970s when, since that time, conditions that negatively impact upon neighborhoods and communities have grown worse, especially since the two terms of Ronald Reagan, the two terms of George Bush, and two terms of George W. Bush? Even under Clinton, political activism, especially as it had to relate to the police and to Clinton's personal issues, was flourishing.

What reasons do Fraser and Kick give for this alleged decline in political activism? Their reasoning is based on their claims that it was because of a global recession, dismantling of welfare and corporations moving offshore. Don't they know that "all politics is local"? Don't they know that the issues they've raised are moot when it comes to the low income because, for the most part, low-income minorities are always living in a "depression" or a "recession." The end to welfare did not hurt, because the money is still coming (if you can find a job), and so is the Section 8 housing subsidy and the food stamps. Poor people are not panicking because they've always been poor; political activism is not waning because the people they advocate for, those same low-income people, remain poor and in need of a voice!

Community-building, as they call it, is a term that places the macro- above the individual needs of residents. How can you build a community without first of all focusing on the individuals, families and neighborhoods that make up that community? Community-building sounds good, but it exists only on the aerial maps and drafting tables of urban planners. They can talk about it in such generic terms because the impact of what is taking place in those neighborhoods and communities *does not directly affect them!*

Since I have refuted the "factors" that the authors claim "shaped current configurations of neighborhood based organizing," then their claim of community building being "spurred" as the dominant type of neighborhood organizing is also incorrect. It may be the preferred type as outlined by the city officials, urban planners, and others, but in the world of application and practicality, political activists are still about organizing small pockets of groups with similar interests and putting pressure on the status quo. It is about confidence-building, coalition-building, and consciousness-raising; if these are successful, *then you have the basis for a grass roots movement* – real community-building.

KEY: CONNECT COMMUNITY WORK WITH "RE-EDUCATION

One of the reasons for the success of the Triple One Neighborhood Association was the subsequent creation of the Triple One Parents' Union, which immediately went to the rescue of black students who were, on varying levels, being abused by the Omaha Public Schools.

The youth are our future and if we defend and develop them, we automatically pave the way for on-going progress. But it has to be done on a playing field that we control and/or have major input into. We have to be able to reject, in detail, defiance and self-determination, the vile and vulgar images and assertions imposed on us by the educational system. They can only teach what they know: and when it comes to cultural inclusion or relativity, they know very little.

Our young people – the students in this educational system - are also victims of stereotype-related maltreatment. **Racism then, perpetuates stigma.** A book titled *Crisis in Black and White* bought out some interesting points in 1964. The author, Charles Silberman, wrote,

> ... For one thing, the children become aware almost from infancy
> of the opprobrium Americans attach to color. They feel it in their
> parents' voices as they are warned to behave when they stray
> beyond the ghetto's wall. They become aware of it as they begin
> to watch television, or go to movies, or read the mass-circulation
> magazines; beauty, success, and status all wear a white skin.
> (Silberman, 1964: p. 48)

Although simplistic, it makes the point. These are issues that far too many of us do not discuss with our kids. When Triple One was going to meetings with teachers and school board members, the parents would be sitting right there, afraid to say much of anything. We had to be their voice because what the children were experiencing is the same thing, to a greater extent, that their parents had also faced when they went to school. And what was that, you ask?

> They learn to feel ashamed of their color as they learn to talk and
> thereby to absorb the invidiousness our very language attaches to
> color. White represents purity and goodness, black represents evil.
> The white lie is the permissible misstatement, the black lie the
> inexcusable falsehood; the black sheep is the one who goes astray
> (and when he goes astray, he receives a black mark on his record);
> defeat is black (the stock market crashed on "Black Thursday"),
> victory white ... (Silberman, 1964: pp. 49-50)

Therefore, to have power, we have to first of all gain power over our own minds and what we "feed" those minds. It is not enough to be in the community organizing while our children enter schools that feed them pablum about how great white people are. This would create conflict within our families and self-esteem issues in the hearts and actions of our future generations. That is why community work, a form of education in itself, has to nevertheless be connected with a "re-education" campaign because the battle for the minds of the people is, as Mao taught, the first half of the struggle.

At the core of community and neighborhood development issues are issues of differing perspectives on what is "good" for our communities. These differing definitions are based on race, and the racial differences are rooted in different types of symbolism. Again, Silberman:

> The symbolism which elevates white and debases black inevitably
> affects the consciousness of every person, white or black ... This
> arrangement of things [is] communicated to all in our culture by all
> its modes and means, passed by osmosis through all the
> membrances of class, caste and color of relationships, caressingly
> and painlessly injected into our children by their school texts and,
> even more, their story books ... (Silberman, 1964: p. 114)

Having been a graduate student in one of the top urban education programs in the nation at the University of Wisconsin-Milwaukee, I learned and studied a great deal about how to change the structure of American education. What they taught me is what I turned around and improved. It was what I learned creating the Triple One Parents Union and organizing in the Omaha community that I wrote about and used in my classroom debates, not the other way around.

At any rate, a key aspect of "re-education" is not only aimed at young people, but also at the teachers themselves – they must be "de-racicized:"

> ... teacher education that embraces an anti-racist perspective
> recognizes that prospective teachers' and teachers' sensibilities are
> shaped by the same forces that mold us in the society at large ...
> However' antiracist educators understand racism as learned

behavior and, as such, it can be unlearned (Ladson-Billings, 2000: 211).

These movements – working in the schools to change the teacher attitudes and the curriculum – can run concurrently with the work being done in the community, just as I did with the Triple One Neighborhood Association and then the Triple One Parents Union, later combining the names (and functions) to become TONAPU -- the Triple One Neighborhood Association and Parents Union.

URBAN MODELS AS A BASIS FOR BLACK POLITICAL ACTION A THEORY AND PROSPECTIVE PARADIGMS

There needs to be some standards for black leadership regardless of the region, the locality, the size of the area, the conditions of the constituency. Black men and women should be just that: "black." And I don't mean "black" in the negative connotation that the white man implies and applies. I mean "black" so that when you hear them speaking, the content of what they are saying clearly distinguishes them from white politicians and leaders, and that means that the solutions that they offer are tailor-made for us, rather than some generic, bland, "one-size-fits-all" strategy that they borrow from their white colleagues.

Since the death of Martin Luther King, Jr., black leadership has, for the most part, been a major disappointment. Some would say that they have been an abysmal failure. They have become to system-oriented, too self-absorbed, too greedy, to obsessed with getting on television or getting their name in the papers, and generally naïve of the issues other than those they glean or gather from the easily assembled facts of the oppressor.

This indictment fits all of them, from religious and civic leaders to political leaders and, in many cases, even the grass roots organizer types. Why these proposed urban models of black leadership? Simply, somebody has to do something. Some kind of standards have to be established so that, at very least, we will be able to see where these people are going, why they chose to lead, how they endeared themselves to the community, how they actually feel about black people (other than their friends and family members) and so on.

At present it seems that anyone can become a leader without actually having to be one. I've seen actual nitwits rise to the level of community wide observance in cities like Dallas, Milwaukee, and Omaha. And I've studied black leadership and their ideas and movements from the days of antebellum slavery up to the present. As a Black Studies scholar and instructor, I make it a point to know more about my history than any white man. As a result, I care more than most people because I've devoted myself to working toward digging us out of this rut that we've gotten ourselves in, mainly because of our police-dog like commitment to the concept of "integration."

Urban Models of Black Leadership, borrowing from three models of urban land use, may sound grandiose. But it gives us a starting point, especially since black people seem to hell-bent on following anybody any place out of some misplaced sense of racial loyalty. That approach worked back in the day when our leadership was accountable to us; that is no longer the case. They now pay homage to white people, money, being on the down-low, crack cocaine and a host of other secondary issues that take precedence over the long-term well-being of black folks. Next, a synopsis and overview of the three urban land use models.

The Three Models of Urban Land/Leadership: Explanation

As an Urban Studies/Urban Planning student (graduate school at the University of Nebraska Omaha and the University of Iowa) I enjoyed this field of study immensely. I learned a great deal about zoning, urban law and legislation, public economy, utilities and how they are determined, construction of streets, tax incremental financing and so much more. As one interview regarding the study of land use informs us:

The study of urban land use, as we learned during courses taken at the Univesity of Iowa, generally draws from three different descriptive models. These models were developed to generalize about the patterns of urban land use found in early industrial cities of the U.S. Because the shape and form of American cities changed over time, new models of urban land were developed to describe an urban landscape that was becoming increasingly complex and differentiated.

These models served as a basis for analysis, and were developed at different times. When placed together, they give urban planners a better understanding of city configurations. But nothing is perfect, and,

> … because these are general models devised to understand the overall patterns of land use, none of them can accurately describe patterns of urban land use in all cities. In fact, all of these models have been criticized for being more applicable to cities in the U.S. than to cities of other nations. Other criticisms have focused on the fact that the models are static; they describe patterns of urban land use in a generic city, but do not describe the process by which land use changes. Despite these criticisms, these models continue to be useful generalizations of the way in which land is devoted to different uses within the city. Below, we will examine the

Concentric Zone Model, Sector Model and Multiple Nuclei Model
of urban land use.

Criticism only serves to make future ideas stronger. This is why I believe that these three models serve as a necessary foundation for the development of what I call generically call "Community Leadership Paradigms" and, more specifically, Urban Models of Black Leadership. Here is why.

To begin with, these models will enable us to establish patterns on the part of those black leaders and those who aspire to lead. These patterns will provide far more stability than anything we have now because for the most part, black people simply refuse to judge or critique black leadership. In recent years, this has served to hurt us, since those who think that they have carte blanche have opted to ignore their constituencies and opt, instead, to carve their own personal niches in the system or seek out riches (or sexual gratification) in some other capacity.

Secondly, like the urban land models, the models of black leadership are more applicable to cities and towns in the U.S. than in other nations. This is not to imply that black leadership throughout the Diaspora cannot be bought off or controlled by outside interests. But the black leadership models that I offer here speak to the unique contradiction that their constituents as well as the majority of people in this country seem to buy into: that being that in America, anyone can "make it," we're all equal, and that all of us have opportunities. These lies, when placed in a real world context, point to many of the problems that black people face: we tend to believe in slogans, phrases, axioms, maxims and catch phrases even when we see the reality right in our face. This is how black leaders can get away with almost anything and yet continue to have large followings, constituencies, congregations and supporters.

Third, like the land use models, these black leaders are a static essence: they seem to act in the same way and there is no process by which their leadership changes or adapts to the needs of the people that they are leading. Almost all of them have Type A personalities and seem to bring with them a "my way or the highway" approach to leadership and community organizing. My models take this into account and do offer some suggestions that offer the masses of black people better options and alternatives when it comes to leadership selection.

Fourth, like the land use models, my models hopefully offer "useful generalizations" of ways in which black leadership assumes and claims to be, as well as what it actually is, when it comes to the defense and development of their followers/constituents/congregants.
In the following section we will examine the Sector Model, Multiple Nuclei Model and Concentric Zone models of urban land use where each will be immediately followed up with my definitions of Urban Community Leadership. Once you get

an overview of what these three models are about, then it will easier to understand the leadership styles that I developed based upon the previously described land use urban planning paradigm.

The Three Models of Urban Land Use/Community Leadership

The first land use form is called the "concentric zone model." This will be explained and then the concept of The Concentric Zone Model Community Leadership Paradigm will be defined and elaborated upon.

<u>Land Use: Concentric Zone</u>

The first land use form is called the "concentric zone model." This will be explained and then the concept of The Concentric Zone Model Community Leadership Paradigm will be defined and elaborated upon.

Envision with me, if you will, a target, with the bull's eye in the middle and rings, white and black, surrounding that bull's eye. This is what the concentric zone model looks like: a central business district in the middle and then a ring around it consisting of neighborhoods, a ring around that consisting of services and then the outer rings, consisting of the suburbs and exurbs. Specifically, Burgess identified five rings of land use that would form around the CBD. These rings were originally defined as the (1) central business district, (2) zone of transition, (3) zone of independent workers' homes, (4) zone of better residences and (5) zone of commuters. An important feature of this model is the positive correlation of socio-economic status of households with distance from the CBD -- more affluent households were observed to live at greater distances from the central city The model was based on Burgess's observations of Chicago during the early years of the 20th century. Major routes of transportation emanated from the city's core, making the CBD the most accessible location in the city.

The Concentric Zone Community Leadership Paradigm

This is the model that describes Omaha the best out of the three in terms of geo-spatial arrangement. It is also the model that offers the potential to be the most far-reaching in terms of political and socioeconomic scope as it relates to the other populations across the city and even the state. However, as a leadership paradigm, I designed something that has never been considered, but if it was, the black community of North Omaha (conceptualized here as our "central business district") would have optimal and far-reaching leadership that would be diverse socioeconomically, but unified in terms of the collective agreement that North

Omaha has to be the focus and fulcrum of attention, resource development and real empowerment.

Two representatives from the four outer rings would be a part of the **Concentric Council of Elders**, a total of eleven representatives (including three from the CBD) that would serve as the guiding/governmental body of the Concentric Zone Community Leadership Paradigm.

With North Omaha as our CBD (central "leadership" district), what each ring surrounding the area would represent would be supportive networks functioning, generally, in leadership specific capacities that, in turn, feed into the CBD thereby empowering and strengthening North Omaha (the CBD).

Directly surrounding and contiguous to the CBD is our **zone of transition**, an area where young leaders that we would be mentored – an area of protégés, close enough to the CBD but serving as a *"learning layer"* that would also be able to deal with the more stable leadership in the next sector. Two leaders from this area sit on the Concentric Council of Elders that serves as the governing body of the centrally located CBD. Mentored by all of the other zones, including the CBD, this is the zone that represents the future leaders of the paradigm.
In other words, this zone of transition would be responsible for learning all they could from the CBD, but also circulating and disseminating information about history, culture, economics, law and other areas, not only within their zone of transition, but also to the third ring of leaders, known herein as "the zone of independent thinkers' homes."

The **zone of independent thinkers** is made up of the intelligentsia, the brain trust for the community. Two leaders from this area sit on the Concentric Council of Elders that serves as the governing body of the centrally located CBD. The zone of independent thinkers is just that: working in the traditional system outside of the community but committing itself to work toward development of the CBD, while also mentoring the protégés from the "learning layer" previously described (zone of transition).

In addition to the zone of transition and the zone of independent thinker's homes, we have the **zone of logistics**. Two leaders from this area sit on the Concentric Council of Elders that serves as the governing body of the centrally located CBD.

The zone of logistics is where the well-to-do members of the black community live, meaning that they have the financial wherewithal to host important meetings and fundraisers to finance the projects aimed at improving the CBD. These are the economic entities that plough monies into whatever is needed by the protégés, the independent workers and, of course, the CBD proper. That is why they are "independent"; they may work in the system but they don't necessarily have to. Because of their financial status, they might be corporate directors or living on an inheritance; at any rate, their location and status serve as a buffer against incursions from the majority community (both financially and physically) and again, they don't have to worry about "retaliation" from an employer or harassment by police because they are system-oriented "negroes" who have the best interests of the CBD and its residents at heart.

Finally is the **mobility zone** (known in urban planning as the zone of commuters). These would be the individuals who would be in charge of "diaspora relations," meaning that black people, no matter where they lived in Nebraska, would be recruited and incorporated into the expansion and beautification of the CBD (North Omaha). Two leaders from this area sit on the Concentric Council of Elders that serves as the governing body of the centrally located CBD. This is the zone where people live who are retired or independently wealthy, many hailing from and regularly interacting with the residents of the zone of logistics.

To recap: we have North Omaha as the central business district; then there is the zone of transition on the inner ring contiguous to the CBD, the zone of independent thinkers, the zone of logistics and finally, on the outer ring, the mobility zone. This then, is the substance and structure of the Concentric Zone Community Leadership Model.

Land Use: Sector Model

Sector model is when the city is cut into different "sections" and the central business district is located somewhere in the middle. Soon after Burgess generalized about the concentric zone form of the city, Homer Hoyt, while recognizing the value of the concentric ring model, also observed some consistent patterns in many American cities. He observed, for example, that it was common for low-income households to be found in close proximity to railroad lines, and commercial establishments to be found along business thoroughfares. In 1939, Hoyt modified the concentric zone model to account for major transportation routes.

Recall that most major cities evolved around the nexus of several important transport facilities such as railroads, sea ports, and trolley lines that emanated from the city's center. Recognizing that these routes (and later metropolitan expressways and interstate highways) represented lines of greater access, Hoyt theorized that cities would tend to grow in wedge-shaped patterns, or sectors, emanating from the CBD and centered on major transportation routes. Higher levels of access translate to higher land values. Thus, many commercial functions would remain in the CBD, but manufacturing activity would develop in a wedge surrounding transport routes.

The Sector Model Community Leadership Paradigm

Transportation routes also serve a key role in the Sector Model Community Leadership Paradigm that I propose. Recall that Hoyt noticed that it was common for low-income households to be found in close proximity to railroad lines, and commercial establishments to be found along business thoroughfares. Black communities are always plagued and divided by some type of railroad tracks; the belief in the '60s was that this was so that if the community had to be divided or trapped, trains could be bought in to do just that.

Just as Hoyt accounted for major transportation routes, North Omaha could do the same thing. Whose community has trucks travelling through it all times of night? Whose community has the concentration of the Metro Area Transit bus routes (and the pollution that it brings)? Whose community has proximity to the river which, in turn, has the potential for the creation of shipping docks for exporting our goods to other parts of the state and region?

Recall also that Hoyt theorized that cities would tend to grow in wedge-shaped patterns, or sectors, emanating from the CBD and centered on major transportation routes. But here is the key: many commercial functions would remain in the CBD, but manufacturing activity would develop in a wedge surrounding transport routes. And this is where the positive productions of what I am proposing is given form and function in terms of leadership

We develop the businesses in North Omaha and bring back the people to improved housing, but use various parts of north Omaha (northwest, east, southwest and the western fringe as out-going (and incoming)transportation routes.

The leadership would function the same way, with the main "sector" being the heart of North Omaha that would be re-named "New Kemet." Kmet is what Egypt was called before the name change, and it translates to mean "land of the blacks." Because of residential and racial segregation in Milwaukee, that is what the central city was – the land of the blacks.

At the basis of my proposed Sector Model Community Leadership Paradigm would be our own City Charter. The preamble, which I developed using Omaha's city charter as a basis, would go like this:

> WE, THE PEOPLE, citizens of Omaha and residents of the
> inner city, In order to form a more symbiotic set of relations,
> increase the prospects for mutual benefit, ensure internal
> stability, increase the area's tranquility, provide for common
> defense and development, promote the general welfare of
> each other, and secure the blessings of liberation to
> ourselves and our Posterity, do ordain and seek to establish,

maintain and enhance the existence of the area of Omaha known hereafter as NEW KEMET.

The Sector Model Community Leadership Paradigm has three leaders of each of the proposed four (4) sectors (northwest, east, southwest and the western fringe) with three representatives from the CBD (North Omaha) for *a Sector Model Strategic Commission* total of 15 persons. The western fringe is bounded by 90th Street on the west, extending from the southwest side to the northwest side.

Every quarter, one of the sectors outside of the CBD hosts a *Strategic Commission Conference* that is open to everyone from the community, with emphasis on each conference revolving around an agenda of items peculiar to that sector. For instance, conference would take place in March, June, September and December. Each conference would address issues of leadership and fundraising with emphasis on empowering North Omaha.

Land Use: Multiple Nuclei

The third and final land use form is called the "multiple nuclei model." This will be explained and then the concept of The Multiple Nuclei Community Leadership Paradigm will be defined and elaborated upon.
In the multiple nuclei model, the city consists of several different areas and as such, there may be more than one business district to serve these various areas.
By 1945, it was clear to Chauncy Harris and Edward Ullman that many cities did not fit the traditional concentric zone or sector model. Cities of greater size were developing substantial suburban areas and some suburbs, having reached significant size, were functioning like smaller business districts. These smaller business districts acted as satellite nodes, or nuclei, of activity around which land use patterns formed.

For instance if we were to use Omaha (which is not typical), the nuclei would be Millard, LaVista, Ralston, Council Bluffs, Papillion and Bellevue. As Harris and Ullman stated, the CBD still exists, but specialized cells of activity would develop according to specific requirements of certain activities, different rent-paying abilities, and the tendency for some kinds of economic activity to cluster together.

The Multiple Nuclei Community Leadership Paradigm

This leadership paradigm develops North Omaha as a collection of "neighborhoods" or "villages" that would be directed by key individuals/representatives. The CBD, in this case, would be 30th and Ames

Streets. The area would be divided into the following five (5) "multiple nuclei:" 68102-east/downtown, 68111-central, 68131-southcentral, 68104-northwest, and 68110-northeast. The leadership directory would consist of three individuals from each of the five nuclei and six from the CBD, for a total of 21 directors.

Each of the areas has more than one business district, which would serve to empower the area with each nucleus working alongside the other four to engage in cooperative buying power and collective fund-raising ventures. Around each business district in each area will be: small parking lots, dotted with apartments and condos, housing surrounding each of these areas and on the outer area, heavy industrial. This offers the potential for close proximity to jobs, cutting down on commute times and addressing the lack of transportation problems that plagues North Omaha (the CBD).

An annual event would be the North Omaha Black Businessmen's Bazaar, with all five areas involve in the planning and implementation. Other collective events on the part of the multiple nuclei would include: (1) the Multiple Nuclei Concert Series; (2) the Multiple Nuclei Lobby, which would include leadership sitting in on the Community Development Block Grant planning sessions, no longer merely responding to the allocations once the decisions have been made; (3) the Multiple Nuclei Education Symposium and (4) the Multiple Nuclei Health and Legal Forums.

CONCLUSION

These then, are the "keys" to empowerment, and they will lead to real empowerment, not the "flunkies fronting as formulators" type of empowerment that is taking place in and around Omaha at the present time. These individuals should actually be ashamed of themselves to have allowed these zany ideas, Neanderthal notions, hack-neyed clichés and foolish conclusions to have ever been put in print. Now their words and lack of insight are in plain view for their progeny to see.

And so is this book.

REFERENCES

Biga, L. (_____). Power players, Ben Gray and other Omaha African-American leaders try improvement through self-empowered networking. **The Reader.**

Edney, H.T. (2004, March 2). Presidential candidates understate extent of poverty. ***The Final Call.***

Fraser, J. & Kick, E. (2005). Understanding community building in urban America. **Journal of Poverty**, 9, (1). 23-43.

Fredericks, S. (2005, June 5). The uninsured in Omaha have "hope." Retrieved from http://www.hopemed.us/news/press_releases/uninsured.asp

Gibbons, Frederick X. "Stigma and Interpersonal Relationships" in Stephen C. Ainlay, Gaylene Becker and Lerita M. Coleman (Eds.) **The Dilemma of Difference: A Multidisciplinary View of Stigma.** New York: Plenum Press. 1986.

Ladson-Billings, G.J. (2000, May/June). Fighting for our lives: Preparing teachers to teach African students. **Journal of Teacher Education**, 51.

Omaha Monitor. (1928, December 14). A city of homes.

Levy, John M. (2000). **Contemporary Urban Planning**. Upper Saddle River, New Jersey: Prentice-Hall.

Omaha World Herald (2004, December 13). Interracial barometer: A horrendous assault brings reminder of decline in one type of racial bigotry.

Omaha World Herald. (2002, July 22). Despite gains, blacks far from parity with whites, report says.

Silberman, Charles E. (1964). **Crisis in Black and White**. New York: Vintage Books.

A Case of Anticipatory Repudiation: *Community Development Block Grant Contractual Violations in Omaha, Nebraska*

INTRODUCTION

Since 1975, the City of Omaha has been the recipient of Community Development Block Grants. Today, in 2017, the city has received more than $275 million during that 42 year period and the black community whose poverty and problems qualified the City for that grant in the first place looks WORSE today than it did in the year1975.

Those funds were used for creating a skyline for the city's downtown, hiring whites to work in the Department, hiring unqualified blacks to work in the department, developing westward expansion of the suburbs, lining the pockets of area contractors and developers and other "pet projects" that promote leisure and frolic for Omaha's population.

A requirement of the CDBG program is that the city that is applying have what is called "a pocket of poverty." In Omaha that pocket of poverty is known as the Near North Side. It is an 8-square mile area on the northeastern sector of the city where 90% of the African Americans in the entire state of Nebraska reside. It has the highest population density, the highest unemployment rate, the lowest median housing value, the highest crime rate, the highest incidences of respiratory ailments and the lowest median income of any community in the city.

Therefore, in order to qualify for CDBG funding, a city has to have at least 50,000 people and what is called a "pocket of poverty." This is the area that qualifies the city for this free money. So what that translates to mean is that some area, some group, some community, *is going to have to remain poor and troubled* in order for the city to get that money on an on-going basis. This pocket of poverty is the Dallas inner city, Milwaukee's central core (North Milwaukee), and Omaha's Northside.

The late Senator Daniel Inoye of Hawaii once informed me of a survey that was given out to the country's mayors. He said that when asked which Federal program they (the mayors) felt that they could do least without, it was the CDBG program that they all wanted to keep the most. And why was that? Because there is limited oversight, no watchdogs and the mayors of those cities have nearly unlimited discretion over how the funding is used.

Therein lies the rub.

<u>Anticipatory Repudiation, Omaha and CDBG</u>

A legal explanation of "anticipatory repudiation", along with my commentary explaining how the concept applies to the City of Omaha, follows. To begin with, an operational definition: "Anticipatory repudiation, also called an anticipatory breach, is a term in the law of contracts that describes a declaration by the promising party to a contract that he or she does not intend to live up to his or her obligations under the contract." (Wikipedia, 2017).

The promising party. That would be Omaha. The promise was to use the Federal funding to improve the lives, life-chances and conditions of the poorest area in the city, North Omaha. And for 42 years they have lied. For 42 years they have placed falsehoods, in writing, on those applications so their violations of the contract are in writing, both pre- and post-allocation. Omaha has not lived up to the claims made on those applications to the government. These violations constitute border-line fraud and as I've written in another work, a case can be made that these on-going violations of the rights of black people in Omaha and the gradual deterioration that they live in because of citywide discrimination and redlining, constitute a RICO violation: organized crime by the so-called "city fathers. (RICO stands for Racketeer Influenced and Corrupt Organizations act).

Now, the specifics. According to an internet legal source,

> A party is considered to have repudiated a contract when they evidence a lack of willingness or an inability to perform their contractual obligations. A repudiation of a contract by one party (the repudiating party) will entitle the other party (the aggrieved party) to elect to terminate the contract. This is based on objective intentions i.e. the repudiating party's words or conduct … This unwillingness or inability to perform a condition must deprive the aggrieved party of substantially the whole of the benefit that they would have received if the remaining obligations were performed under the contract (Wikipedia, 2017)

To begin with, lack of willingness. These Omaha white people in the City Planning Department live nowhere near North Omaha. During a September 17 meeting with the director and six of his "planners" I made the statement that, "You are neglecting North Omaha but you live in the suburbs." The director became adamant and nearly shouted, "You don't know where I live!" I shut him up quickly with my response: "I know where you DON'T live." And this was the point I was making. These white people and their black flunkies make decisions about the state's only real black community and then at the end of the day head as far away from the area as they can get. This "white flight" attitude is a key part of Omaha's racial history.

Secondly, the repudiation of the contract. It is not a verbal repudiation – it is a repudiation by the lack of action and compliance. It is repudiated "by the repudiating party's words or conduct." The key word is conduct, and the evidence is in the 42 years of non compliance by the City of Omaha.

Third, the clincher where it makes clear that, "This unwillingness or inability to perform a condition must deprive the aggrieved party of substantially the whole of the benefit that they would have received if the remaining obligations were performed under the contract." It is more of an "unwillingness" to perform, but in Omaha, because of the hickish and hillbilly nature of these white men (despite the suits, ties and white shirts that the planners wear to work each day) it could also be an issue of inability to perform. After all, for years the director wore a pony tail down his back as did his assistant, another white man who was taking prescribed Quaaludes as he helped make funding allocation decisions that would impact on the black community. Many of them have been alcoholics, on the job and off. Check the record.

Omaha does not deserve any more CDBG funding, and the following passage proves my point:

> When such an event occurs, the performing party to the contract is excused from having to fulfill his or her obligations. However, the repudiation can be retracted by the promising party so long as there has been no material change in the position of the performing party in the interim. A retraction of the repudiation restores the performer's obligation to perform on the contract (Wikipedia, 2017).

Omaha should be excused because the city has not performed to the benefit of the poorest community. Transforming the black community's "street of dreams" into an "urban village" where the city now owns or controls all four corners of 24th and Lake Street is nothing more than a land grab by the city and its lead money provider, Susie Buffett, daughter of Warren Buffett.

Another violation can be found in the following fact:

> Another rationale for the doctrine of repudiation is based on the breach of an implied term not rendering future performance futile: "[O]ne essential promise which is implied in every contract is that neither party will without just cause repudiate his obligations under the contract, whether the time for performance has arrived or not" (Wikipedia, 2017).

The City is in violation of its long-time and continual promises to fulfill the CDBG contract. And that is why the relationship between CDBG and the city should be extinguished – and damages should be rewarded to North Omaha for the City's decades of neglect, abuse and fraud:

> Repudiation of the contract by one party entitles the other party the right to terminate and claim for damages. However, it is possible that the repudiating party does not repudiate the entire contract but only certain obligations. In this case, the aggrieved party will only

acquire the right to terminate if the repudiating party repudiates an obligation which, if breached, would grant a right to terminate (Wikipedia, 2017).

The Office of the Inspector General for HUD is nearly worthless, and justice cannot be expected. The OIC does not do inspections on these programs and allows city after city – Omaha, Milwaukee, Dallas, etc. – to continue their flagrant abuse of CDBG funding.

Evidence of the Failures of CDBG in Omaha

Allegations of abuse of CDBG are stacked a mile high. But as a scholar, I believe in contextual appraisals that outline the conditions surrounding the need for CDBG, community reactions to those conditions, and other sociocultural factors that clearly show the NEED for the grant funding.

Stevens (1981) sheds light on what little concern there was for North Omaha long before there was even a CDBG program:

> In 1946, the members of the Housing and Slum Area Elimination Committee recommended urgent action to reverse the deterioration in some neighborhoods north and south of the central business district. They asked financial institutions to formulate a mortgage plan which would enable the poor residents to obtain funds for home improvements. Also, they noted that the municipal government had neglected the North Omaha area, which housed most of the city's black population, and urged the City Commissioners to provide better services. Yet no altruists emerged to undertake the corrective measures … (pp. 36-37).

Promises were made, lies were told. The method was not a new one. In fact, it represented what now, in retrospect, appears to be an historical tendency, documented in a work written in 1971 called, *Odyssey: Journal Through Black America*. In one segment, long-time Omaha dentist Earle Person had this observation:

> "When the whites put together their new downtown area, their slogan was: "Can do." We [blacks in Omaha] saw that the slogan for the Near North Side was: "Won't do." The prime movers just say, "Well, we'll try a few little things, form a committee, call in an outside research organization, make a study." And they do survey after survey after survey, and al of them get stuck away in some file..." (Selby & Selby, 1971: 290)

Omaha had four riots during the 1960s and still refused to do much more than build recreation centers. They simply refused to do anything for the black community with existing taxpayer dollars; if it couldn't be done off the government dole, with free money from the Feds, then racist Omaha wasn't going to direct any money toward its ghetto

According to the "State of Black Omaha 1978" report by the Nebraska Urban League, the ghetto was an area that they even referred to as such. Black Omahans , with few exceptions, have very low self-esteem and apparently do not care what takes place in their community. Whites have traditionally known this, and they knew it as far back as 1977. The Urban League quotes "one city official who has boasted that 'Omaha today is host to one of the neater, more law-abiding black ghettos in the country." (Urban League of Nebraska, 1978: 7).

While the City continued to abuse CDBG funding, commissions, reports and programs were put into effect to pacify the Black community. For instance in 1999, a Commission was so limited in their research skills that they attempted to masquerade their shortcomings with irrelevant quotations, outmoded data and generic conclusions. An example lies in the following 1999 passage from the city's so-called "racial study" put together by the Omaha Commission on Community and Race Relations:

> Since the spring of 1998, volunteers from across this city
> have been actively engaged in research, analysis and
> assessment of race relations in Omaha, Nebraska ... Racism
> in all its manifestations is an emotional topic for many, and is
> extremely difficult to talk about. Members of the committees
> experienced this as they strived to create actionable
> recommendations organizations, government and even
> individuals can embrace and implement. (p. 3)

Also in 1999, the lies continue to mount, as the need to cover up the shabby work increases. Take note of the following attempt at an explanation:

> Cross sections of people from across the metropolitan area
> participated in the Omaha Commission on Race and
> Community Relations. Individuals from all walks of life were
> actively involved in all subcommittees. This means that
> leaders from community organizations, private and public
> sectors as well as front line concerned individuals were
> actively engage in the work of the commission. (p. 3)

This is a lie. Ultimately however, what they really mean is that everyone involved was selected, picked or recruited by someone else. And this means that what you ultimately had was a "clique of the unconscious," a coterie of kooks, a circle of pseudo-intellectuals. By banding together, they make it appear as if the issue of race is so complex and that they do not know what the problem is. The more people they recruited, the bigger the problem became because when it comes to race relations in Omaha, white people are the major problem, and their handpicked flunkies of color make solving the problem even more difficult.

By 1999 – 24 years after the first CDBG grant was allocated to Omaha – the black community continued to deteriorate and black residents continued to die. The reason why nothing was ever done was offered in the 1999 report. Check out the following:

> … **The original purpose of the commission was to assess the status of race relations in Omaha – not "fix" the problem** … The gathering of this diverse group of people to discuss the nature of race relations in Omaha, Nebraska is **a strong first step.** Many recommendations for improvement of race relations in the seven target areas have been made from the best efforts of this Commission … (p. 4—emphasis original)

They admitted it, and this is par for the course of Omaha in all that they do when it comes to race. They want black people learn to "suffer peacefully." And this is the same attitude they had when the CDBG checks arrived; they didn't want to "fix" anything as they had promised to do. They wanted to "assess" the situation, spend some chump change on a few ghetto still corporations that would rubber stamp the (false) attempts at progress of the City, and then spend the overwhelming majority of the money on a city whose median income, median housing value and general state of life are far above the national average.

As it was reported in the August 4, 2000 edition of the *Omaha World Herald* in an article titled, "Omaha Race Poll Still Unfinished:"

> A controversial $40,000 survey to gauge racial attitudes in Omaha remains on hold … Most of the funds for the poll, which was to be conducted by the Gallup Organization, are in the hands of the city's Human Relations Department. But disagreement remains over whether a survey exploring race relations would do any good. About 12 members of the city's race relations commission gathered this week and discussed, among other items, the poll's fate … [Kellie] Paris-Asaka [the city's human relations director] said she is optimistic that the final $10,000 can be raised. The other $30,000 is coming from

the United Way of the Midlands, the Lozier Corp. and a
federal hate crime grant.

Years passed and CDBG funding kept coming. Mayors Mike Boyle, PJ Morgan, Mike Fahey, James Suttle, all got their piece of the pie and watched while the City Planning Department constructed a master plan that offered nothing but bright painted sidewalks for North Omaha, two postage stamp sized parks and massive expansion for other parts of the city.

For years I have been writing articles documenting the lies and deception of the Omaha City Planning department, some of which I have provided in this book. Now, with CDBG funds about to dry up (few people know about this), the World-Herald comes forth with an article on January 17, 2011 under the headline, "Changing Broken Promises of Past Economic Development." The article, which features testimony from a number of black people who don't know what the hell is going on, tries to relieve the City of its responsibility for the on-going decline of North Omaha. But the recipe or formula is so simple.

Now, for the article, and my analyses will filter in and out.

Promises, Promises, Promises. That seems to have been a common theme over the years in North Omaha when economic development has been the discussion. Today, another announcement of a new employer locating to North Omaha, but this time the promise is expected to stick. Mary Parker likes what she sees. So much so that she's opening a regional headquarters for her multi-million dollar Atlanta-based security business, All (N) 1 Security, in North Omaha. "If we're coming in to a community, unlike other businesses it behooves us to come in and invest in the residents of this community," she said (Hamer, 2011).

Mary Parker was deceived and almost as soon as this article appeared she packed her shit and her successful Atlanta business and headed back. She found out, just in time, that she was dealing with duplicitous, lying white men who, as the First Nation people warned, "speaks with forked tongue."

The promises were really lies from the get-go. In fact, I wouldn't be surprised if the writer of the article just quoted stole concepts from articles I had published in the state's only African-American newspaper, the Omaha Star. I had well documented the promises that were made and were included in headlines in the major newspaper, a rag that continually worked in collusion with the City Planning Department, area developers and contractors and anyone interested in encroaching on North Omaha. Ms. Parker was just the most recent black business victim of Omaha, a city that went so far as to ram a freeway through the heart of the area and therefore destroyed almost every black business in existence.

A former pawn and another unwitting victim of Omaha's racism was Jim Nelson. He thought he was in the "inner circle" when he, the mayor and a black city councilman closed down the black "people of color station" that Cox Cable had provided for years. The exposure of the people who colluded with the city was more than these "negroes" could stand, so they closed it down and turned over the decision making to the trusted "negro," Jim Nelson.

Here is Nelson in his own words:

> Jim Nelson invested his own money in a video production facility at 24th and Lake about eight years ago. He's heard this talk of economic growth before. "What's happening and has always happened in North Omaha is imagery and that image has always been one that it's not a good investment," he said. But, he believes this one's different. "We've seen the dog and pony shows," he said. "The difference now is that we see people coming in from the outside...people of color." (Hamer, 2011).

This negro didn't even live in the black community. He was a coon who worked for racist Cox Cable and his business wasn't flourishing. In fact, it was attached to a so-called business incubator that has violated every rule of business incubation that I ever read. I created two when I lived in Dallas and one thing I know is that the businesses who are allowed in have to leave within six months to a year and head out on their own. But in Omaha's version there are businesses in there that have been around for over twenty years! Nelson was "paying" the way he makes it sound and he sure wasn't making any money. He was a thrall for Cox Cable and his office was out in the western suburbs.

He passed away recently without a whimper.

Next comes testimony from one of the biggest exploiters of property in North Omaha, a former school board member and city council person, who also ran and won a seat in the legislature, none other than Brenda Council. A woman with a gambling addiction, she lost her seat in the Legislature after embezzling $60,000 from her campaign fund. So with that in mind, remember that her credibility is questionable:

> There are other reasons economic growth has sputtered here. "Is it discriminatory lending practices? or is it lack of people with the potential and ability to move the business forward," Nebraska State Senator Brenda Council said. "I'm suggesting to you that its not the latter." "We've done it backwards in North Omaha," Mayor Jim Suttle said. "We've tried to put commercial service

> jobs here with no customers...therefore it won't work. To get
> customers you've got to have industry and the in-between
> companies like Mary Parker." (Hamer, 2011).

Anything that appears to be "going wrong", akin to what Ms. Council said and also the remarks by Suttle, are not mistakes. They are by design and they bring pain to North Omaha.

For instance when Suttle talks about putting businesses where there are no customers, he is telling a half truth. That may be the way it is NOW, but there is a relocation strategy taking place and in a few years, what was once a black community and a "street of dreams" is going to be populated by the children of the same white people who cut and ran during the "white flight" of the 1960s and 1970s. So those businesses serve a purpose: just not an *immediate* one.

Ms. Council is also correct but again, this is by design. Indeed, she's capitalized on the availability of abandoned properties by buying them up. She and her husband own property in North Omaha and haven't paid taxes. One of the charges against her during the time she got busted for her gambling habit was the fact that she owed tens of thousands in back taxes. The man who succeeded her, Ben Gray, also came into office with tens of thousands of dollars in back taxes owed. So the people chose to lead North Omaha are lacking in character and conviction themselves. They are in no position to criticize the white man if what is in their power they do not do.

And speaking of Ben Gray, pay close attention to the following:

> "We are going to make a significant difference in this
> community," Omaha City Councilman Ben Gray said. "We are
> going to keep moving forward in spite of those who want to say
> something different. We are talking the talk and walking the walk
> and we are going to get business done." Jim Nelson shares Mary
> Parker's vision of Omaha. "This is a gold mine and those
> businesses on the outside that are coming in here that are seeing
> that aren't just looking at North Omaha they're looking at
> Omaha," he said (Hamer, 2011).

Who is the "we" that Gray was referring to in 2011, some six years ago? Because North Omaha actually looks worse, and the "street of dreams" that existed when Gray was a camera man for a local TV station is now an "urban village" under Gray's watch. He boasting about bringing Wal-Mart to town as if he did it by himself. He is not "talking the talk and walking the walk"; he is squawking and balking while the white man just gawks.

And how foolish was Nelson with his claim that businesses outside are not just looking at North Omaha but at Omaha." Bullshit. Steering and redlining are still in full effect in Omaha so any black business that seeks to relocate to Omaha is going to be "steered" to the ghetto area. Those peckerwoods out west aren't going to support a black man or woman in their quest for success. Such an action would run counter to the history of race relations in Omaha!

The article concludes, thusly:

> Mary Parker mentioned that it's all too fitting that the announcement occurred on Martin Luther King Day. And the hope is that as time goes by those barriers holding back economic development in places like North Omaha will soon disappear. One reason Omaha targeted Atlanta is that city has a successful model of black-owned businesses. Because Mary Parker's business is nationally certified, Atlanta banks say she's worthy of financial backing. The North Omaha business community wants to build the same climate here. The security company could provide up to 100 jobs over a three year period (Hamer, 2011).

That poor sister didn't realized that she was being used. The announcement being made on King's birthday is a vintage Omaha scam. Just like that shrunken park named after King, just after the center on Bedford named after King. If they loved King so much, why don't you name something in the white community after him? I think you know the answer.

Besides, the announcement of her short lived business coming to Omaha was made for another reason. One of the major scams you can run on someone who you want to propose to is to make that proposal on Valentine's Day, Christmas or some other major holiday. In that way, you have no choice but to remember it!

Sis. Parker was in charge of a security company and should have known better than to fall for the okey doke. She's based in Atlanta; what on earth would possess her to want to come to a hick-ass cow town like Omaha in the first place?

Again, Omaha is guilty of an anticipatory breach of contract. Omaha had no intention of living up to any promises it may have made to Ms. Parker. It had no intention of caring about bringing a security firm to North Omaha when it's own police force can't be kept busy and is therefore over-used in North Omaha. The leaders claiming that things were going to change should have warned this black woman. I was in Dallas at the time and didn't learn about Ms. Parker until after I returned in 2013.

For more than 30 years I have fought the racists in the Omaha City Planning Department over their on-going, perennial abuse of CDBG funding. They would fill out their annual applications, attach the negative demographics generated by an intentionally segregated black community, make claims about needing the money to make improvements, and send in that application. A lax Office of the Inspector General and HUD Undersecretaries who were too busy chasing skirts and getting drunk to pay attention, simply rubber-stamped each application. At the same time the city marches out their token shills like North Omaha Community Development and Omaha Economic Development Corporation to make it appear as if all is well and that the "negroes are involved in citizen participation".

But the struggle must continue. The money is beginning to dry up and most black communities today look as bad as they did back in 1975 when the CDBG funding first began being dispersed. As Ralph Waldo Emerson once said, "Every thought which genius and piety thrown into the world alters the world." Forget about the piety because I believe Marx when he said that, "Religion is the opiate of the oppressed masses." But I'll settle for genius any day.

After all, I fall into that category.

REFRENCES

Selby, Earl and Marian Selby. **Odyssey: Journey Through Black America.** New York: Putnam Publishing. 1971.

Urban League of Nebraska (1978). **State of Black Omaha, 1978**. Omaha, Nebraska: Urban League of Nebraska